PROPERTY

Rowan Moore is the award-winning architecture critic of the *Observer* and author of *Slow Burn City* (2016) and *Why We Build* (2012). He was formerly director of the Architecture Foundation, architecture critic of the *Evening Standard* and editor of *Blueprint* magazine.

Further praise for *Property*:

'An ambitious book that examines our global obsession with home ownership . . . After we put aside self-interest, the first thing we need to do is at least believe that a different way of living and of organising and funding society is possible.'

FINANCIAL TIMES

'Wide-ranging and readable . . . For anyone interested in the ideas and interests that have shaped property and its preeminent impact on our modern world. With examples across the globe, his always judicious account acknowledges both its benefits and costs but ultimately reminds us that it is – or should be – a means not an end, one whose possession (in common or private) should secure our social well-being, not obstruct it.'

JOHN BOUGHTON

'Rowan Moore is funny and insightful as he sets out on a mission to liberate us from the madness of our fatal addiction to property . . . An urgent message for all those who care about the way that we can live together.'

DEYAN SUDJIC

T0323172

'An absorbing and enriching read. Moore steps well back from real estate hysteria to revisit and question the fundamental theory and practice of property. He seeks out examples not only of the terrible abuses that property has motivated, but also of cases where well-motivated alternatives show glimpses of potential better ways.'

DR BARNABAS CALDER

'Moore's fabulous new book tells the sorry tale of the UK government's mismanagement of the land economy. He argues really convincingly for an interventionist government.'

PETER BARBER

ROWAN MOORE

PROPERTY

The Myth That
Built the World

faber

First published in 2023
by Faber & Faber Limited
The Bindery, 51 Hatton Garden
London EC1N 8HN
This paperback edition first published in 2025

Typeset by Faber & Faber Limited
Printed and bound in the UK by CPI Group (UK) Ltd, Croydon, CR0 4YY

A CIP record for this book
is available from the British Library

ISBN 978–0–571–35010–0

Printed and bound in the UK on FSC® certified paper in line with our continuing
commitment to ethical business practices, sustainability and the environment.
For further information see faber.co.uk/environmental–policy

2 4 6 8 10 9 7 5 3 1

To the Irish tsunami

Man did not make the earth . . . It is the value of the improvements only, and not of the earth itself, that is the individual property.

Thomas Paine, 1797

Real estate is a mind game.
I Bobby-Fischer the shit out of situations like this.

Christine Quinn, *Selling Sunset*, 2019

The land is our mother, nourishing all her children, beasts, birds, fish and all men. The woods, the streams, everything on it belongs to everybody and is for the use of all. How can one man say it belongs only to him?

Massasoit, Wampanoag leader, 1620s

Own your own home.

Proposed licence plate slogan for New York state, put forward by Fred Trump in 1939

With the abolition of private property, then, we shall have true, beautiful, healthy individualism. Nobody will waste his life in accumulating things, and the symbols for things. One will live. To live is the rarest thing in the world.

Oscar Wilde, 1891

Land monopoly is not the only monopoly which exists, but it is by far the greatest of monopolies – it is a perpetual monopoly, and it is the mother of all other forms of monopoly.

Winston Churchill, 1909

CONTENTS

Introduction 1

The World According to Property

1. The Miracle Ingredient 13
2. The Property-Owning Democracy 35
3. The Values of Value 59
4. The Reality of Realty 79
5. Developer Kings 99
6. City of Monads 117

The Philosophy of Property

7. Property Is Heft 139
8. A Convenient Fiction 161
9. Possession and Domain 181

What Else Could There Be?

10. Life in Common 197
11. Community and Cooperation 209
12. The Visible Hand 231
13. Imagine a Country 253
14. How to Solve a Housing Crisis 271

Conclusion 283

Notes 291
Select Bibliography 315
Acknowledgements 319
Image Credits 320
Index 321

INTRODUCTION

Property, natural and imprescriptible human right, foundation of freedom, engine of wealth, maker of peace and law. The concept that runs through Western democracy like steel through reinforced concrete, that wrote the code for the formation of the United States, that underwrote the expansion of great cities, which has been embraced by developing economies as the means to prosperity and private fulfilment, and without which neither industrial nor post-industrial society, nor uncountable cultural, social and economic benefits that follow, would exist.

A good craved by individuals, that converts personal effort into permanent achievement. A foundation for a good home, for the shelter and setting of your life and the repository of your dreams.

Property. Which also has a way of making the world go mad.

Many millions are dispossessed, dislocated and excluded by the manipulations of big property. It is a currency of kleptocrats and gangsters, the medium of their transactions, the means by which they dispense patronage, entrench power and accumulate and conceal wealth. Recent years have seen a breed of developer kings – Erdoğan of Turkey, Putin of Russia, Aliyev of Azerbaijan, Mohammed bin Salman of Saudi Arabia, Trump of America – for whom property and politics have been mutually reinforcing implements of power.

And the idea of property has physical effects on the places where people live their lives. The investment mechanisms of real estate rebuild cities into large and controlled enclaves of profit. In Gurugram, India (formerly Gurgaon), it is considered an asset that your child can go to school without contact with the outside world. In the same city, outside the protected boundaries of individual apartment complexes, basic systems of electricity, sewage and transport break down.

My own country of Britain has played a starring role in the adventures and misadventures of property. Over the last four or five centuries it incubated modern ideas of private ownership and exported them to its colonies, such that they reshaped continents. It is a society where home ownership is particularly prized. It is also one where rising prices forced large sections of its population into tiny and insecure homes, lightless and airless, creating new divisions of class, age and region based on ownership or otherwise of your home.

House price inflation creates a property-based social order that affects security, quality of life, prospects, even health, and can cause cities to atrophy, if the young, the public-spirited and the creative are shut out – a story that has played out with similar results in Sydney, Paris, New York, Tokyo.

And then come the crashes, which bring their own miseries: negative equity, repossessions, over-leveraged owners stuck in homes they can't sell, shocks to national economies, drastic falls in the building of new houses. These collapses, if the ability to buy is simultaneously weakened by high interest rates and a weakening economy, in practice don't make homes much more affordable.

Much of this property-based economic activity takes a form, the extraction of rent, which tends to attract investment away from more productive uses of capital, and so threatens the success of the economies concerned. Rent-seeking directs energy, as the economist Joseph Stiglitz put it, 'toward getting a larger share of the pie rather than increasing the size of the pie'. In which case such activity is a decidedly mixed blessing.

––––––

The Western idea of private property makes a promise – to both individuals and nations – that it will make you happy and rich and free. It is meant to be a reward for hard work, and the device by which the fruits of endeavour and effort are protected. Often it achieves all these things, but it has also been a tool of appropriation, exclusion and enslavement. In which case it is not an absolute good in itself but a means, that can be judged against others for its effectiveness in achieving its ends.

This book aims to show that this theory of ownership – so ubiquitous and normal that it is taken for granted, barely noticed, treated as natural – is neither inevitable nor preordained. I argue that, if property is seen as social, it can do a better job of providing shelter and security than if it is treated as purely private. If it is seen as a human instrument, and not as something given by nature, it will be more practical in serving human needs.

I start by telling stories of the triumphs and mishaps of private property – in the predominantly black city of Kinloch, Missouri, in the suburban Levittowns of New Jersey and Pennsylvania, and in Britain's forty-year pursuit of what Margaret Thatcher called the 'property-owning democracy'. I explore what ownership does to your mind, its impact on the lives and values of both haves and have-nots. I describe the role of fantasy and illusion in sustaining real estate markets in Los Angeles and Las Vegas, the attractions of property deals to kleptocratic rulers, the effects on the citizens of Gurgaon of living in a city built at high speed by giant property companies.

A powerful myth lies behind the creations of these worlds, going back to the seventeenth century, which holds that property is 'natural' and a 'natural right'. The middle section of the book examines this philosophy, and its physical and human consequences: the ways in which grids of property boundaries were laid onto the United States of America, and the accompanying removal of native populations.

A myth, though, is what it is. Property is better understood as a tool, a convenient fiction, sometimes a weapon. And it was fundamental to these theories of natural property that there was a place called America with apparently limitless vacant land, one with unbounded opportunity for pioneering individuals to acquire territory through enterprise and endeavour. Since this infinitude of space has turned out not to be the case, where does this leave the philosophy that depends on it?

The middle section of the book examines both this faith in the natural quality of property and its alternatives. It outlines different beliefs of what can and cannot be privately owned – all land absolutely, according to some; that it cannot be owned at all, according to others, any more than air. Or that you can own the produce earned from it, but not land itself.

As several thinkers have observed, property is social as well as private: it cannot be held without relationships with others, and to laws, customs and states. Its wealth is based not only on the works of individual owners, but also on those of neighbours, businesses and governments, through the building of infrastructure, for example. The actions of others will affect property owners, whether they like it or not: pollution and climate change have no respect for title deeds.

Given which, it becomes valuable to see what land and property look like when they are not purely private, which is the subject of the book's third section: common land in medieval Europe, for example, or squats in Berlin during and after the Cold War, or the 'wild settlers' who formed self-governing communities around Vienna in the aftermath of the First World War, or the gigantic Co-op City in New York. There are no utopias in this section, but there are ideas and places that work. The rise of public housing is described – a once radical alternative to private ownership that is now ubiquitous – and the idea of the garden city, realised in post-war British new towns, which is based on the belief that uplifts in land values are shared property.

I conclude with Thomas Jefferson's statement that land should 'belong in usufruct to the living' – that what matters most is the ability to benefit from it, while passing it on in good shape to future generations. This ideal requires both that property is social and that it is a means to an end, rather than the end itself. The aim here is not to annihilate the idea of property but, through a better understanding of what it is, propose how its wondrous promises might be fulfilled.

'Property', for the purposes of this book, is land and buildings – real estate – rather than personal belongings such as jewellery or furniture, or intellectual property. It is this sub-category of the larger term, the one that has effects on food and shelter, that has most exercised philosophers and politicians, and has had the greatest effect on the world as it is now. My focus will be on the concepts of ownership that were developed in particular in Europe and North America in modern times.

The subject requires me to explore areas of expertise that are not my own – philosophy, economics, law. I don't claim original thought in these fields and I apologise in advance to true experts for the inevitable simplifications. My aim is to bring these ideas back to lived experiences and physical spaces. Since property is not universal, but varies from place to place, I offer no universal solutions. I hope to show, rather, that there are many productive ways of dwelling on land and in buildings.

———

Although property is not natural, it has roots in nature. While it is a cold word – impersonal, unemotional, technical – it is an abstraction of something which an animal understands – territory – and for which humans and beasts sometimes fight to the death. Property relates to land, and land relates to food, and food relates to survival. Property, as a means of perpetuating the gains of one lifetime for the benefit of others, is a weapon against mortality, and therefore charged with emotions of fear and love. So property is a matter of life and death conducted with technical language, a struggle for existence fought with spreadsheets, instinct made into law.

You, dear reader, might be a winner or a loser. You could be an owner who has seen your capital treble or quadruple or more, or have bought at the wrong time and be left with nothing but debt. If you live in a city like San Francisco or London, you may have reason to believe that you will never own a home in your life. If you live in one of those European countries where rented accommodation is a more reasonable proposition than it is in Britain, you might have a calmer relationship with the space you inhabit. Even so, under the widespread influence of the Anglo-Saxon model, your situation may be less stable than you thought.

Whatever your situation, you will have been affected by property one way or another. You might well have been obliged to become a player in the turbulent and irrational markets on which that fundamental need, for a home, is traded. Perhaps you have changed your life, your location, your career, in search of a place you can afford, or found your relationships coloured by your material prospects, as a couple, of finding a place together. You might have found yourself stuck with a partner you no longer loved, for the reason that you owned something together and couldn't afford to live apart.

Property does things to your mind. It will have an effect on your happiness – probably negative, if you are shut out of the magic kingdom of ownership and do not live in well-managed rental accommodation. You might be insecure, be brought into poverty by high rents, and/or forced into the lousy living conditions that renters have to accept in an owners' market. You might be frustrated by your lack of control – your reliance on indifferent landlords and apathetic agents, your limited power to decorate and improve your home in ways that meet your needs and express your identity. You may feel understandable fury and envy that you pay more in rent than an owner would on a mortgage for the same property, which rent is gone for ever once it is paid, whereas the landlords who receive it funnel it into their ever-enlarging capital.

The effect of property is possibly positive, if you have watched zeros adding to your fortune, simply through owning something for a long period of time. But even then your pleasure may not be unalloyed. Unearned wealth brings its own anxieties: a lurch in the stomach at the thought that large numbers are at risk, a lurking suspicion that you don't deserve it. You might fear the next crash in prices. And the thing about profit on your home is this: you can't spend it. Or rather, it can generally only be realised if you sell up and move somewhere cheaper, in which case you will be stepping off the property escalator. You and your heirs can only get on again at a lower level. It is a weird sort of wealth that means so little, in practical terms, to those who have it, and so much to those who don't.

You may, if you are an owner, have built your financial planning around your property. It might add to your pension pot. Perhaps you plan to give tax-free portions to your children so that they too can be among the residential haves, not the have-nots. This may be a rational response to your circumstances, but it means that you are now treating your home, with all the personal and emotional significance of that word, as a financial asset. You are made a player in a volatile market, for which you may not have much skill or liking, in order to achieve simple human wishes. Feelings are made into numbers.

You may, if you own, be a good citizen, as conservative politicians have argued that you will be. If you have a stake in society you will strive to maintain it. You may be motivated to behave well and encourage good behaviour in others, to report vandals and troublemakers to the police, to press the local council to keep the street clean. You might become a governor of a local school, to help raise its standards, and support societies dedicated to the betterment of the neighbourhood.

But ownership can also make you selfish. You might oppose wind turbines, or a treatment centre for people who use narcotics, or low-cost housing being built nearby, or indeed any housing that affects your view. You might discourage those whom you consider to be the wrong sort of people from coming to your street. This notional you may even want to exclude people on the grounds of race. In some places, at some times, this is exactly what has happened, with deliberation and method.

You are just as likely to be a good and active citizen if you rent. You don't have to own property to be prejudiced, but property values can multiply pettiness. If the cost of something or someone thought undesirable can be measured in figures – 'it/they will take £50,000 off the value of my property' – it can lend both impetus and bogus justification to excluding them.

If you don't own, but want to do so, the experience may not bring out the best in you. Since you are told that ownership makes good citizens, you may not feel fully part of the society that delivers this message. Or you might be magnanimous enough to overcome discouragement and make selfless contributions to public life. If so, your actions will be despite the conditions in which you live, not because of them.

Wherever you are on property's wheel of chance, you are likely to be powerfully affected by it. In which case you might want to know: what is this idea that is so important? Where did it come from? How does it work? How can it work better?

THE WORLD ACCORDING
TO PROPERTY

1

THE MIRACLE INGREDIENT

> The inhabitants of the English colonies in North-America, by
> the immutable laws of nature, the principles of the English
> constitution, and the several charters or compacts . . . are
> entitled to life, liberty and property.
>
> **Declarations and resolves of the First
> Continental Congress, 1774**

In Kinloch, Missouri, a little over a century ago, a Mrs B and
her husband bought a house. There was nothing unusual about
that: they were acting like countless other citizens of the United
States of America, a country where private property was fundamental to its constitution, economy and self-perception, whose
land was marked from coast to coast by the gridlines of property
boundaries. The nation's philosophy had been captured before
its formation in *Letters from a Farmer in Pennsylvania*, written
in 1767 and 1768 by John Dickinson: 'We cannot be happy,
without being free,' he wrote. 'We cannot be free, without being
secure in our property.'

Kinloch was an attractive but affordable new suburb of St
Louis that was growing up around a streetcar and a railway that
gave easy access to the centre of the city. So there was nothing
unusual about this purchase except that Mr and Mrs B were
black. The theories of freedom, happiness and ownership at the
time of American independence hadn't been constructed with
people like them in mind. Rather, as slaves, they were themselves
viewed as property. But by the turn of the nineteenth century
there had been a civil war, followed by emancipation, and in
theory Mrs and Mr B were entitled to own land.

So they did. They bought the house from some white friends. Then, when white residents discovered the skin colour of their new neighbours, they sold their plots. More black people moved in. *Kinloch, Missouri's First Black City*, a brief history published in 2000, describes what happened next: 'Within a few years, 30 or more black families came to occupy five or six blocks in the extreme southeast portion of the area.' They began to build schools and churches, found businesses, form clubs and associations, start sports teams. 'The good coloured people' of this area, to quote a condescending advertisement published by the Olive Street Terrace Realty Company in 1917, 'have built themselves a little city of which they have a right to be proud'. The term 'city' is used loosely here, but in 1948 Kinloch was incorporated as such.

There were struggles, as in practice black people's entitlement to property was more obstructed than white people's. Resources were limited. Some roads went without paving or street signs for decades. But according to John A. Wright Sr, the author of the history, it was 'a community where neighbours once all knew each other and looked after each other, where children grew up knowing they could be a business owner or an elected official, because they saw those role models every day'. Crime was almost non-existent; doors could be left unlocked. It was 'a place in time where there was hope and an opportunity to dare to dream of unlimited possibilities'. 'You didn't have to leave Kinloch, they had everything,' recalled an ex-resident recently, 'and I'm talking about the nineties.'

This, in a nutshell, is the promise of property. You buy land and build a house, or you buy something already built, and possibly improve it. Confident that the law protects your plot from appropriation, you make a life there. You invest your hopes, effort and money in it. Your neighbours do the same. You share with them

The St. Louis Argus

St. Louis' principal negro newspaper.

And now we are giving land to a certain number of white people of good standing at a nominal price because we believe their money, their influence and their good will are going to help South Kinloch Park.

—

Olive Street Terrace Realty Company

—

LOTS WHITE MEN BUY DOUBLED IN PRICE TO NEGROES

Realty Company Engages to Resell Sites in New South Kinloch Park Subdvision.

Map Showing Kinloch Park's New Negro Subdivision and Its Relation to St. Louis

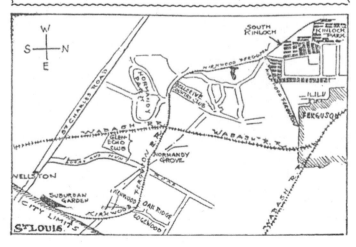

an interest in the well-being of the community, which you help to shape with them. There may also be conflicts with neighbours, but both law and collective interest help to resolve them. Multiplied many times, these actions help to make a town or a city.

Which is a dream pursued and played out times without number.

Consider, for example, the inhabitants of Levittown, New Jersey, a twelve-thousand-house suburban community developed in the 1950s by the private company Levitt and Sons that was entirely composed of homeowners. Then the largest builder in the eastern United States, the Levitts (the company's founder Abraham and his sons William and Alfred) based their success on making house-owning affordable and accessible, often to people who had never owned before, many of them war veterans, through the use of mass-production techniques developed from the construction of navy housing during the Second World War. 'The General Motors of the housing industry', they called themselves, capable of completing one house every sixteen minutes. As with cars, choice was rationalised to a range of models, reflecting the buyers' budgets and wants – the 'Cape Cod', the 'Rancher' and the 'Colonial', their prices ranging from $11,500 to $14,500. At the same time the Levitts wanted to create communities, to which end they provided village greens, neighbourhood shops, swimming pools, playgrounds and schools.

The New Jersey Levittown was the subject of a famous sociological study, *The Levittowners*, published in 1967, whose author Herbert Gans bought a house in the development and lived there with his wife. His aim was to oppose the assumption that life in these new suburbs was as dull and repetitive as the standardised factory-made houses dotted along their endlessly curving roads, described by the urban theorist Lewis Mumford as a 'uniform environment from which escape is impossible'. 'Suburbanites

One of four different styles of the Jubilee

One of four different styles of the Colonial

Levittown — IN 1957

One of five different styles of the Pennsylvanian

One of four different styles of the Country Clubber

SHEET MUSIC AND SONGBOOKS

BRILL BUILDING

were incapable of real friendships,' was how Gans summarised the critique he set out to challenge; 'they were bored and lonely, alienated, atomised and depersonalised.'

Gans found ample evidence for his belief that Levittowns were in fact sociable and lively. New residents, he discovered, made friends, founded or joined voluntary groups and churches, had family lives as successful or otherwise as those of people who lived elsewhere. 'Suburban life', he wrote, 'has produced more family cohesion and a significant boost in morale through the reduction of boredom and loneliness.' Some proclaimed themselves happy with 'quiet things . . . visiting, sitting out front in the summer, having people dropping by'. 'Every weekend a party,' reported one: 'barbecues, picnics, and things like that. I really enjoy it.' 'We have a new house and want to keep it up nice,' said another; 'this is not work but enjoyment. I've never been more content. In the city, we looked forward to going to the shore; here my mind is occupied all the time.'

Similar views are expressed by a fictional character, the narrator of W. D. Wetherell's 1985 short story 'The Man Who Loved Levittown'. 'You talk about dreams,' he said; 'hell, we had ours. We had ours like nobody before or since ever had theirs.' Like Gans's subjects, Wetherell's narrator found community spirit: 'There wasn't anything we wouldn't do for each other. Babysit, drive someone somewhere, maybe help out with a mortgage payment someone couldn't meet.' He was also untroubled by the unexciting architecture of the houses: 'Sure they were little boxes when we first started', but 'the minute we got our mitts on them we started remodelling them, adding stuff, changing them around.'

Again and again, across decades and continents, you can find tales of the bounties of property, the security and prosperity it brings, the joys, the freedoms. A dweller in a London inter-war suburb found that homeowning there 'adds a thrill and zest to life.

It is an experience in having no traditions to live up to.' In 2018 the twenty-six-year-old Pan Jingyuan told *The Economist* that she was planning to buy a flat in Shenzhen so that she could live away from her parents and free herself from traditional expectations of marriage. For other young Chinese people the attraction might be the opposite: a home helps them to attract a spouse, raise a family and shelter their parents in their old age. The point is that property gives them the choice.

Whatever their motivations, these buyers share the belief that property will make them free. It will emancipate them. It will enable them to live their lives as they want. They also believe it to be a good investment – 'There is no way the government would ever let prices really fall,' said Pan. And then these individual blessings breed and multiply until they build cities, power economies, enrich cultures and empower nations.

You could look, for example, at the Brill Building, which the economist Edward Glaeser picks out in *Triumph of the City* as an example of urban creative energy. Close to Times Square in New York, it is an art deco block through whose black granite and brass-garnished portal passed what has been called 'an evolving roster of songwriters, booking agents, vocal coaches, publicity agents, talent agents, and performers', and from which emanated hundreds of hits. At its peak it housed 165 music publishers and related businesses, a competitive-creative hive where the likes of Carole King would, as she put it, be 'squeezed into our respective cubby holes with just enough room for a piano, a bench, and maybe a chair for the lyricist if you were lucky. You'd sit there and write and you could hear someone in the next cubby hole composing a song exactly like yours.' The pressure, she said, 'was really terrific'. It contained clubs where Glenn Miller, Ella Fitzgerald and Dizzy Gillespie performed, and the Turf restaurant, a favourite of Duke Ellington's.

The edifice gave its name to a musical style, the Brill Building Sound. It was the creation of Abraham E. Lefcourt, described at the time of his death in 1932 as 'one of the greatest builders in history since Louis XIV and Sir Christopher Wren', a former newsboy and bootblack who made his first fortune in the garment industry, and who then in a twenty-year career as a property developer led the way in reshaping midtown Manhattan. He was one of the builders, as Glaeser put it, who turned 'the New York of slums, tenements and Gilded Age mansions' into 'a city of skyscrapers'.

Lefcourt wouldn't have intended the Brill Building to make such a contribution to the culture of New York, America and indeed the world. He didn't mean to create the unofficial centre of pop music, as it has been called, in the United States. He had announced, three weeks before the 1929 Wall Street crash, a plan to build the tallest building in the world on this site. Even after the project had been scaled back to a mere eleven storeys, the idea would still have been to house financial businesses there, but the onset of the Great Depression meant that the building was let to whoever could be found, which turned out mostly to mean music businesses. (Nor would Lefcourt, who liked to add his name to his works, have wanted this one to carry that of the Brills, the clothiers and haberdashers from whom he had subleased the site. It seems that, with Lefcourt's business collapsing, the property and the naming rights reverted to them.)

Private property ownership – with its paraphernalia of law and finance, its risks and gambles, its twists of fortune – didn't write the tunes that came out of the Brill Building, but it created the spatial conditions for their creation. It drove the upward expansion of the district, the island and the city around it. It led the way (albeit with help from regulators, planners and public investment) in giving New York its world-famous urban form.

The story keeps repeating. If the developer-led explosion of Manhattan was spectacular in its time, so has been that of Chinese cities in this century, such that China came to have the world's highest rate of home ownership among millennials. A comparable expansion, also based on private property, enabled the population of nineteenth-century London to multiply by nearly six. The serried skyscrapers of one and the brick terraces of the other are only different clothes on the same phenomenon.

The Pennsylvania farmer's point, that freedom and ownership go together, has been repeated over and over. 'Property must be secured or liberty cannot exist,' said John Adams, the second president of the United States. 'A nation of homeowners,' said Franklin Delano Roosevelt, 'of people who own a real share in their land, is unconquerable.' 'You cannot, in my opinion, have a truly open and free society,' said the twentieth-century free-market economist Milton Friedman, without private property. The kind of freedom that it fostered was specifically seen as liberal and capitalist. 'No one who owns his own house and lot', said William Levitt, who took over from his father as the main driving force behind the construction of the Levittowns, 'can be a communist. He has too much to do.'

The liberating power of private property has been seen as a particularly American phenomenon. As George W. Bush said of his Cuban-born housing and urban development secretary Melquiades R. Martinez: 'He understands American values. He's grown to appreciate them. And there's no greater American value than owning something, owning your own home and having the opportunity to do so.' It was a model that other countries wanted to emulate. Meng Xiaosu, a Communist Party member, former Red Guard and president of the China National Real Estate Development Group, put it like this: 'In the 1950s and 1960s, the American dream was to own a private house and a private car.

Now the Chinese have the Chinese dream.'

He said this in 1998. In the same year Yukon Huang, then the chief representative of the World Bank in China, said that 'the most important issue in China today is housing reform. It triggers reform in almost every sector of the economy.' It was a prophetic description of China's prolonged economic boom, in which property development has played a leading role. For prosperity as well as freedom is part of the bounty attributed – often truthfully – to private property.

Nor, in theory, does ownership have to be a privilege only of the better off. Hernando de Soto Polar, a Peruvian economist celebrated by both Margaret Thatcher and Bill Clinton, and a candidate in his country's 2021 presidential elections, has argued that squatters in informal settlements all over the world should be granted legal title to the land they occupy, which would give them freedom and security, and would release (he estimated) $9.3 trillion of untapped capital. If you give slum-dwellers legal title to the land they occupy, he proposed, they can raise loans and build businesses. They will be happier, more secure, more prosperous and better citizens. 'When people have legally documented property and make deals according to accessible laws, they follow the rules.' De Soto's theories have not been entirely borne out in practice, but they express an idea of enduring appeal, the empowerment of the smallholder.

And so private property might help the people of Kinloch to build a community, and the Levittowners to have their barbecues and home improvements, and young Chinese women to dream of independence, and de Soto's squatters to be secure and prosperous. It helped Carole King to write her music and made mighty cities soar. It has made whole countries rich and powerful. And if some of these goods might in theory be achieved under some other dispensation of inhabiting land, private property seems to have done a pretty good job of it. 'The rapturous idea of property' is what a promoter of Kentucky land called it in 1775. Added to the 'beauty and excellence' of the region's undeveloped terrain, it offered 'so glorious a prospect'.

———

The miracle of property, by the time that the people of Kinloch sought it for themselves, had some centuries of practice and theory behind it. The fact that its land was even available to be subdivided and sold to individual property owners was due to the Public Land Survey System, started in the infant years of the American republic, which over decades mapped and appropriated the best part of a continent. The survey enacted the belief of Adams and the other founding fathers of the United States in the liberating power of ownership. They in turn drew on the writings of the seventeenth-century English philosopher John Locke, for whom people had a right to retain whatever they acquired through their labour. 'The great and chief end', Locke also said, of people 'putting themselves under government is the preservation of property.'

Locke lived in a country where the idea of private property – the legally protected right of individuals to hold and dispose of land as they please – had supplanted feudal forms of tenure with an effectiveness unmatched in any other country. Its consequences were phenomenal: the nature of ownership in Britain was a significant reason why industrial and agricultural revolutions happened there first, rather than in other countries also blessed (as Britain was) with natural resources and human skill, such as China or France. Landowners, secure in the knowledge that their property would not be removed, were both incentivised to maximise its profits and confident that the benefits of investment would remain theirs.

Private property ownership in Britain, as one historian puts it, 'brought into existence a widely dispersed, politically powerful, highly capitalised class of property owners. It offered an incentive to obtain profit from the land and from innovation. And most amorphously but recognizably, it fostered a highly personalized, self-motivated outlook on the use to which possessions might be put.'

In agriculture, private ownership – and with it the ability of a single owner to enclose land on which a number of people might previously have had rights of access and use – facilitated more efficient practices, with such things as easier management of livestock, less labour-intensive methods and therefore lower labour costs, and greater incentives for the owners to invest. In industry, security of tenure and the concentration of resources provided the stability needed to pay for the high up-front costs of machinery and factories, on which a return might not be immediate.

'Nothing but real and well-known landed property joined with ministerial connections', wrote one eighteenth-century industrialist to another, was essential to the success of a bank they were proposing to found in Birmingham. The first major canal of what became a national network, which before the railways came was crucial to moving raw materials and goods around the country, was commissioned by the owner of large estates, the Duke of Bridgewater, so he could transport coal from them to the city of Manchester. He secured a loan of £25,000 against his property for the purpose. Early ironworks, leadworks and textile factories, along with the innovative machinery that served them, were also financed against land. It helped too, in the time when water was a bigger source of power than coal, if you had an estate whose rivers could supply free energy to your mills.

Efficient agriculture and productive industry drove people from the countryside to cities, where the mechanisms of private property were the principal provider of homes for the new populations. Thirty to forty per cent of the population of Britain, at the beginning of the nineteenth century, lived in towns, compared with 4 per cent in Russia, 7 per cent in China and 15 per cent in France. The population of London grew from about 750,000 in 1760 to nearly three million in 1860 to 6.5 million in 1901. The lords of the great estates – aristocrats lucky enough to own the rural land into which the capital expanded – grew richer through raising crops of houses on their fields, in the form of the Georgian streets and squares now generally admired for their elegance. The less gracious parts of industrial cities were the work of both large and small landowners, of old families and entrepreneurial speculators, each trying to maximise the opportunities of their roods and acres of land.

Not that protection of individual property should be confused with equality: it was a central aspect of the rise of private property in Britain that it was often achieved through the enclosing of commons and other types of land on which non-owners had had rights for such things as grazing livestock, gathering firewood and collecting building materials – the means of their livelihood – which rights were often brutally removed. Part of the seeming productive miracle of enclosed land came not only from more efficient methods of farming, but also from the transfer of resources from those newly excluded to the private owners.

As those Birmingham industrialists said, legal ownership was not itself enough to make property truly lucrative. Landowners also benefited from their political connections and clout, through which they could get the legislation passed which would entitle them to enclose land – and four thousand 'Inclosure Acts' were passed by the British Parliament between 1700 and 1830 – or (as was the case with the Duke of Bridgewater and his canal) would enable them compulsorily to purchase land they didn't own for the purposes of their projects.

And, if developments in farming meant that the average English family was better fed and better off than its counterparts elsewhere in Europe, enclosures and land clearances also created a class of the dispossessed. People who had lived off land that was now in the exclusive control of single owners became vagabonds, subject to severe punishments for the crime of having been deprived of the means of their existence. This established a pattern that continues to be a feature: although there is nothing in the theory of private property that says it must inevitably create extreme consequences for those excluded from it, such consequences repeatedly occur. These historical English experiences also established the poles of debates about property ever since: on the one hand the manifest cruelty of expulsion and exclusion, on the other the argument that such things are regrettable but necessary prerequisites for the prosperity and freedoms that accrue from private property.

From the seventeenth century on, England exported its property formulas to its North American colonies, a territory far less constricted and constrained than the small island of the old country. (And the process of colonisation was accelerated by those dispossessed by enclosure in their homeland, who arrived either as transported convicts, or as desperate seekers after new livelihoods.) These formulas included the idea that land that seemed to belong to no one in particular, or was held in common, might be enclosed and cultivated or built on by those with the energy, will and might to do so. Here the clear losers were the native inhabitants of the continent, who, despite periodic hand-wringing about their plight, were over the centuries progressively displaced.

The liberty and happiness arising from the 'preservation' or 'securing' of property, of which Locke and Adams wrote, was, then, more to the benefit of some than of others. It is clear that, for the framers of the United States constitution, the concept of 'freedom' was mostly for white property-owning males. In the early United States, indeed, you had to own property (as well as be white and male) to be able to vote. In Great Britain the right to vote was subject to property qualifications until 1918 (for men) and 1928 (for women).

It should also be noted that property requires government. Enthusiasts for the small state, for whom private property is usually a hallowed concept, have to make it the one exception to their belief in freedom from government interference. In practice public entities – like the Birmingham industrialists' ministerial connections, and the obliging legislators who assisted the Duke of Bridgewater's canal – repeatedly intervene on behalf of landowners and potential buyers. The division of the North American continent into private lots by the Public Land Survey System is a spectacular example of this. The Levittowns, apparent beacons of free enterprise, owed their 'very existence,' as Colin Marshall put it in the *Guardian*, 'to a rare act of American socialism: the 1948 Housing Bill, which loosened billions of dollars in credit and gave every American the chance to get one of those five-percent-down, 30-year mortgages in the first place'.

The alliance of property with political power, and the assumption that ownership was only for whites, did not disappear with the emancipation of black slaves. If black people were now in theory allowed to play the property game, in practice the rules were stacked against them. They were forbidden from buying in many areas. They found it hard or impossible to get loans. The practice of 'redlining', whereby financial institutions denied mortgages and insurance in districts designated as black, was commonplace. The Home Owners' Loan Corporation, a federal agency designed to protect homeowners from eviction during the Great Depression, would later develop a rating system that would grade white districts higher than black, which shaped both house prices and potential buyers' ability to raise mortgages.

The instrument of eminent domain, the compulsory purchase by government of large tracts of land for developments supposedly in the public good, was wielded disproportionately against black neighbourhoods. In the 1950s, for example, the District of Columbia Redevelopment Land Agency wiped out much of the south-western quadrant of Washington, dislocating twenty thousand predominantly black residents. The area suffered from 'blight', they said, using a vague, much-used and easily weaponised term; the clearances were necessary for 'renewal'.

And homes in the Levittowns of New Jersey, New York and Pennsylvania, celebrated by Gans for their friendly neighbourliness, came with the condition that their residents 'agree not to permit the premises to be used or occupied by any person other than members of the Caucasian race'. After this clause was struck down in court as unconstitutional, William Levitt continued to operate a de facto whites-only policy.

When in 1957 a black middle-class war veteran and his wife, William and Daisy Myers, managed to buy a house in the Pennsylvania Levittown, they and their children faced threats, violence and angry mobs gathered outside their house, both by day and at night, throwing stones through windows and burning eight-foot crosses in their yard. Confederate flags were waved from a daily parade of cars past their home. Confederate anthems were blasted out. If post-war American suburbia 'offered growing families a private haven in a heartless world', as the urban historian Kenneth Jackson put it in his 1985 book *Crabgrass Frontier*, such peace and security was very much more available to some than to others.

In Kinloch black residents' pursuit of the American dream encountered obstacles that would ultimately prove insurmountable. From the beginning banks wouldn't accept their credit notes as collateral, which caused the realty company that owned the plots to set up a scheme whereby white citizens could buy plots, underwrite the credit and sell them on to black buyers, who would have to pay double or more what the whites had paid. The banks got the collateral they wanted, the realty company sold the lots and the white intermediaries made a handsome profit. The blacks got their houses, but at inflated prices.

In 1938 a new municipality, Berkeley, was set up by whites unhappy at sharing schools with blacks. This move made Kinloch into a racial peninsula, surrounded on three sides, and reduced the tax base from which schools and roads might be funded. But the heaviest blow came from the hand of eminent domain. In the 1980s the City of St Louis started buying up and emptying land in Kinloch, as part of a noise abatement programme for the nearby St Louis Lambert International Airport, which destroyed most of the private homes in the city, made businesses unsustainable and devastated the community.

In 2014 the neighbouring city of Ferguson, which joins Kinloch on the side where it is not encircled by Berkeley, achieved unwelcome fame for the fatal police shooting of the eighteen-year-old Michael Brown and subsequent unrest. Much was made of Ferguson's dangers and poverty, but 'compared to Kinloch', according to a *Vice* reporter who went there in 2015, 'it's absolutely thriving'. The first black city in Missouri was, he said, 'in danger of falling off the map – literally. A whole grid of streets in the southwest part of town are unlabelled on Google Maps. When you take a real-life trip to visit them, you see power lines and paved streets there, but the homes are now rubble, and wilderness has overtaken nearly everything.' Ferguson's population had dropped from ten thousand to fewer than three hundred. Once there were 'barber shops, chicken shacks, pharmacies, a YMCA, turkey farms, and even a cab company. B. B. King played a club here, called 12 Oaks, before it closed in the 50s. But now, beyond a salvage yard and an auto body shop, Kinloch doesn't have a single business, according to its city manager.'

It was a terrible outcome for a place in which so much aspiration and courage had – for a while successfully – been invested. But its failure does not disprove the miracle-making powers of property. Rather, through negative example, it affirms them. What went wrong at Kinloch was the deprivation of the full rights, protections and freedoms of property as imagined by John Locke, the founding fathers and any number of philosophical, economic and political champions of private ownership.

At the same time the Kinloch story demonstrates an important truth about property. It is not, as its greatest enthusiasts claim, automatically benign, unlocking prosperity and freedom wherever it goes. It is rather a tool, an instrument, a weapon, capable of great things for those who can wield it, but also of inflicting damage on those who find themselves on the wrong side of it.

It embodies a classic liberal dilemma: if you believe in freedom and prosperity and opportunity for all, achieved through the unfettered operations of private ownership and enterprise, how can this belief be reconciled with outcomes of manifest injustice? Are they just regrettable necessities, unavoidable collateral damage?

This is not a remote historical question but one that affects billions of daily lives today. The last forty years have seen private property become an ever more powerful force – socially, economically and politically – in the world's largest and richest countries. A pioneer of this tendency was the British prime minister Margaret Thatcher, whose pursuit of what she called the 'property-owning democracy' was a defining feature of her career.

Her government successfully brought home ownership to millions who would not previously have thought it possible. It helped make fortunes, large and small. But her ideas and policies, as continued by other governments in Britain and elsewhere, have also created new inequalities based on tenure. They have come to defeat their own stated objectives: rates of ownership have gone into reverse, dividing society into those who own and those who have little hope of doing so.

2

THE PROPERTY-OWNING
DEMOCRACY

Imagine a country where homeless individuals and young families are sent to live in office blocks badly converted into homes, some in high slabs, some located in business parks, surrounded by polluting and dangerous roads, far from shops and public transport, in flats so small that, according to one mother, 'My eldest daughter has to read her school books in the toilet so she doesn't wake the little one.' Where children arrive at school exhausted by their long journeys there, and where they are stigmatised for where they live. 'Office-block kids', they are called.

In which drug dealers trade and fight in the corridors and lobbies on the other side of flimsy front doors. Where it is too dangerous to play among the turning trucks in the industrial roads that make up the external space and where infestations of rodents make parents nervous to leave their children to play on the floor inside. Where families are housed in shipping containers, stifling in summer and freezing in winter, a rain of condensation falling on them every night. Where a family with four young children might be rehoused thirteen times in eighteen weeks. Or where an estimated two hundred thousand children live under threat of eviction and 125,000 live in temporary accommodation. All with consequences for mental health, education, physical health, employment prospects and all-round well-being. In the same country it has been legal for developers to build homes that have no windows or that are, at thirteen square metres, little bigger than a standard parking place. If you have a job, you might in the worst cases have to spend 60 per cent of your income on rent. If you are old and rent you might be among the 25 per cent who live in fear of losing your home. If you are in an abusive relationship you might find it impossible to escape. If you are in theory well off, say a professional aged forty, you might still have no prospect of owning your own home, and face a lifetime renting overpriced, poor-quality and insecure accommodation.

You might postpone starting or enlarging a family, perhaps indefinitely, if you can't afford the space for children. Housing markets, according to a study for the Adam Smith Institute, 'have substantial effects on fertility: rising house prices may boost fertility for homeowners, but slash fertility amongst renters – between 1996 and 2014 157,000 children were not born due to the cost of living space . . . If current trends are maintained we may expect fertility to fall even further.'

The average new home costs many times annual average earnings. If you're not helped out by your parents, and don't have inherited wealth, you'll be hard pressed to get on the first rung of the property ladder, a construction that has become as unreal as a magic beanstalk. In which case, pretty stories of homemaking told in movies and media and advertising are a cruel joke.

This country is Britain, fifth or sixth richest in the world, depending on which measure you use. It is a place where the romance of houses and gardens is strong, where the Englishman's home is reportedly his castle, a country famous for its domestic architecture. The British inventions of the garden suburb and the Georgian townhouse have been exported around the world, and you can find Tudor manors, country houses, Scottish castles or arts-and-crafts cottages in California and Shanghai and Buenos Aires. In 1904 a German architect and diplomat thought new British houses so exemplary that he published a book, *Das englische Haus*, so that his own country might learn from them. In 1934 a Danish architect, Steen Eiler Rasmussen, wrote that 'the one-family house, open-air life and all that we others admire and are fain to imitate, is inseparable from the English mode of thought of life'.

Rasmussen dreamt of a 'Town of the Future', inspired by English examples, made up of houses and gardens where 'children can be out of doors and enjoy the sun and air as soon as they can notice anything at all. They crawl about in the grass, stand up and try to touch the flowers, birds and insects, make unintelligible remarks to them, and try their strength in a hundred harmless ways.' The same gardens would give adults 'exercise and relaxation after the drudgery of the day, the joy of creating'. They would 'provide space for a healthy development – right up until the old people are led out into the garden for the last time that they may drink in the sun and air, the songs of the birds and the scent of flowers, just the same as the tiniest human being'. He described precisely those joys and fulfilments from which millions are now excluded.

Britain is also the country that has led the world, these last forty years, in a social, political and economic experiment called the 'property-owning democracy'. It was based on the idea that property would make you a better and happier person. It responded to the simple, reasonable and powerful desire of very many people to own their own home. The property-owning democracy would make you prosperous. It would set you free.

The phrase was coined in 1923, by the Conservative Member of Parliament Noel Skelton, for whom private property was a kind of magic potion. Its benefits were economic, moral, social and political, and worked to the good of both individuals and the state. 'The beneficent effect upon human character,' he wrote, 'both of the effort to acquire private property and of the opportunity, after it has been acquired, for its wise or foolish use, can hardly be over-estimated.' Ownership, he said, gives a 'sense of

responsibility, a wider economic outlook, a practical medium for the expression of moral and intellectual qualities'. The wage-earner 'appreciates the security and economic freedom which the possession of private property gives'. The 'stability of the State' depended on 'the possession of private property by the people'.

There was, for Skelton, an urgent need to counter the 'intellectual appeal' of socialism with a Conservative 'view of life, a statement of fundamental principles'. There was, he believed, a new era, shaped by universal education and suffrage, in which the economic emancipation of widespread ownership lagged behind. He therefore proposed that workers should be made co-partners in the companies for which they worked, or at least share in their profits, and that farm workers should be enabled to acquire small holdings of land.

This was, for the Conservative Party of the 1920s, radical. Skelton's dream of worker-shareowners and agricultural smallholders never became a central part of Conservative policy. His concept, however, was picked up by the future prime minster Anthony Eden, who in 1946 spoke of 'the distribution of ownership over the widest practicable number of individuals'. The phrase 'property-owning democracy' remained in use, until it was dusted off and polished up by Margaret Thatcher, prime minister from 1979 to 1990, for whom it became a defining statement of her philosophy. She used it in her first conference speech as leader of the Conservative Party in 1975, and in her last as prime minister in the House of Commons.

Like Skelton she spoke of the liberating and transformative qualities of property. Her support of private ownership was, she said, a 'crusade to enfranchise the many in the economic life of the nation'. 'Ownership', said one of her ministers, Michael Heseltine, 'stimulates the attitudes of independence and self-reliance that are the bedrock of a free society.' Thatcher also shifted from

Skelton's interest in the workplace: her version of the property-owning democracy was focused on the home. With home went family, which gave another moral pillar to her idea of property.

'The family is the basic unit of our society,' she said in 1981, 'and it is in the family that the next generation is nurtured. Our concern is to create a property-owning democracy and it is therefore a very human concern. It is a natural desire of Conservatives that every family should have a stake in society and that the privilege of a family home should not be restricted to the few.' A good society, she suggested, depended on good family life, which in turn depended on – or at least was greatly helped by – private home ownership. And Thatcher's policies were effective. From 1980 to 1990 rates of home ownership in Britain rose from 55 per cent to 67 per cent of households. Millions of people could fulfil their dreams of owning their own home. The effects were transformative, liberating, empowering.

Her most famous housing policy was 'right to buy', under which tenants of 'council houses' – public housing let at subsidised social rents – could buy their homes at discounts of up to 70 per cent. The proceeds would go back to the Treasury; the local authorities who had owned them could not invest in their replacements. In this way 1.5 million homes were transferred from public to private ownership between 1980 and 1990. One of the first was 39 Amersham Road, Harold Hill, Essex, where Thatcher was photographed handing over the keys to its tenants-turned-owners, Maureen and James Patterson. 'She was an icon to me,' said Ms Patterson, years later, 'she was a lovely guest. I gave her a guided tour and she said, 'This is not just a house – it's a home.' I was so proud. She had Downing Street and Chequers but no. 39 was just as special to me.'

Thatcher's government deregulated and liberalised mortgage markets, for example pushing back against lending limits, which together with her political rhetoric enabled and encouraged people to buy homes, financing them with mortgage debt. There was an incentive to spend as much as possible on your home – the more you invested, the greater the return, so long as prices kept rising – which both pushed buyers to the limit of their abilities to borrow and drove up prices, which created yet more reason to borrow and buy.

You were pushed, in pursuit of the simple human desire for a place you could call your own, to become a micro-tycoon, to bet on the fluctuations of the market, to wheel and deal, to leverage your assets, to expose yourself to risk. Some took to it, some didn't – there is no reason why a teacher or a factory worker or an office administrator should also have the skills of an amateur property speculator. Among the losers were the Pattersons of Amersham Road, who could no longer afford their mortgage repayments when interest rates went up. The stress helped to end their marriage, they sold the house, and after staying for a while with her sons Maureen Patterson went to live in a mobile home.

––––––––

In general Thatcher's government prided itself on fighting inflation, inflicting heavy costs on employment and growth in order to bring the annual rate down from 14 per cent to 5 per cent. But with property it was different: the price of the average home trebled during her eleven-year term. Owners could make as much money (on paper at least) watching the value of their homes go up as they could from their salaried jobs. Inflation, when it came to homes, was to be celebrated. It was a sign of economic virility. Tabloid front pages started trumpeting price increases, as they have continued to do until recently. As late as 2014 a Conservative housing minister would celebrate inflation:

'I bought a house and I expect the value to rise,' he told a BBC presenter, 'and I'm sure you did as well.' It was natural, part of the order of things, that prices should go up.

Inflation made homeowners feel good, both prosperous and clever, and inclined to push their luck by investing still more heavily – buying a bigger home or a second home, or enlarging what they had. It made people who didn't own ever more desperate to do so. The straight line of the property ladder curved 360 degrees into what the social geographer Danny Dorling called a 'hamster wheel', on which buyers had to run faster and faster to keep up. A phenomenon became commonplace, that of regarding your home as an investment, of making the haven of everything dearest into an abstract calculation, of blurring the distinction between what economists call its 'use value' and its 'market value'. This phenomenon has never gone away.

Property became a Ponzi scheme, reliant on ever-increasing prices and on continuous input of funds from newcomers at the bottom of the expanding pyramid. It became an addiction, not only for individual homeowners but for the economy as a whole. Mortgage debt, as a proportion of income, grew. Financial institutions made lending to residential property an ever larger part of their portfolios. Governments became reliant on the tax revenues that came with property-based wealth. In a 2017 book, *Rethinking the Economics of Land and Housing*, the authors describe 'a feedback loop, with ever-rising house prices and ever-increasing household debt making our economy highly vulnerable to economic shocks'. For whatever was the case in the 1980s became more so later, albeit with hiccups along the way.

There are also crashes, as Ponzi schemes eventually fail. These might be seen as necessary adjustments, as evidence that the markets are successfully correcting themselves. If it's a problem that prices are high, then falls should be beneficial. But in practice crashes hit hardest those owners least able to withstand them – those who arrived late at the house inflation party, failed to build up the value of their property, maxed out their debt, took on mortgages they were stretched to afford or unexpectedly lost their jobs. And if prices fall because buyers are less able to afford them (because the employment market has worsened, or because interest rates have gone up) then home ownership is no more accessible than it was before.

In the recession of the early 1990s, just after the end of Thatcher's time in office, house prices fell, pushing a million or more of the eager new converts to ownership into negative equity, where their homes were worth less than the loans they had raised to pay for them. Repossessions rose: 345,000 homeowners lost the sure-fire investments that they had been so strongly encouraged to acquire a few years previously. They were ejected from those nests in which they might have nurtured the wholesome family life celebrated by Thatcher. Heseltine's 'bedrock' crumbled. Their tickets to being full members of the property-owning democracy were torn up.

Yet the inflation of the Thatcher period proved only to be a prelude for three more decades in which her model continued to be pushed by governments of both right and centre left. The Labour governments of Tony Blair and Gordon Brown, as Thatcher's Conservative administration had done, fuelled the economy and the exchequer with the debt raised on increasing property prices. Upward pressure was intensified by the restricted supply of land: Britain is a densely populated country, especially in the prosperous south-east, with a complex planning system designed (among other things) to protect the countryside from development. The system also tends to protect the interests of existing homeowners against construction that might harm the value of their property, such as new homes appearing in their view. It can be difficult, expensive and risky to get permission for new development, for which reason (and some others) the number of homes built per year repeatedly falls below the targets set by government.

Values trebled between Blair's coming to power in 1997 and 2007. The early 1990s recession became a dimly remembered blip. The same period saw the rise of 'buy to let', whereby private individuals became landlords, buying homes as investments, seeking high returns both from the rents paid by their tenants and from the rising value of their properties. Margaret Thatcher had relaxed rent restrictions in 1988, making it easier to evict tenants, which, when combined with both generous tax incentives and helpful mortgage products offered by banks to individual investors, made this proposition hard to resist. Why would you not take advantage if you could? By 2014 there were almost two million such landlords owning 4.9 million properties, with a combined value of nearly £1 trillion. But the buy-to-let phenomenon fuelled yet more inflation, and made it still harder for those outside the magic circle of ownership to get inside.

Meanwhile, in the United States, parallel property speculations flourished, most notably the plays on sub-prime mortgages that led to the 2008 crash. But not even this financial catastrophe could permanently alter the trajectory in Britain: according to *Rethinking the Economics of Land and Housing* the economy was now too much hooked on high land values to allow them to crash, so both government and banks worked to make sure they didn't. It wasn't until 2013 that prices regained their 2007 levels, but it remained the policy of the government (by now led by Conservatives) to boost private property ownership by whatever means necessary. So powerful was the mystique of the homeowning market that it was inconceivable, if it wasn't working well, to consider alternatives. The only option was to inject it with performance-enhancing financial drugs. Nothing could be imagined except more and more and more of the same.

So in 2013 the British government introduced 'help to buy', whereby it lent buyers up to 20 per cent of the equity of their homes (40 per cent in London), interest-free for five years. The idea was to help people access properties they wouldn't otherwise have been able to buy, but the policy had the predictable effect of boosting housebuilders' profits and pushing up prices still more. The housebuilders Persimmon, who by 2019 sold almost half their homes with the support of help to buy, nearly tripled their profit on each home between 2013 and 2018. In 2017 they awarded their chief executive Jeff Fairburn a bonus of £110 million, later reduced after a public outcry to £75 million. In 2019 they reported annual profits of £1 billion, the first British housebuilder to do so. Help to buy also made the government into a stakeholder in the property market, with an interest in continued inflation: should prices fall, it was in danger of not getting its loans repaid.

Quantitative easing and low interest rates, measures introduced to stimulate the post-crash economy, had the side effect of increasing the attractiveness of property as an investment asset, with a further upward push on inflation. Foreign capital, seeing British property as a safe haven, also poured in. From 2013 to 2019 prices rose by 40 per cent. During the early days of the COVID-19 outbreak in 2020 the government boosted the market again, by reducing tax on transactions, with a resulting jump in prices. Over the whole forty years of the grand Thatcher property experiment the prices of houses have outstripped earnings. In the 1980s the average house price was three or four times average annual income – to be more than that was considered a sign of dangerous overheating. In 1997 the figure was still 3.5. By 2021 it was 9.1, and more in parts of London.

All of which was good news if you were old enough and lucky enough to get on the property escalator early. A house bought in 1980 could, in parts of London, be worth twenty, thirty or forty times as much by 2020. In Bishops Avenue, a North London street sometimes called 'billionaires' row', where houses could be bought for £1 million in the 1980s, prices reached £65 million by 2014. This long boom was less wonderful if you were aspiring to grasp your first morsel of ownership, to stop burning a large part of your income as rent and start putting it into something you could have for life.

Eventually the property-owning democracy started to eat itself. Home ownership in the UK reached a peak of 73 per cent in the mid-noughties, since when it has declined to 63 per cent. As the economist and journalist Liam Halligan points out in his 2019 book *Home Truths*, this figure puts Britain, the promised land of home ownership, behind the EU, the USA, Canada and Australia. The legendary 'Englishman's home', for an increasing proportion of the population, is now an insecure and inadequate privately rented flat. Rasmussen's word-pictures of domestic gardens, where people from the tiniest to the oldest could drink in the sun and air, the songs of the birds and the scent of flowers, have become for many a distant fantasy.

This decline was particularly marked among young adults, who, according to Halligan, 'have less chance of owning than any post-war generation'. In 1996 one in ten thirty-year-olds were privately renting; by 2019 the figure was four in ten. They were also paying more for the privilege – approaching 30 per cent of income on average, compared with the 15 per cent paid by baby boomers – and for worse conditions. The result is what he calls 'limiting life chances'. Where in 1996 8 per cent of babies had been born to parents in private rented accommodation, that figure rose to 40 per cent two decades later – rarely out of choice but because there were no other options. The 'nurturing' of the next generation of which Thatcher spoke, to which home ownership was so important, would be that much more difficult. The mutual support of your own family and your own home would be denied. People as hard-working and as responsible as a previous generation would, through no fault of their own but the timing of their birth, be shut out from the benefits that Thatcher had considered so important to full membership of democracy.

But the dysfunction of the market in buying and selling houses is only half the story. The other is the decline in publicly funded social housing. 'Council housing', as it was called, was built in the post-war decades at rates of up to two hundred thousand homes per year. The numbers fell almost to zero in the 1980s after Margaret Thatcher took away local authorities' ability to fund them. Housing associations – not-for-profit organisations that provide affordable homes, usually with the help of government support – increased their output, but at nothing like the numbers once provided by local authorities. Meanwhile homes sold under right to buy depleted the stock available at affordable rents. The outcome of all these factors was that the number of socially rented homes fell from over 31 per cent of the total in 1979 to 21 per cent in 2021.

A perverse outcome of these changes, which were carried out in the name of shrinking the state and reducing public spending, was that the government's bill for housing benefit – the payments made to people who otherwise could not afford a home – shot up. As the number of publicly owned homes shrunk, more benefit had to be paid to private landlords, who as property prices rose could charge ever higher rents. In an attempt to cut these costs the Conservative-led coalition government of 2010–15 placed limits on the amounts tenants could receive – which, given high rents, meant that some could no longer afford their homes. The government also introduced the under-occupancy charge or 'bedroom tax', whereby any recipient of housing benefit who was deemed to have a spare room would receive lower payments.

As predicted by housing charities, these changes pushed up homelessness. The number of households living in temporary accommodation in England rose from 48,240 in 2011 to 94,780 in 2022. Local authorities in London resorted to increasingly desperate measures to find homes for the unintentionally homeless whom they are obliged by law to house, for example sending them to distant locations where they would be cut off from friends, family and prospects of employment.

Thus anyone seeking a home, unless they had a high income or access to significant amounts of capital, found themselves stranded between two vanishing sources of shelter. On the one hand home ownership was being priced out of reach; on the other hand publicly subsidised housing was receding, which left paying rent to private landlords as the only alternative.

This is a social, political and economic failure of colossal proportions. It creates individual frustration and misery. It stultifies mobility. It nullifies any increase in your standards of living, if with your largest single item of expenditure, rent, you are paying more for – in terms of size and quality – less. It creates generational divisions, between those lucky enough to get early onto the property escalator of the last forty years and those who were not. It creates social divisions between those who can be helped by their parents (who might well have been among the aforementioned lucky winners) and those who cannot. It creates regional divisions, between areas of high and low property values.

Such problems have been obvious for a long time. 'There is, to put it simply, a shortage of adequate housing for the demand now being placed on the capital,' I wrote in the London *Evening Standard*, in 1999. 'It is a crisis that damages lives, affects relationships, chokes business and threatens the smooth running of the capital. It burdens the city's transport systems with people commuting long distances from cheap areas to their places of work, and means schools and hospitals can't find the teachers and nurses they need.' In 2004 the economist Kate Barker, in a report commissioned by the Treasury, predicted 'problems of homelessness, affordability and social division, decline in standards of public service delivery and increasing the costs of doing business in the UK – hampering our economic success'.

'House prices are currently the main obstacle to stable family life and stable parenting,' said Alan from Sheffield, an interviewee in a BBC vox pop in October 2007. 'Home ownership, once seen as a ladder out of poverty,' wrote the columnist Hugo Rifkind in 2013, for the right-wing magazine *The Spectator*, 'has become a millstone of the middle. It's where all our money goes, meaning that it can't go anywhere else.' By 2016 the Conservative prime minister Theresa May had got the message: 'High housing costs – and the growing gap between those on the property ladder and those who are not – lie at the heart of falling social mobility, falling savings and low productivity.'

But, throughout the years and decades in which these issues have been apparent, government has failed to address them, preferring to use its power and resources to push up prices still higher. The well-founded warnings of economists and people in the street and journalists and experts, and the intermittent acknowledgement of such warnings by politicians, have achieved more or less nothing. Rather, the problems that could be spotted a quarter-century ago have mostly got worse.

A fundamental reason for the lack of change is what Liam Halligan calls the 'iron triangle' of vested interests. One corner is made up of a few large companies that build most of the new houses in Britain, another of the individual homeowners who still make up the majority of the electorate, the third of the banking sector, three-quarters of whose outstanding UK bank loans are property-related. All have an interest in seeing property values continue to rise.

So reasoned proposals for stabilising prices, or for such things as a public housebuilding programme to complement that of the private sector, founder. In 2020 the prime minister Boris Johnson announced that his government would 'help turn generation rent into generation buy, not by endlessly expanding the state, but by giving power back to people – the fundamental life-affirming power of home ownership, the power to decide what colour to paint your own front door'. He was right that many people would love to own if they could, but his proposals had nothing for those who cannot. His main idea – to support low-interest and low-deposit mortgages – would, like help to buy, only increase the value of houses and therefore be self-defeating. Again, the only cure on offer for the addiction to house price inflation is yet more of the same drug.

There are physical and human effects to these failures. The average new-built home in Britain is smaller than at any time since reliable records began in the 1930s. In a period that has seen unimaginable transformations in the quality and affordability of cars, of technology, of entertainment, of access to good food and cheap clothes and foreign travel, in which almost every necessity and pleasure has become better and more accessible, with more choice, new-built homes for sale have gone in the opposite direction.

———

Older readers may remember the hundred-foot Stay Puft Marshmallow Man in *Ghostbusters*, the animated giant of white goo that endangered New York in the 1984 film. The property-owning democracy has become similar, something once sweet and likeable bloated into a life-threatening monster. At its most grotesque it creates the world in which children have to live in office blocks and do their homework in toilets, and play in car parks and on industrial access roads. For here an extreme form of free-market ideology has combined with the rise in homelessness to toxic effect.

It started with some reports by the right-wing think tank Policy Exchange in 2011 and 2012. What, their bright sparks wondered, if the planning system was deregulated, such that owners of office buildings could convert them into flats without going through the usual procedures of applying for planning permission? Local authorities would have no power to stop them, or to insist on minimum standards for the size of rooms and flats, or push for good design, or receive the contributions to such things as affordable housing and street improvements that developers usually pay when they are given planning permission.

'No one is going to mind if an office becomes a home,' said Policy Exchange. 'We need to systematically change the planning system. Our current planning system, designed as part of a socialist utopia in the 1940s, has to be modernised for a 21st-century economy.' Leading figures in Policy Exchange got jobs in David Cameron's government, and in 2013 their ideas became law.

The effects were predictable. Developers made flats as small as possible, some barely larger than the 11.5 m^2 British standard car parking space. Some, until the government closed this particular loophole, had no windows. Conversions were as basic as possible. There was little or no attempt to domesticate the pre-cast concrete or the glass panels of old office buildings, to modify the window types or the exteriors such that they were more suitable to people's homes.

These conversions would go wherever there was under-used office space, which might be nowhere near a residential area. Often they were in satellites of London, some of them towns built or expanded after the Second World War – Harlow, Crawley, Croydon – where the 1960s had left a legacy of under-used and ageing office stock. And so came into being places like Shield House in Harlow, whose residents found themselves 'really isolated' (as one said), forty minutes from schools or shops and other places of habitation, in mould-prone flats whose large windows – suitable for offices but not homes – caused overheating in summer and cold in winter, where it was hard to get away from the 'shouting and arguing' in the narrow corridors, where dwellers on the ground floor, looking onto the car park, were too frightened to open their windows at night.

Developers made these places because they could, and because they could make more money that way. Permitted development (as this policy was called) was in effect a free gift from government to the owners of such blocks, many of whom saw their values double as a result. One justification was choice: if people wanted to spend less on rent by living in such a flat, why shouldn't they? 'People are actually choosing to come here,' said the manager of one such block, by way of defence against accusations that it was a 'human warehouse'.

The other justification was numbers. In 2018 the policy was said to be a 'strong success' on the basis that in the previous year the creation of tiny units in old office blocks had pushed the number of 'new homes' over the government's target of 200,000. All questions of quality or suitability, or of providing the kinds of homes that were most needed, were sacrificed to meeting a somewhat arbitrary official number.

It is a poor response to house price inflation to encourage smaller and lousier flats. It hardly addresses the underlying causes. And the libertarian argument – 'if you don't like it you don't have to live there' – ignored the fact that many people had no choice. Thanks to the decline of social rented housing, local authorities resorted to increasingly desperate means to house homeless people in their territory. Several London boroughs despatched them to converted office blocks in places like Harlow and Crawley. If they refused, they would be deemed to have made themselves intentionally homeless, in which case they would lose their rights to be housed.

So they were removed from the support networks of family and friends: it might take a round trip of three or four hours, plus hard-to-afford train fares, to visit them. Some had to take their children out of school. 'It's like an open prison,' said a man moved from Newham in London to Harlow in Essex. 'I've been in prison so I know. It's hard, hard, man, very. I don't know no one, there ain't much to do round here artistically and culturally. It's a different kind of area, hardcore Essex.'

Some had problems with mental health, or substance abuse, or criminal records, or were escaping domestic abuse, none of them problems created by the office-block conversions, but which could be made considerably worse by the cramped and sometimes isolated places that were created. The policy also put the property companies that owned the converted office blocks into a role for which they were ill suited, that of caring for their sometimes troubled tenants.

'People treat us like we're a support service and we're not,' said the manager of several blocks in Harlow. 'The biggest issue is we shouldn't have to do what we do, truthfully we shouldn't, and if there was enough social housing we wouldn't have to be news.' But there was news. TV and newspapers recounted disturbing tales of what they called 'rabbit hutches'. Ex-employees of property companies reported that, for example, if people didn't have drug problems when they arrived at these densely populated blocks, the amount of dealing inside meant that many of them soon did. 'There were two instances', said one, 'where babies were taken off their mothers because they had overdoses.' A woman with mental health issues, agoraphobic, uprooted and stranded and unable to go out to register with a local doctor and get medication, killed herself.

In the 1980s, when Margaret Thatcher attacked council housing, she drew on a widespread backlash against the failings – some real, some perceived – of the public building programmes of the previous decades: tower blocks, 'concrete monstrosities', 'sink estates'. Not all council housing was in fact in the form of towers, nor made of concrete, and whether or not it was, it was often successful at providing decent homes. Most council estates did not become sinks. None of it was as mean and shabby and damaging as the worst of the office-block conversions formed in the name of deregulated free enterprise.

Despite these well-documented horrors, ministers declared the policy a triumph and, in 2020, decided to expand it. It would now be possible not only to convert office blocks into flats, but also to knock them down and rebuild them. The government did at least promise to ban windowless flats (it was hardly a mark of a civilised country that they were ever possible) and to insist that flats be a bit bigger than parking spaces. Over other issues of quality and location there would still be little control.

Certain assumptions underlie the concept of permitted development. One is that homes are like any other product – vacuum cleaners or tins of tomatoes or underwear – and can be traded in a free market. If the market doesn't work well, the only conceivable option is to deregulate, to free up supply to meet demand. The other assumption is that high property prices are natural. If the only way to make a home affordable is to make it tiny and shoddy, that is considered part of the order of things. The economic model that created this situation is not called into question, but treated as invisible and inevitable.

But homes are not like tins of tomatoes. They require land. The supply of land, especially in a crowded island like Britain, is restricted. This is why there is a planning system – to manage this finite resource and to mitigate conflicts that might arise from competing interests within this limited space. It is a fantasy to think that planning can be deregulated into non-existence. It will always be there. Existing landowners, whose property is protected against sudden shocks by planning, would be among the first to complain if it were removed.

Land is not portable. It cannot be put in a truck and driven to a supermarket. It cannot, on the whole, be manufactured. It is also spoken for, its owners registered and protected by law, its boundaries defined. Thanks to house price inflation, which is really land price inflation, it is hard for newcomers to access it.

High prices are not natural or inevitable. They are made by policy, which reflects political interests. Different policies would produce different prices. Nor is property ownership itself natural. It is a human device for organising land, often useful and effective, but not unique or unalterable.

The current concept of the property-owning democracy assumes otherwise: it tends to take it for granted that the market in land is open and free and that whatever prices follow from it cannot be questioned. Perhaps, too, high prices are thought a reward for the wisdom (or, rather, luck) of those who invested early. For very many people the consequences of these misconceptions are the opposite of the emancipation and civic virtues of which Noel Skelton dreamt, and which Margaret Thatcher and her ministers promised. They create frustration and division, not freedom and cohesion. The plight of the office-block kids, shocking in itself, is an extreme sign of a larger failure.

The peaks and troughs of the property market also have powerful effects on heads and hearts. Its magical bounties – sometimes unexpected, in some senses unearned – can make its recipients defensive. Their gains, having come easily, might easily go. So they want to fortify and amplify them. For those on the other side, the insecurities and dysfunctions of renting can dominate their lives. In both cases the concept of home as a place of shelter and identity gets twisted out of shape. In the next chapter I'll explore some of the ways in which the property-owning democracy affected ideas of domestic and neighbourly life.

3

THE VALUES OF VALUE

'He is probably a nice guy,' said one of the mob who in 1957 attacked the Pennsylvania Levittown house of William and Daisy Myers, 'but every time I look at him I see $2,000 drop off the value of my house.' Property prices, for him, legitimised violent racism. This was a circular argument: prices fell because white owners feared living near black people like the Myers family, which fear could be excused on the basis that it brought values down.

William Levitt, the developer of the town, put it like this:

> As a Jew, I have no room in my mind or heart for racial prejudice. But I have come to know that if we sell one house to a Negro family, then 90 or 95 percent of our white customers will not buy into the community . . . We can solve a housing problem, or we can try to solve a racial problem, but we cannot combine the two.

His attitude was supported by the US government's Federal Housing Administration, whose underwriting of loans was crucial to the success of the Levitts' empire, and which encouraged restrictive covenants that excluded black people from ownership. The National Association of Realtors, the trade association for the real estate industry, also endorsed segregation at the time. They all saw integration as bad for business.

Racism, of course, can exist without private ownership. But the question of value adds motivation and an illusory justification to prejudice – 'It's not that I'm bigoted, it's just that that person's skin colour is costing me money. It's devaluing my home!' It is telling that an organisation set up to drive out the Myerses called itself the Levittown Betterment Committee, as if it were campaigning for improved pavement repairs or waste removal or some other unarguable enhancement of amenities and values.

Such interactions of property prices and social conflict don't only apply to race. In Hampshire, England, in 2017, a businessman was issued with a restraining order after he had allegedly played 'When a Man Loves a Woman', on repeat for an hour, at a lesbian couple living nearby. He was also said to have called one of them 'a fucking lezza'. He claimed, it was reported, that the crowing of their pet cockerel had taken £50,000 off the value of his million-pound house.

In such stories there is both aggression and defensiveness. There is territorial instinct. There is a preoccupation with the individual sphere at the expense of the shared. There is a tendency to make property ownership into both fortification and trophy. There is a desire to give maximum value to the private benefits of a home and minimum value to the communal – or else, as in Levittown, to define 'community' so narrowly as to exclude people unlike yourself.

If you own something and if you are honest, you may well find similar instincts in yourself. Hopefully you can manage them in such a way that you remain a functioning member of society. If you continue to be honest, you may also find that these instincts do not inevitably contribute to the benefits you may have hoped for from ownership – freedom, perhaps, or happiness, or peace.

Versions of this behaviour take place, with varying degrees of extremity or justification, every day. They are amplified in places where a high premium is placed on ownership and where high prices are correspondingly paid for homes. When your home is also your primary speculative investment, perhaps the basis of your pension planning, when a significant proportion of your lifetime income has been derived from its increase in value, it can do something to your head and your heart.

That something might be positive. It might give you the generous desire to share your good fortune with others. It is an important part of the Myerses' story, one that they themselves were later keen to emphasise, that some of their fellow citizens rallied to their support, organising patrols, babysitting for their children and clean-ups of the damage to their home. But unearned property wealth might give you a sense of entitlement which, perhaps insecure that you fully deserve it, you defend with all the more belligerence.

In Britain, four decades of inflation made property into a cultural obsession. It was already noticed in the 1980s that house prices had become a dominating topic of dinner party conversations, with tales of amazement that a house once worth x was now worth $3x$, or that a slum area had become a trophy neighbourhood. There were boasts of brilliant coups, fears of making ruinous mis-steps, anxieties about being left out or left behind by the ever-accelerating property train.

The press latched on. A recurring headline was that of the Knightsbridge broom cupboard, 6 × 12 feet or thereabouts – sometimes these reports seem to be about the very same unfeasibly tiny space, sometimes about different ones. In 1987 one sold for an outrageous £36,500. In 1994, a crash having intervened, the price was £30,000. In 2010, now called 'the London flat that's smaller than a SNOOKER TABLE', the legendary broom cupboard was worth £200,000. In 2017 the reported price for a relatively ample 14 × 13 foot 'ex-broom cupboard' was £225,000.

The earlier reports have a well-I-never-the-world's-gone-mad tone. The later ones begin to accept these prices as a fact of life, and to focus on the ingenuity of the individuals who were trying to make the best of these bonsai residences – canny buyers who had turned a profit on them, designers who had squeezed the most out of minuscule space. *Metro* quoted the two architects who renovated the 2017 example. 'These spaces really excite me', said one of them, 'because I know [we] can work wonders. Just because it is small doesn't mean it can't be luxurious.' 'It's the same principle I apply to larger projects,' said the other – 'maximise every inch.'

Here the broom cupboard theme joins forces with a parallel and larger media phenomenon, that of the home makeover. There has long been a never-ending supply of advice on ways to Increase the Value of Your Home. 'A bit of wow factor', we're told, 'will set it apart from others for sale in the area and will add a significant premium to your sale price.' Add a conservatory. Join rooms together (to make an open-plan living space!). Separate them again (so you have an extra bedroom!). Convert the loft. Install a new kitchen. Install a new bathroom. Get a wood-burning stove. Upgrade the taps. Highlight the period features. Redecorate, but not in strong colours that might put off purchasers. Bake bread and brew coffee when potential buyers come round, so that your property is suffused in enticing aromas. Scatter some cushions. Put cut flowers in vases.

Such improvements would hopefully make a home more attractive for its inhabitants, but they are primarily aimed at someone else, an abstracted stranger known as the potential purchaser. Your tastes and desires are subordinated to a wider notion of appeal, one that is inevitably generic and probably conventional, as the individual characters of these people are not known. You make your choices not just for yourself but for this unimaginative and rather boring phantom. The idea that your home expresses your identity is supressed. It's all about resale value, resale value, resale value. Idiosyncrasy and eccentricity are risky; conformity to the look of other properties on the market, and to the pictures in magazines, is good.

For week after week, decade after decade, the property supplements of newspapers have published articles remarkably like one another, telling similar stories about couples happy in much the same way. We turned our dingy basement into a light-filled garden room. We opened up and knocked through. Our clever architect transformed the interior by turning the staircase round. It's bright and airy. Our kids can run about. None of which should be denigrated – historians of the future might well identify this period as a golden age of interior design, one preferable to the dampish drear of previous decades. The pleasure that many of those couples get from their makeovers is genuine. Such spaces might be thought a positive by-product of high property prices, without which it would have been hard to justify the investment in planar glazing and in the engineering necessary to prop tottering Victorian bricks above open-plan living zones. But there is still a marked conformity.

———

In 1998 the conjoined preoccupations with property prices and home improvements bore upon grave matters of state. Peter Mandelson, reputedly the most powerful minister in Tony Blair's cabinet, certainly the most talked about, had a house in Notting Hill, London, a district in the middle of its ascent to what it is now, the world's ultimate example of property-driven gentrification. In the 1950s this was the area where the property tycoon Peter Rachman owned hundreds of tiny and squalid flats, 'an empire' according to a tabloid of the time, 'based on vice and drugs, violence and blackmail, extortion and slum landlordism the like of which this country has never seen'. Rachman's Trinidadian enforcer Michael de Freitas (later known as Michael X, eventually hanged in Port of Spain for murder) would write of the area:

> It was impossible to believe you were in twentieth-century England: terraced houses with shabby, crumbling stonework and the last traces of discoloured paint peeling from their doors, windows broken, garbage and dirt strewn all over the road, every second house deserted, with doors nailed up and rusty corrugated iron across the window spaces, a legion of filthy white children swarming everywhere and people lying drunk across the pavement.

By the 1970s Notting Hill was celebrated by the writer Jonathan Raban as a shabby bohemia, 'a ruined Eden, tangled, exotic and overgrown'. In the 1980s the police still classed it as an area of high crime. In the late 1990s it would give its name to a genteel romcom starring Julia Roberts, with Hugh Grant as an unprosperous bookseller. The film was unrealistic in two distinct ways – while it portrayed an ethnically diverse area as almost all white, it also failed to notice that the Grant character was the sort of Raban-era small trader who by then was getting squeezed out – but the movie could only be beneficial to the Notting Hill brand.

In the next decade, as the *Daily Telegraph* would breathlessly report:

> The bankers have moved in, along with film stars, music makers and heads of television channels . . . bringing in high-spend refurbishments, rare hardwoods, pressurised water systems, roof terraces and a craze for minimalism. You can afford to do fantastic things because people want smart, they want contemporary, they want spectacular. It almost doesn't matter how much you spend because you know you can always recoup it.

Mandelson's house was in a street called Northumberland Place. This address, as it happens, means something to me, as it was where my parents lived when they were newly married, in a house that they sold in 1960 for £5,000. In 1974 they heard to their chagrin that it had just been resold for £45,000. Mandelson's different but similar property cost him £450,000 in 1996. He also spent a reported £50,000 on getting the Victorian house 'minimalised' (as one newspaper put it) by the architect Seth Stein – white walls, limestone, oak, stainless steel. The space was part of the minister's persona, as an embodiment of 'cool Britannia' and of 'new' Labour, a political party that was no longer grimy and industrial but forward-looking and design-conscious. He was photographed there, seated in a stylish contemporary chair, emanating Britannic coolth.

But there was a snag. The price of the house, at the time that he bought it, was beyond the reach of the salary he was then receiving as a Member of Parliament. To bridge the gap Mandelson cadged a favour from a multi-millionaire colleague and party donor, in the form of a loan of £373,000, which – Mandelson having failed to declare it as he should – led to his resignation from the cabinet. He managed at least to sell the house for a profit, at £780,000, although he might have been galled to know that it was on the market at £1.3 million in 2004. At the time of writing houses in Northumberland Place are listed at about £4 million, which as it happens is at the cheaper end of Notting Hill property.

If the Mandelson affair was emblematic of the status of property at the time, we hadn't seen nothing yet. As a supermassive object in space bends light, the sheer density of pounds-per-square-feet was enough to warp everything around it, especially ordinary ideas of what a home might be. The second decade of the twenty-first century, for example, would bring the phenomenon known as the Iceberg House, in which colossal basements would be hollowed out beneath the rickety brick-and-stucco terraces of which Victorian London was made.

These basements would be filled with whatever might (a) communicate status and (b) not require natural light: swimming pools, private cinemas, private art galleries, gyms, spas, wine cellars, climbing walls. Rather than making space to serve a function, it seemed that functions had to be invented to fill space. For these basements went as deep as they could, eighteen metres in some cases, and as far as they could to the property line – out underneath the back garden, under whatever bit of pavement might be included. Often the basements would be several times the volume of the old house that floated above them, hence the 'iceberg' in their name.

The logic was simple. Expensive though it was to build these underground structures, high values would deliver a profit when it came to selling the property. If it cost x per square metre to build a basement, and residential space was worth y, there would be a return of $y - x = z$ per square metre. The old houses would usually be subject to planning policies designed to protect their historic interest – they would be listed buildings or in conservation areas – which limited the potential for expanding them above ground, so their owners decided to dig.

The apparatus of extraction became a common sight in the smarter parts of London, especially in the west of the city, with Notting Hill again at the forefront. There were long segmented plastic tubes for the passage of earth, skips in which to collect it, hoardings, mechanical plant – in effect compact mineshafts were built, with the difference that the thing being excavated was not gold nor coal but empty space: three-dimensional, measurable, priceable real estate. It looked perilous, and it was. The original houses, thrown up none too carefully by nineteenth-century speculators, were, despite the reverence often accorded to domestic architecture of this period, somewhat jerry-built. Their foundations might be a few bricks deep, their skinny walls and their timber roof beams leaning on their neighbours for support, held up with inertia and hope. They were never intended to have major engineering works going on underneath.

Many of those neighbours who were not building such basements themselves (and some who were) would object vociferously. They argued that worrisome movements and cracks occurred in nearby houses when such basements were built, and that unknowable consequences would flow from the disturbance of the water table. Then, in November 2020, their fears were confirmed. Two adjoining Chelsea town houses, where basement redevelopments were reportedly in progress, collapsed into rubble. Only a cornice at the top of their four-storey facades remained miraculously in place, spanning the void like the crossbar of a goal, forming with the adjoining houses a picture frame around an unintended view of the sky, a tree, the backs of houses beyond.

The time of Peak Property (if that is what it was, if that time is not still to come) bred other prodigies. There were 'ghost streets', made up of houses that were left empty most of the time, while their super-rich owners visited other properties in their global portfolio – St Moritz, Monte Carlo, Miami, Moscow, wherever. At the other end of the market, in less glamorous neighbourhoods, there were 'beds in sheds', where structures in back gardens were illegally made into dormitories, often for migrant workers. There were 'hidden favelas', where twenty or thirty people might be housed in a three-bedroom house.

These phenomena together demonstrate a radically unequal distribution of space: so much in an iceberg house that you have to invent uses to fill it; so little in a bed in shed that a bed is almost all you have. They also twist and pummel and stretch beyond recognition the familiar idea of home. This, as represented for example by the traditional London terraced house, might be an amount of space roughly suitable to your needs, in which you might invest your personality and memories and some hopes for stability and continuity, while allowing the possibility to move on elsewhere. It might also carry some ideas of neighbourliness and privacy, of the ways in which you are and are not part of a wider world. The architectural form – the roofed masonry object with front and back and enclosure and openings – is an expression, setting and vessel of these needs, desires and ideas. With the iceberg house it becomes a bauble, a figurehead on the great submerged ship, a bonnet mascot for a luxury car. With the hidden favela it is more like a shipping container, finite dividable space to be packed efficiently with people.

And these examples are not the end of the distortion of the domestic by property inflation, not by any means. The London boom also created the phenomenon that the leading planner Peter Rees called 'safe deposit boxes in the sky', towers of apartments sold as investments, often to overseas buyers, sometimes left empty. Their primary design consideration is not to form part of a congenial neighbourhood where you might want to live, so they don't. Such things as external landscape and harmonious relationships to neighbouring buildings are desultory. Their lobbies and lifts and corridors and even the flats themselves are not really places where, if you thought about it, you would want to spend your days.

Their primary design consideration is to get sold, to which end they have the accoutrements necessary to justify the adjectival noun 'luxury' – spas, gyms, screening rooms, residents' lounges, composite stone worktops, concealed LED lighting, lacquered full-height handle-less wardrobe doors – plus whatever branding and styling helps them stand out in the fuzz of property websites and in marketing events thousands of miles away. The Dumont, the Corniche, Vista, they get called, or Merano Residences, Atlas, Spire London, the Madison, the Landmark Pinnacle, the Flower Tower, Newfoundland. Their shapes might be bulbous or crystalline or swooping or floral or stepped or criss-crossed with steel bracing.

Alternatively, new residential blocks go for a plain functional look, which when practised by 1960s local authorities would have had them branded as 'Stalinist', but here makes a business proposition: you know and I know that we're trading living space as if it were futures in pork bellies or industrial plastic, so let's just get on and make a deal. But at least these investment vehicles have reasonable standards of space and basic amenities, which is more than can be said for the places where millions of renters actually live.

———

Grace is a university graduate, London-born, in her mid-thirties. She and her husband Cody have two children. Her grandmother Rose enjoyed a secure tenancy in public housing for forty years. Her parents Kathy and Eddie benefited from both Margaret Thatcher's right-to-buy policy and four decades of house price inflation. They too were tenants of a local authority, but were able to buy their home in the 1980s. In due course they sold it and bought a larger home in a cheaper area, which is now worth several times what they paid for it.

But where her parents and grandmother had lived securely in homes that met their needs, whether as renters or owners, Grace and her family have struggled to do the same. Now, driven by their search for a better place to live, they have gone to live in another country. Collectively, the three generations have experienced the vicissitudes of private and public property ownership, with contrasting effects on the quality of their lives. They happen to have lived through sixty years of shifts and switches, from a time when state-funded public housing was ascendant, to the rise of private ownership under Margaret Thatcher, to the time when high prices put ownership out of reach for many, while a contracted public sector made alternatives less accessible. Theirs is not an exceptional story, but it is a vivid microcosm of the experiences of millions.

In the years after leaving university, Grace at various times lived with her parents and with Cody in privately rented accommodation. Eventually they found a place that suited them. They decorated it, improved it and transformed its garden. 'Because we had grown up in a house that was our house, I never felt insecure,' she says, so she was happy to put time and money into making it better. But then they got a 'bombshell letter' from their landlord, announcing that he was selling the property and that they would have to move out. Grace was by now pregnant with their second child, as a consequence of which they were given an extra two months to find a new home.

By now the 'hard moment of truth' had dawned on Grace and Cody that 'actually home ownership is really difficult and really unlikely to happen'. Whereas, with some assistance from their parents, her older siblings had bought houses a few years previously, the upward ratchet of the market had made the prospect, even with help, more remote. Grace and Cody both had health problems, which knocked them back further.

They moved back into two rooms at Grace's parents' house – 'a really stressful time . . . things started falling apart'. They considered an option whereby they could part-own and part-rent a home, which turned out to be a 'really terrible deal'. Eventually they found temporary accommodation on a large public housing project which was in the process of being redeveloped. A nearby block had been emptied of residents in preparation for demolition. 'There were gangs and drugs. The bottom of our communal staircase was effectively a twenty-four-hour pharmacy – if I'd ever wanted to take crack or heroin, all I'd have had to do was go down there and look like I wanted something.'

After that there was a period when they rented from friends, from where they and their children went to a privately rented two-bedroom flat above a kebab shop on a noisy and busy road. The shop was open until 3 a.m., sometimes twenty-four hours, and 'it is no exaggeration to say that there was a stabbing every week' on or near the road. Grace and Cody were both in full-time employment, but they still needed state benefit to help pay the rent, to do which they claimed that Grace was a single mother, and Cody absent. They committed benefit fraud, in other words, without which they would have had to live somewhere worse.

They believe they were far from unusual: 'There are so many people doing that, and necessarily so. People not doing it are extra fucked over – if everyone is robbing and you're not robbing, you're extra worse off.' But as well as being a crime, their deception took its toll. 'You're always looking over your shoulder,' says Cody. 'You have to make sure kids don't say "Daddy" when you're on the phone.' Not doing that 'means that you have to leave the country' – and so they did.

The contrast is striking between Grace's experiences of property and those of her parents and grandparents. Rose, who worked as a waitress, never had much money – she owned £700 when she died – and her home was modest. But it gave her everything she needed and wanted and she had no fear of losing it. She was, in Cody's view, effectively 'a member of a big cooperative that was called the council – she was not beholden to them, not scared. It was like she owned her flat.' She was supported by a welfare state that would take care of her health and basic well-being. She therefore had the freedom and resources to help others, to help look after her grandchildren, to build friendships with her neighbours, to contribute to her community. She felt no need to hoard capital as a defence against the future.

Kathy and Eddie, as a result of right to buy, found similar freedoms by a different route – owning rather than renting. Buying, they say, was 'a landmark in our lives'. Their motivation was to 'support our family'. They were 'almost obliged to do it', as it was so much preferable to the available alternatives. Their home was to be a place where their children could grow up. They never saw it as an investment – they didn't mind when a price slump soon after they bought it knocked a third off its value. Yet thanks to the house price inflation of the intervening years, it is now worth seven or eight times what they paid. It remains a haven of family life. It is also security for their old age, and – as they can borrow against the equity they hold in it – a way of giving financial help to their children.

Rose, who had almost no capital, and Kathy and Eddie, who came to possess quite a lot, all felt both safe and in charge of their own destiny. For Grace and Cody, renting from private landlords, this was not the case. 'You're in a market,' Grace says. 'Your tenancy is a product. You're competing to be the least annoying tenant, the one best able to look after the flat – which also means the least vulnerable.'

They hope, having moved to another country, to buy there. 'People like me', she says, 'so want to own their home, to get that one golden ticket', but she'd prefer a world in which there were other ways to live well. In all her family's housing adventures, she says that the happiest time was on the social housing estate condemned for demolition. There was, she says, 'a sense of community – possibly a community of misfits and deplorables, but there was some kind of warmth, a consciousness of a shared experience. Which is not the case living in a street in a house where everyone is in a bubble.' It helped that they paid a low rent, that they weren't spending most of their income on housing costs. It also helped that, as tenants of a local authority, 'we never felt pressure from a private landlord; we were at liberty to put pressure on them – that sense of agency adds to our sense of well-being.' The only trouble was, that this relative contentment was only available in a place that wouldn't be there for long.

———

For seven years up to 2023 *Vice* magazine ran a column by Joel Golby called London Rental Opportunity of the Week, in which he highlighted particularly egregious offences against living standards from the listings on property websites. Examples included a shower located in a kitchen; a garden shed erected in a living room, with a mattress inside, to make a bedroom; something marketed as a 'one-bedroom semi-detached house' that was actually a conservatory; 'a fire escape that someone put a bed in'; and a kitchen with two beds in it.

As with the iceberg houses and the hidden favelas, there is polarity between luxury apartments in the new towers and Golby's 'rental opportunities'. On the one hand there is under-inhabited luxury, on the other overcrowded squalor. A yawning void opens up between them where you might look for both an equitable society and a modicum of domestic happiness, but find neither.

Sympathies in such circumstances are not naturally with the property owners. 'Landlords', says Golby, 'are robots designed to spot how to turn slivers of potential space into a semi-liveable but fully rentable opportunity', and he speaks for many. But it is worth considering what unearned property wealth can do to people, if only because everyone, owners or not, gets to live with consequences.

For property inflation has made homeowners, whether they like it or not, into micro-tycoons. They have found themselves, from the moment that they started contemplating their first purchase, trying to read the market, to assess risk, to calculate their leverage. Is this a good time to buy? In this area? Should we stretch ourselves to the limits to get the largest mortgage we possibly can? The answer to this last question is usually 'yes', because the conventional and rarely disproved wisdom is that property investment always wins and that you therefore can't have too much of it. Also because in many cases stretching to the limit is the only way that buyers can get a home even slightly resembling their needs and wishes.

They might then experience some stresses – the near-collapse of their purchase before it completes, the risk of falling prices and negative equity, a dip in their income, a rise in interest rates and therefore mortgage repayments, some unexpected building repairs, the ever-nagging feeling that they didn't make the smartest possible move, that someone else has made £££££ by buying earlier or elsewhere, a someone else who might be their theoretical wiser selves. They might make some sacrifices, sticking with a job they don't like so that they can service the mortgage, denying themselves luxuries and expensive treats, sticking with a partner that they don't like.

They might, assuming they survive these hazards, start reaping some rewards. They might watch with satisfaction as tens or hundreds of thousands are added to their notional wealth. They might find that they now have good collateral for further loans, which might help them to fund a buy-to-let property, which might be their pension. They have a taste for this tycoon thing now, and they want more of it.

Some (not all) will be tempted by the fact that they can squeeze out some more hundreds of pounds per month by renting out the deformities of the domestic – beds-in-kitchens, beds-that-aren't-beds, beds-in-sheds-in-living-rooms – that Golby documents. Enough money for a dream holiday or some lovely clothes or (following the failure of those relationships overly based on ownership) alimony, and if there are punters who will pay the asking rate for such places why should anyone turn them away? These home buyers, once blameless people who started out just looking for a home for their family, are now landlords.

These micro-tycoons might think that they are clever. They might believe that, due to their stresses and sacrifices, they have earned what they have. They would not be entirely wrong on either count, although they will probably underestimate the amount of luck that came with living in a time and place that made their windfalls possible. They might continue to feel insecure, both because property is an uncertain business and because it is hard to dispel the feeling that wealth that has easily come could just as easily go. They might feel guilt, which would then have to be justified away.

Insecurity breeds defensiveness. Defensiveness feeds entitlement. Property owners (some, not all) want to fortify their winnings. They want to draw up the drawbridge. They become nimbies, opposing affordable housing or a mosque or a centre for people with learning disabilities in their metaphorical back yard – anything that endangers their property values. Or they might want to close or limit a pub, a music venue or the activities of a popular park even if such things were already there when the property owner in question moved into the area. Such things happen.

I might be stressing the negatives here, and underplaying the many stories of contentment and decency enabled by the transaction of property, but I am nonetheless describing the real and lived experience for very many people. It is a situation that brings out the best in no one, in neither the guilty-but-entitled owner nor the exploited and resentful tenant. It doesn't necessarily make either particularly happy.

And then there is the phantasmagoric quality of property, the way in which something as physical as a house, and as heartfelt as home, can become a financial abstraction, an investment above all else, one which starts to tell you how to live your life, how to interact with other people and about the nature of the society in which you live. Linked to this quality is the nature of property as a business, one in which it is possible to do very well even if you have no particular skill for making things or for managing organisations or for understanding your customers' desires. You just have to market and to trade, to sell illusions, to gamble and to get lucky, to bully and to manipulate, to know how to play those entities that will help you get what you want: the public authorities who regulate, the corporate investors who lend, the private individuals who buy or rent, the contractors who build. Which (the illusions, the gambling, the bullying, the manipulation, the organisational incompetence) is a fair summary of a modus operandi that has become widespread in society and in politics in recent years, in several parts of the world.

These industries of fantasy have flourished in Californian sunshine and the heat of Nevada, where the transformation of dreams into real estate is serious business. Las Vegas, outlandish and extreme as it might seem, has had a profound influence on the buying, selling and building of cities worldwide. If you want to understand property's altered versions of reality, the western side of the United States is a good place to look.

4

THE REALITY OF REALTY

'Real estate is a mind game. I Bobby-Fischer the shit out of situations like this.' So says Christine, an agent at the Oppenheim Group, the self-described 'most successful real estate agency in West Hollywood', just after she has taken two prospective buyers around 'five thousand square feet of absolute zen' of the kind that the company sells. The viewing couple are picky. 'I wish it was a gas stove, though,' says one of them. 'Bitch, you don't even cook, OK?' says Christine to camera, later.

This is *Selling Sunset*, the Netflix reality series about the short and bald if gym-fit twins who run the Oppenheim Group and the fleet of model-tall, lush-maned women whom they employ to sell houses. Here glamour, celebrity and property fuse. A world unfolds of five-bedroomed, nine-bathroomed, two-hot-tubbed homes with the views over canyons and city and palm trees, furnished with spas and infinity pools and 'the largest rooftop deck of any property ever listed in the Hills' or some other such uniqueness to distinguish their otherwise uniform modernist-style radiance. California sunshine bounces around white surfaces and glass walls, off the ten-thousand-dollar Calacatta Gold marble slabs on the kitchen islands, the Jeff Koons balloon dogs and the Design Miami and pimped-Bauhaus chairs.

This is Hollywood, and the shine of the dream factory backlights every scene. Some of the agents date men who have been seen on screen. The success of *Selling Sunset* will make them famous themselves. The homes they sell are like film sets, locations where you can imagine that a film star has just ascended the crystal staircase, or is about to dive into the pool with a crisp cinematic splash. This is the dream that the Oppenheim Group are selling, for which buyers pay millions. Then Netflix makes these spaces, literally, into film sets. For, although *Selling Sunset* is in the category of reality TV, it is high theatre.

The realtors' arts include what they call 'staging', where homes for sale become sets dressed by professionals – 'creating an environment where a client will envision themselves living in a home', as one of them puts it. 'Things to kind of contemporise it a bit,' says another. They import furniture and artwork and house plants and fabrics. 'This will be a really fun stage,' they say: 'I want the vibe to be for a couple and more of an entertainment home, not so much family vibe . . . we're on Sunset so we're more of a lifestyle, entertainment . . . I want the vibe to reflect that.'

'All that is solid melts into air,' wrote Karl Marx, and he might as well have been thinking of *Selling Sunset*. For if property is an essential part of the American dream, it is indeed dream-like. Much of the trade in homes is based less on the needs, dignity or personal fulfilment of their inhabitants than it is on display and shared illusion. This is not to deny the uses of the latter – they are part of being human, too – but it is important to know the appeal of ownership for what it is. Land and buildings are material, hard to move, and require heavy labour to construct and cultivate – yet property has a striking affiliation with fantasy.

Among the philosophical enthusiasts for the liberating and enriching powers of private property, there is a striking lack of agreement about its essential character. Many, John Locke included, have argued that property is 'natural', 'a natural right', an extension almost of the human body, a thing based on productive toil and honest work. According to Hernando de Soto Polar, however, 'property, like energy, is a concept; it cannot be experienced directly. Pure energy has never been seen or touched.

And no one can see property. One can only experience energy and property by their effects.' De Soto advocates spreading property rights as widely as possible, but he sounds quite Marxist in his description of property's lack of substance.

So there is divergence between the view of property as a thing of earth and body and de Soto's almost mystical belief that it is intangible and invisible energy. Property, it seems, can be perceived in different ways. Other views are also available – you might, for example, consider property to be invented by humans as a convenient tool or instrument. In this case there would be another kind of divide between the Lockean faith in property as an act of nature and its reality as useful artifice or fiction. If something assumed to be natural is actually contrived, you might expect some kind of dissonance or strangeness to result, some sort of mismatch between expectation and experience.

In this case fantasy might be an effective way of bridging or blurring the gap. It would be a way of describing what is actually going on – a trade in abstractions – in terms of what is supposed to be going on, which is humanity's 'natural' search for shelter and security. It is as if the fictional aspect (to look at it another way), which is suppressed by the description of property as natural, reappears in exaggerated form.

Whether property is natural, mystical or artificial, the real estate business is characterised by the striking contrast between the financial abstractions with which it is conducted and the unarguable physicality of the buildings and land that it describes. Here too fantasy helps to reconcile and obscure the divide, or to give you something altogether different to look at, so you don't pay so much attention either to the abstract or the physical.

Readers of *The Big Short*, Michael Lewis's account of the subprime mortgage crisis that precipitated the 2007–8 financial crash, or viewers of the film made from it, might remember the head-spinning financial instruments used to gamble with people's mortgages. The synthetic sub-prime mortgage bond-backed CDO, or collateralised debt obligation, was, for example, so 'opaque and complex', in Lewis's words, that investors and rating agencies would struggle to understand it. Wall Street liked it that way, as complication and lack of transparency increased the opportunities for making money.

These instruments made it possible to hide risk by complicating it. CDOs were vast bundles of bonds, which were in turn vast bundles of mortgages, the risk on which, with the help of devices called credit default swaps, could be passed from one financial institution to another. $20 billion of such risk ended up with a single company, AIG FP. The CDOs, through some questionable financial alchemy and the indulgent attitudes of the credit rating agencies, helped to turn bad loans into good ones, transforming them from a triple B rating to a triple A.

Vast sums could be made – roughly $400 million a year in 'riskless profits' by Goldman Sachs alone – with the result that packaging mortgages became Wall Street's most profitable business. Half a trillion dollars of sub-prime mortgage-backed bonds were issued in a single year, 2005. An insatiable appetite for loans developed, fed by aggressive salesmen, who lured individuals with little creditworthiness to sign up for too-good-to-be-true deals, incurring debts that they would probably be unable to repay. The US mortgage bond market came to depend on the unending rise of house prices. They had to rise, what's more, at a certain rate: the housing market didn't have to collapse, only to slow down, for the precarious whirligig of financial instruments and eleven-figure risks to fall to pieces. Which it did – as is well known – with devastating consequences not only for American homeowners, but for the global economy.

CDOs and credit default swaps were abstractions of

abstractions: absurd, like the conception of a Dadaist dramatist, but with vast effects. Their unreality was ultimately based on reality: real people with real homes on real land, who paid real consequences when it all went wrong. That the base of the speculations was the fundamental human need to find a place to live appears to have assisted the financial phantasmagoria: the more grounded the product might seem to be, the more extravagant the instruments that might be developed from it. The fact that this was to do with homes, among other things, brought politics into play: politicians like to be seen to be helping people get homes; they don't like to be seen to be making them homeless, even though that was the eventual outcome of the process that they assisted. The presence of homes in the equations raised the stakes still higher: it made government more likely to intervene to prevent complete catastrophe. Which probability was something that could be gamed by the speculators. It gave them a safety net for still riskier financial acrobatics.

If abstraction and distance from physical reality are aspects of most forms of capitalism (a trader in bauxite may never have seen such a thing in his or her life), they are particularly characteristic of property. Property interacts with such fundamental parts of life as home and community, which means that there are profits to be made in the spaces between abstract and concrete, and between numbers and emotion, by selling image and aspiration as well as physical fact.

Property also tends to involve interaction with public authorities – for example to get planning permissions, tax incentives or infrastructural investment in a location – which means that appearances can be useful. Politicians have a common interest with property companies in convincing the public that a given urban transformation really will be as great as they claim. The long timespans of construction mean that developers have to bridge the credibility gap between conception and achievement, to persuade funders and buyers to invest in something that doesn't yet exist. They have to act almost as if a planned building is already there. Sometimes it never in fact appears, or not in the way promised, but if a site can be flipped or sold on, or its permissions renegotiated, at least some of the parties will go away satisfied. They will feel a job has been well done. If reality – actual, real, lived reality – is not essential to the deal, it can be dispensed with.

———

The spiritual heart of this version of real estate (if it could be said ever to have had spirit or heart) is in gaming cities, centres of themed entertainment like Las Vegas and Atlantic City, where money that was sometimes dubious in origin was transmogrified with illusion and fantasy. Las Vegas's founding deity, its Romulus, was Bugsy Siegel, a gangster. As with Romulus, his role was wrapped in myth – he wasn't the first to build a casino there, nor was he the sole creator of the Flamingo, the development that made him famous. But with its scalloped-edged Olympic-sized pool, its pink upholstery and metal–glass facades and imported greenery, the Flamingo brought glamour and attention to this desert settlement. Its eventual success proved that ambitious gambling resorts could work there. Its *moderne*-style architecture, unlike anything Las Vegas had seen before, demonstrated the power of both novelty and spectacle.

Siegel was assassinated a few months after the Flamingo's opening in December 1946, seemingly because his investors were disgruntled by his questionable management of the project. But he planted a seed that blossomed into an ever-growing, ever-mutating jungle of constructional stimulation and simulation,

one that like an invasive species eventually found fertile ground in other cities and countries and flourished there. What at first seemed an exotic and rare desert bloom became as ubiquitous as turf.

Competing casinos, seeking new markets and new ways to outdo their rivals, fuelled an endless production of imagery, in which punters were lured inside with appropriations of Hollywood's changing scenarios. Pre-Flamingo, the El Rancho (1941) and Last Frontier (1942) casino complexes conjured Wild West themes, dressing their staff as cowboys and cowgirls and inventing nineteenth-century frontier histories for a city that was only founded in 1905. Later there was outer space (the Stardust), Arabia (the Dunes, Aladdin), ancient Rome (Caesar's Palace) and clowns and acrobats (Circus Circus).

By the 1990s, seeking to attract the family tourist market, developments would borrow freely from the Disney Corporation's genius for drawing people to its theme parks. The casinos were by now 'resorts' offering shopping malls and rides and entertainment as well as gambling. Excalibur, a medieval-style development that opened in 1990, didn't try very hard to conceal its debt to Cinderella's Castle at Disneyland, there being no copyright on battlements and turrets. Luxor, with its big dark pyramid, 150 per cent-scale Sphinx and chlorinated Nile, did Egypt. Further conceptual evolutions led to resorts based on famous cities: New York, New York; the Venetian; Paris Las Vegas; the Monte Carlo. Later again developers attempted parodic versions of the iconic museums and landmarks created by more culturally respectable cities: art by Picasso, Jenny Holzer and Maya Lin; architecture by Rem Koolhaas, Rafael Viñoly and Norman Foster. Daniel Libeskind applied his architecture of anguished angles, originally conceived for the Jewish Museum in Berlin, to the Crystals mall at MGM Mirage's CityCenter resort.

With the promiscuity of imagery went continuous innovation in the technology of attraction. El Rancho put neon on its Western-style windmill, the start of the city's fascination with coloured light that would lead to the eight miles of luminous tubing that wrapped Binion's Horseshoe Club twenty years later. Casinos would build and rebuild their signs, always taller and more extravagant than before. Creation came with destruction: the detonation of structures that had lost their allure was a recurring sight of Las Vegas. In 1989 the casino magnate Steve Wynn brought the game to a new level with the eight-storey, hourly-erupting, piña-colada-scented volcano that he installed outside the Mirage. He would raise the game again with battling pirate ships outside Treasure Island (1993) and once more with musical fountains at the Bellagio (1998). 'It's what God would have done,' said Wynn of his volcano, 'if He'd had the money.'

More subtle devices were used. The Flamingo excluded daylight and clocks from its casino, and made its layout disorienting, dissolving space and time so that gambling could become the only reality. These tricks became standard in Las Vegas for decades. Casinos would later develop ways of tracking customers' movements, their shopping preferences, their choice of drinks, by means which – if now the common practice of tech companies – were advanced at the time.

Fundamental to the success of Las Vegas was that there was no 'there' there, that it started as almost empty and valueless land, minimally encumbered by custom and law, its plots delineated with the simple rectangular logic of the Public Land Survey System and therefore easily acquired and developed by investors. Something that speculators particularly liked about the Strip, the four-mile length of road along which the most famous casinos stand, was that it was outside Las Vegas's city limits, and therefore free of whatever taxes and regulations the city might impose. Nevada's libertarian laws, which made it for forty-five years the only state to have legalised casino gambling, were also fundamental to the city's success.

Las Vegas was never a location where, according to the traditional vectors of urban growth, you would expect a city to flourish. It lacked such assets as a river, a natural harbour, an intersection of major trade routes or a fertile hinterland. Nature gave it violent heat and little else. 'I thought I would die in that desert,' said the crime boss Meyer Lansky. 'Vegas was a horrible place.' It was as near as possible nothing, an arid abstraction, but one that could be irrigated by speculation. Its formula was this: sand + electricity + water + air conditioning + minimal regulation = a boom town. Fantasy, in such mathematics, would be a multiplier.

At the same time, like many seeming triumphs of free enterprise, it couldn't have happened without public investment – in this case the nearby Depression-era Hoover Dam, which brought water and electricity to the desert, as well as hordes of construction workers looking to let off steam, who gave the city's gambling and sex-work businesses an early boost. Federal investment in defence, based partly on the Nevada desert's attractions as a nuclear testing zone, would later bring further tax dollars to the region.

————

If Las Vegas seems like a whimsical sideshow, it was anything but. It was big business. Forum Shops was the most profitable mall in the United States. Hotels reached unprecedented sizes: five, six and seven thousand rooms. The Venetian would overtake the Pentagon as the United States' largest building. Its figure of eighteen million visitors in 2006 was about the same as that for the entire Italian city that inspired it. The Bellagio would make it onto lists of the American public's favourite buildings. From

1990 to 2010 Las Vegas was the fastest-growing city in the United States, its population more than doubling. And its influence would extend beyond its boundaries. Cruise ships would take Vegas-style theming and entertainment onto the high seas. The companies who made belle époque ornaments and fake skies for casinos started applying their skills and products to private houses. 'Casino chic', as the *New York Times* called it, 'may be coming to a home near you'. 'Belle epoxy' was another name for the style.

Sheldon Adelson, the mogul behind the Venetian and Sands resorts, successfully exported his concepts to Macau, as part of a Vegas-inspired transformation of the Chinese city which by 2008 would enable it to achieve double the gaming revenue of its Nevadan model – if Macau had been called 'Asia's Las Vegas', observed Adelson, Las Vegas should now be called 'America's Macau'. He also realised the $5.9 billion Marina Bay Sands complex in Singapore, now that city's most conspicuous landmark, famous for its infinity pool 650 feet in the air, where a casino and hotel are embellished with art by Anish Kapoor, seven celebrity-chef restaurants, a convention centre, mall, theatres, ice rink and a lotus-shaped museum with musical fountain, lasers and holographic mermaids.

The Strip's factories of escapism are prototypes for the contemporary metropolis. Around the year 2000 a poll of Chinese citizens found that the American city that they would most like to visit was Las Vegas. It is not surprising that, since that poll, many Chinese cities have been redeveloped with similarly comprehensive and still vaster developments. And not just in China: in the Gulf states, in Russia and – adjustments to the historic fabric permitting – London and New York, cities are rebuilding with typologies forged in the Nevada desert.

Some developments are themed in the Las Vegas way. In

China – before the government banned 'copycat behavior' – developers built an Alpine Village in Guangdong province, an English-styled Thames Town near Shanghai, and Tianducheng, a wannabe Paris that includes one of several Eiffel Towers to be found in the People's Republic. In Burj Al Babas, Turkey, there is a speculative development of three hundred close-packed miniature French chateaux.

Some Vegas-esque developers opt for making buildings that look like something that is not a building: in Baku, Azerbaijan, there is a trio of flame-shaped towers and a crescent moon hotel. Others choose the more abstract and theoretically more sophisticated approach of using 'iconic' architecture, as seen at the Strip's CityCenter resort – extravagant-looking forms generated by celebrated architects or their imitators. In all the aim is the same: image, branding, fantasy, marketing, the need to stand out while trading chunks of city.

Nor was Vegas's influence only about imagery. The Strip also helped to incubate what the architect Stefan Al calls 'holistically designed and multisensory environments', all-encompassing zones where every paviour, shrub, artwork, light fitting and architectural flourish conspires with menus, retail and entertainment options to address all their punters' wants of body and spirit. They are typically large: in Las Vegas, Circus Circus put together a mile-long, 230-acre string of resorts, connected by private walkways, moving beltways and escalators, such that you could go from one end to the other without leaving their property.

The ideal is to allow no stimulations that are outside the control of the management, to own your desires for the duration of your visit. These places are, says Al, 'technologically wired and "smart"'. They function inside and out, drawing the sidewalk into their universes with landscaping and spectacle and streetmosphere. In so doing they have made Las Vegas, whose 1950s and 1960s iterations were structured around the capabilities and requirements of cars, pedestrian-friendly.

Such domains are found not only in entertainment-based complexes like Marina Bay Sands, but also in those that are more residential and office-based, such as the twenty-eight-acre, $25 billion Hudson Yards development in New York. They don't have to put on a show (although Hudson Yards does include the $200 million artwork-cum-visitor-attraction known as the Vessel) to achieve a Vegas-like totality of environmental and aesthetic control.

And the cultural and social effect of Las Vegas would go beyond style and urban design. The city was closely implicated in the growth of high-risk financial gambling – casino capitalism, it is sometimes called – of the kind described in *The Big Short*. Much of the early success of the volcano-building Steve Wynn was based on his business relationship with Michael Milken, the junk bonds specialist imprisoned in 1990 for a number of financial crimes. Milken backed Wynn's Mirage project, which opened in 1989, with $535 million of bonds. 'They made me,' Wynn said of Milken's firm, Drexel Burnham Lambert.

Milken, it would later turn out, was a pioneer. As ingenious as his devices were at the time – and collateralised debt obligations were invented under his direction at Drexel Burnham Lambert – they were made much more so by the further development of financial alchemy. As spectacular as the excesses of the 1980s seemed at the time, they were trivial compared to those of the years before the 2008 crash. And Las Vegas went along with the ride: the $2 billion cost of the Bellagio, which opened in 1998, was financed with CDOs. In 1996 banks lent a total of $10 billion to major Las Vegas developments.

With the help of highly leveraged loans, Las Vegas continued to flourish. Room numbers and room rents kept going up, and the city's population kept growing. Plans were made and construction started on more ambitious resorts. The city was hailed as 'a triumph of post-industrial capitalism'. And then, from 2007, it crashed. Building work stopped on half-built towers. Banks foreclosed. MGM Mirage stock dropped 94 per cent, Las Vegas Sands 99 per cent. The city's homeowners, who like millions of other Americans had bought into the dream of ever rising values, were also hit: in 2009 *Time* reported that it was in 'the deepest crater of the recession' with 'the highest foreclosure rate of any major metro area'. Las Vegas, more than any other city, personified the boom and bust of the American economy.

Post-war Las Vegas was built on criminal money, its casinos being perfect for both laundering and skimming cash. 'We owe a debt of gratitude to the Mafia for developing Las Vegas, and there's nothing to be ashamed of,' a former state archivist called Guy Rocha has said. 'It was the mob that moved (Las Vegas) forward, with the good, the bad and the ugly.' It three times elected as its mayor Oscar Goodman, a lawyer who had previously represented a number of organised crime figures, and then elected his wife Carolyn, who at the time of writing continues in office – which suggests that the city's citizens are quite accepting of its past.

Las Vegas was built again with the help of casino capitalism. In both cases there was an interplay of the visible and the invisible, and of the intangible and the physical, that was mediated by fantasy. The criminal nature of criminal money is not meant to be seen, but the tall neon pylon of the Flamingo demanded attention. Few things are more opaque and abstracted than the financial instruments of casino capitalism, but few things could be more visible – they insist that you look – than the volcanoes and waterworks for which those instruments paid.

Alternative realities were created, both in financial engineering and in theming, albeit in different ways: a synthetic sub-prime mortgage bond-backed CDO doesn't look much like a Venice-themed leisure resort, but both are in the business of distraction. These distractions come with their special languages: as in *Selling Sunset*, words are neologised, parts of speech hop their species barrier, nouns and verbs are adjectivalised. New realities need new vocabularies, new syntax.

One way of looking at the Strip, indeed, is as a set of built adjectives. Each theme, from Arthurian to iconic, modifies the underlying sameness of the basic product, which is composed of slots, shows, rooms, shops, food and drink. The beauty of adjectival architecture is that it is relatively cheap – it costs less to make something look like a palazzo than it does genuinely to emulate Venetian quality and craft – but it can change perceptions, and it is in perceptions that the profits are made.

The role of property in these transactions is multiple. It does such simple things as provide the physical location without which the whole game of speculation could not be played, and can act as collateral to loans. It is the thing whose value can be multiplied by fantasy and construction and adjectives, whose initial emptiness and uselessness make it all the more amenable to the conjurations of developers. It offers conceptual as well as financial collateral: land and buildings look substantial and grounded and in some sense 'real', even though their financial values might be evanescent, a fact which makes a solid-seeming base for the financial phantasmagoria and architectural fabrications that play around them.

We have seen similar phenomena in modern politics. Donald Trump brought his real estate techniques to the White House, including the blurring of substantial fact and outrageous fantasy – what his book *The Art of the Deal* called 'truthful hyperbole'. As a developer he gave the number sixty-eight to the top floor of the Trump Tower, even though it is only fifty-eight storeys off the ground. As president he built some of a wall. He created a vast fiction of a stolen election. Between his actual and imaginary constructions he made a large space for the operation of his power and for the sometimes criminal actions of his associates. These patterns of behaviour, whether by himself, his children or his imitators, are likely to persist into the future. It may be significant in this respect that Trump's largest single donor was Sheldon Adelson, the magnate behind the Venetian and Marina Bay Sands. Vegas values have, in any event, reshaped not only cities, but also the government of the United States.

For the fantastical and illusionary qualities of real estate, which enable wealth and power to be both displayed and concealed, make it favourite instrument of kleptocratic governments the world over. One is spoilt for choice as to which one to pick as an example, but the former Soviet republic of Azerbaijan is a good place to start.

5

DEVELOPER KINGS

'I love you Bak-uu-uuuu,' mouthed Loreen's kiss-shaped lips to camera, as the inky lighting of her soulful performance dissolved into the orange zigzags and flame motifs with which the Baku Crystal Hall was decked out. Baku, the capital of Azerbaijan, loved Loreen back, or rather the electorate of the 2012 Eurovision Song Contest did, as the Moroccan–Swedish singer went on to win that year's first prize.

The Crystal Hall itself, built in nine months, hundreds of homeowners and residents having been evicted from its site with what Human Rights Watch called 'wilful disregard for their dignity, health, and safety', is a striking – indeed crystalline – object on the shore of the Caspian Sea. It is part of Baku's version of the now familiar cityscapes formed when the global pipelines of murky finance are tapped, whether in Doha, London, Miami, Moscow or Shanghai, and slimy money coagulates into the depthless digitised fantasies of their architects' computers. Always ostensibly different, always profoundly repetitive. In the case of Baku: a threesome of flame-shaped skyscrapers, a mirror-glassed horns-downward crescent moon that houses the seven-star Crescent Hotel, a carpet museum in the shape of, yes, an unrolling carpet. Also a 130-metre-high structure, somehow resembling both vulva and phallus, that was going to be the Trump International Hotel and Tower Baku, and the Heydar Aliyev cultural centre, the money-no-object masterpiece of the late architect Zaha Hadid, whose swooping forms aspire, in the words of her practice's official blurb, 'to express the sensibilities of Azeri culture and the optimism of a nation that looks to the future'. The prestigious Design Museum in London gave its Design of the Year Award to this 'clear vision of a singular genius', as one of the judges put it.

Azerbaijan is particularly carnivalesque in its property dealings. It ranked 157 out of 176 in Transparency International's 2022 Corruption Perceptions Index. Its ruling family, the Aliyevs, in power since the ex-KGB officer Heydar Aliyev became president in 1993, have developed a knack for mixing politics with business. The current president, Ilham Aliyev, was, leaked US diplomatic cables suggested in 2010, Azerbaijan's richest person, running a 'feudal' political system in which 'a handful of well-connected families' control most of the economy.

In 2017, the 'Azerbaijani Laundromat' was revealed, a mechanism for buying influence with corrupt money, whose picturesque side effects included the awarding of UNESCO's Mozart Medal, usually awarded to legendary musicians like Elisabeth Schwarzkopf and Mstislav Rostropovich, to Mehriban Aliyeva, vice-president and first lady of Azerbaijan. In 2010 it was reported that the president's then twelve-year-old son had bought $44 million of property on the legendary Palm Jumeirah island in Dubai. The president's spokesman said: 'I have no comment on anything. I am stopping this talk. Goodbye.'

In 2017 the *New Yorker* exposed the dealings around the putative Trump Tower, whose site was cleared by government order of the houses that once stood there, their owners receiving in compensation a fraction of the true value of their homes. The role of the Trump Organization was to license the use of its valuable brand name, potentially to manage the completed hotel and, under a technical services agreement, to take a close interest in such things as the Macassar ebony ceiling of the lobby and the book-matched walnut doors of the ballroom. 'Trump

International Hotel & Tower Baku represents the unwavering standard of excellence of The Trump Organization and our involvement in only the best global development projects,' said Donald J. Trump, chairman and president of the Trump Organization in 2014. 'When we open in 2015, visitors and residents will experience a luxurious property unlike anything else in Baku – it will be among the finest in the world.'

It didn't open in 2015, however, and the Trump Organization withdrew from the project in December 2016. Until then their partners – the people who were actually building the tower – were a nexus of businesses belonging to a family called the Mammadovs, who were also closely involved with the extensive property-development interests of the Iranian Revolutionary Guard, the immensely powerful military organisation charged with protecting Iran's Islamic republican political system from external and internal threats. The business of the future president of the United States was, in other words, one degree of separation from the regime that he would call the 'biggest sponsor of terrorism around the world'.

As well as their building projects in their own country, there is another use of property by Azerbaijan's ruling elites: the purchase of overseas real estate with their considerable wealth. Luke Harding of the *Guardian* has reported that Leyla and Arzu Aliyeva, daughters of president Ilham Aliyev and vice-president-cum-award-winning-musician Mehriban Aliyeva, had decided to spend £59.5 million on two luxury flats in Knightsbridge, London, including £3 million to convert them into a single home. The press usually describes the sisters as 'socialites', though Leyla also calls herself an artist. The device chosen for their acquisition by this renaissance woman and her sister was Exaltation Ltd, a secret offshore company in the British Virgin Islands set up to help manage their British assets.

The Aliyev sisters appear to have backed out of their purchase after it was reported in the press, but the family retained an extensive global portfolio, a portion of which was revealed by the Organised Crime and Corruption Reporting Project in 2016. It included a house in Hampstead, North London, a flat overlooking Hyde Park, nine waterfront mansions in Dubai, a dacha near Moscow and a villa in the Czech spa town of Karlovy Vary.

Property is the currency of the Azerbaijani elite, their manifestation and their disguise. The lavish monuments allow these dominant families to express their power and vanity in a way traditional to dictators, and the investment of illicit funds in construction helps enrich them. The forced clearances of sites for development are the actions of political and commercial interests inextricably combined.

The real estate of the Azeri elite, both at home and away, could not be more visible, yet it conceals as much as it shows, in particular the origin of the money that might pay for it. As the *New Yorker* put it, 'money launderers love construction projects. They attract legitimate funds from governments and private investors, and they require frequent payouts to legitimate subcontractors.' An overseas property, once purchased with the help of a shell company in the British Virgin Islands, or St Kitts and Nevis, or wherever it may be, cleans the cash with which it was bought. It can be traded again, as a decreasingly tainted piece of wealth. Those Knightsbridge flats and Hampstead houses, being in some sense homes, can exploit the wholesome, heart-warming associations that the word 'home' evokes.

Property fortifies what might be the fleeting advantages of position and influence. It solidifies the transient and the intangible. For courtiers like the Mammadovs it provides a refuge for their money and their own persons when the time comes for their downfalls, as it did for them. It is both safe deposit box and bolthole.

The Aliyevs are spectacular examples of a flourishing twenty-first-century type, the Developer King, the ruler for whom the property business is both instrument and symbol of political and economic power. Other examples include Mohammed Al Maktoum of Dubai, former Mayor Yury Luzhkov of Moscow and his wife Yelena Baturina, and Recep Tayyip Erdoğan of Turkey. Donald Trump, by going from property development to presidency, reversed the usual trend, but he was in a similar game.

Baku is no more than a gaudy and burlesque vision of one way in which the world is going. The direction of travel is towards the takeover of politics by property. It is not only dictators and egomaniacs who embrace property development – mature democracies use it too, to fund affordable housing, public space, concert halls and other social and political goods. They run their economies on house price inflation. Political leaders point to swinging construction cranes as evidence of prosperity.

Wherever big business and big government combine, chances arise for abuse. The state and the property business tend to become indistinguishable, dictators become tycoons, and laws invented for public benefit – such as those on compulsory purchase and tax incentives – are turned to help favoured developers. Public works – an airport, a highway, social housing – become enmeshed with the development opportunities they bring.

———

In 1976 Donald Trump handed to the city government of New York a document that confirmed an option agreement between himself and the owners of the Commodore, a clapped-out 1,600-room hotel next to Grand Central station. Or rather, it would have confirmed the option, had the document been signed by both parties. But, as no one chose to notice that it wasn't, the city proceeded with negotiations with the young developer about possible tax incentives, which helped to convince the Hyatt hotel chain that they could go into partnership with him for the new hotel Trump wanted to create there, which unlocked a forty-year tax break worth $4 million a year, gave Trump his foothold in Manhattan, and later led to the creation of the legendary Trump Tower (also with generous help from the city), fame, celebrity, the scattering of Trump-branded buildings around the world and, eventually, the presidency of the United States of America.

The year is significant. In 1975 the city of New York had almost gone bankrupt, as years of generous spending on public services had collided with a declining economy and the flight of the tax-paying middle classes out of the city. It was rescued, but at the cost of handing control to financial institutions, in what is now seen as a turning point in the switch from the social democracy of the 1960s to the market-led policies that have prevailed since. From now on a city's job would be above all to attract investment and stimulate growth. The result is what we see now in cities like New York and London, cleaner, safer, more prosperous, more entertaining, more populous than ever, but increasingly inaccessible to citizens on middle incomes and more a playground, as has been said of Manhattan, for *Economist* readers.

The shift was expressed through property. Property was a way to draw investment, generate activity, demonstrate progress and grow confidence. Richard Ravitch, who as chairman of the New York State Urban Development Corporation is the man usually crediting with rescuing the city from its financial morass, was a property developer. Provisions intended to encourage such things as affordable housing were repurposed to incentivise the property business. So when Trump asked for help with rebuilding the

Commodore Hotel, he was asking a city desperate for anything to happen at all. It helped too, according to Trump's biographer Michael D'Antonio, that the then mayor Abe Beame was close to Trump's father, Fred. Both had built their careers in Brooklyn, getting to know each other in the borough's intertwined worlds of business and politics. 'Whatever my friends Fred and Donald want in this town, they get,' Beame is reported to have said. When Ravitch tried to oppose the extent of the city's largesse to Trump, Trump told him he could have him sacked.

It is easier to see what the young Trump didn't bring to this particular table than what he did. He had little track record in development, beyond managing some of his father's extensive rental properties, let alone at the scale of what the investigative journalist Wayne Barrett has called 'the city's only major ongoing development deal' at the time. Trump had little money of his own to put in, and limited ability to raise finance – although he claimed to have the backing of Equitable Life, they had refused his request for $75 million and gave no more than an indication that they might put up $25 million, conditional on his finding more substantial support elsewhere. He had no organisation – at the start of his involvement with the Commodore, his office was his apartment – and little expertise in construction. There was no certainty that his offer was the best available. Yet he secured an extraordinary array of favourable conditions without which his Manhattan career – at least on this occasion – would have gone unlaunched. For our knowledge of these favours we are indebted to Wayne Barrett, who was the first to report on Trump's rise in the 1970s, and who until his death on the day before Trump's 2017 inauguration continued to be one of the more revealing writers on his business affairs.

If Trump lacked expertise, organisation, experience, skill and finance, what he did have was connections, combined

with a genius for manipulating officials, politicians and lawyers through combinations of favours, inducements and threats. He owed both his connections and his networking skills to his father Fred, who four decades earlier had launched his career by buying the mortgage-servicing subsidiary of the Brooklyn-based J. Lehrenkrauss Corporation, a once famous company destroyed in the Great Depression. As with Donald's Commodore adventure, Fred wasn't the best-qualified or best-resourced contender for the deal, which among other things would give him the ability to foreclose on homes and resell them at a profit. But he exaggerated and falsified his credentials.

He also knew how to work the power structures of Brooklyn politics, the 'machines' of the dominant Democratic Party, through which powerful individuals dispensed favours and traded influence. Fred Trump's intimacy with these political networks was the basis of the fortune that he built up over his lifetime, which would become the launchpad and often the safety net of his son's turbulent career. The discreet background presence of Fred, with his millions and his contacts, reassuring to nervous investors and officials, was one of several crucial factors behind the Commodore deal.

Property converts the intangible – influence, connections – into something material and permanent. It fortifies advantage. It creates a visible shiny object (literally so in the case of the glass-clad ex-Commodore) that distracts from the convolutions that brought it into being. Look! the politicians could say (and they did), we have brought this glittering example of progress and economic growth to a city gasping for life. For the passers-by in Forty-Second Street, and for the guests at the hotel and restaurants, the Commodore became another striking building, part of the urban furniture of the city. An architecture critic could write with perhaps naive enthusiasm that the overhanging Garden

Room restaurant would be 'one of the city's most appealing public gathering spaces, a sidewalk café in the air'.

Property can cleanse and launder. It can offer a route from insecurity to stability, as with Trump's journey from his distinctly shaky position pre-Commodore, based on networks and front, to celebrated ownership of some New York landmarks. Land once grabbed is not easily reclaimed. To be sure, it is not completely invulnerable, as Trump found when his Atlantic City casino empire collapsed in 1991, but even then his buildings constituted facts on the ground that played a role in his escape from catastrophe.

Neither Fred nor Donald Trump had some special skill at delivering projects more efficiently or at better quality than their rivals. They were not particularly good at making things. Their genius – and it was genius – was at manipulation. They understood how to play politics and law to their advantage, by working on the susceptibilities of the individuals who operate the institutions of civil society. Their tools were inducement, bullying, deception and self-promotion. It was crucial to success that all involved should believe that they were part of an inexorable force, one that would crush its opponents and buoy its allies.

They created coalitions of mutual self-interest that might rise as they rose. They would fall if the Trumps fell. This, famously, was how Donald Trump escaped the wreckage of his Atlantic City casinos in the early 1990s: the financial institutions that had lent to him were in so deep that it was not in their interests for him to fail completely.

———

In his home in Ayvansaray, Istanbul, a seventy-eight-year-old man drank some pesticide and lay down to die. He could see no other choice. His wooden house, with the accumulations of his forty-five years of living there, its ornate chairs and frail wall hangings, was to give way to 'urban renewal'. He feared he would be pushed out of his home, as his neighbours had been out of theirs, by a merciless machine of property and politics, a public–private state + business beast whose limbs and organs included, as the man's suicide note said, not only property developers but also the mayor of the local municipality and the president of Turkey, Recep Tayyip Erdoğan, for whom the redevelopment of Ayvansaray was a morsel in a $100 billion banquet that included shopping malls, tower blocks, a development-lined Bosphorus canal and the new Istanbul Airport, intended to be the busiest in the world.

Actual and prospective sacrifices to this property and construction beast included many more houses like the old man's, thousands of acres of protected forest and wetlands, the fragment of green space that prompted the Gezi Park protests of 2013, and much of the historic fabric of Istanbul: also protected natural environments in Ankara and by Lake Van where, in defiance of court rulings that they should not be built on, Erdoğan pushed ahead with gigantic presidential palaces.

For Erdoğan property development is entwined with government. It is means and end, an instrument in enhancing the power and wealth of himself and his allies, an emblem of economic progress and national pride. With the help of a large public deficit Erdoğan inflated a property-generated economic bubble, whose collapse in 2018 – alongside less picturesque casualties – resulted in Burj Al Babas, the estate of three hundred make-believe French chateaux, being left incomplete.

With due allowance for differences in personality and national politics and law, Erdoğan operates in ways similar to the Aliyevs and the leaders of other kleptocratic regimes. They use public funds and powers to further private property interests, especially their own. State and real estate merge, dictators are tycoons, and laws invented for public benefit, such as those on compulsory purchase and tax incentives, are turned to help favoured developers. Public works – an airport, a highway, social housing – become enmeshed with development opportunities and the lucrative contracts that they bring. Property is a means of patronage, of dispensing favours to family and allies.

In Trump's case, as president there seemed to be correlations between his foreign policies and his overseas business interests. The president's former national security adviser John Bolton, according to the *New York Times*, observed that the president often confused personal relationships with national relationships. Or, as a former minister and ambassador in the Bush administration put it, 'He replaced formal relations among nations in several cases with family-to-family relationship, or crony-to-crony relationships.'

The *New York Times* also pointed out the ways in which Trump 'confounded his fellow Republicans in Congress' by unusually favourable dealings with Turkey. He slow-walked legally mandated sanctions against the country for installing Russian missile systems. His administration 'balked at aggressively punishing a state-owned Turkish bank for evading American sanctions against Iran'. He agreed during phone calls with Erdoğan to withdraw American forces from northern Syria, thereby betraying US allies in the region, and their years of heroism and endurance in helping to defeat ISIS.

His friendliness to Turkey, the *Times* argued, had something to do with what Erdoğan called the 'bridge' between the sons-in-law of the two presidents, the property developer and political adviser Jared Kushner and the Turkish finance minister Berat Albayrak. A crucial intermediary in their discussions of missiles, sanctions and other subjects was Mehmet Ali Yalçındağ, chairman of the Turkey–US Business Council, which lobbies Washington on behalf of Ankara. He was another son-in-law, in this case of the property tycoon Aydin Doğan, developer of the twin Trump Towers Istanbul, which were opened in 2012 by Erdoğan, with Donald and Ivanka Trump and Kushner in attendance. 'I have a little conflict of interest because I have a major, major building in Istanbul,' was the way Trump himself described the situation in 2015, when interviewed by his future chief strategist Steve Bannon on a Breitbart radio show. 'It's a tremendously successful job. It's called Trump Towers – two towers, instead of one, not the usual one, it's two.'

There is, in other words, fraternity among developer kings, and real estate lubricates their political and financial transactions. It makes unlikely associates of the pre-presidential Trump, the court of the Aliyevs and the Iranian Revolutionary Guard, creating in effect an informal transnational network of property deal-makers, closely linked to political power, who operate with zero or few degrees of separation from corruption and theft. The property-political complex, you could call it. Its structures and operations survive changes of personnel. Trump is out of office, Erdoğan won't last for ever, but there will be others like them. All those sons and daughters and sons-in-law, for a start.

———

What this means for everyone else depends partly on who you are and where you live. In Baku and Istanbul it might mean forced removal from your home, to make way for an icon of national progress like the Crystal Hall or for a real estate opportunity for your country's rulers and their allies.

A regime unconcerned with law and its citizens' rights won't be greatly troubled by such things as ecology and heritage, either, so the property-political complex will wreck them if they get in the way. A free press, which might expose developer kings' dealings, is also an obstacle to be removed. Almost without exception, they like to bully and constrain the media and suppress dissent.

Their kingdoms tend to be characterised by the contrasts between the glitter of the rulers' icons and boondoggles, and widespread shabbiness and poverty. For if the primary objective of both public investment and public planning policy is to enrich the ruling elite, it's likely that anything outside these objectives will be neglected.

Even if you don't live in one of the states ruled by developer kings, you might well feel their effects. They like to launder and export their cash, in particular by investing in real estate abroad, which means that cities such as London or Miami or Sydney feel the weight of their wealth. Development in these places begins to bend to the will of the people helping to pay for it. It begins to reflect their tastes, needs and fantasies. The political and legal systems of the host cities feel their pressure.

———

Private property, as conceived by liberal philosophers of the seventeenth and eighteenth centuries, and by classical economists of the nineteenth and twentieth, wasn't meant to be like this. It was supposed to defend the individual, resist tyranny and generate wealth. Those philosophers and economists, along with their modern followers, could justifiably blame the heavy hand of the state for the failings of the property-political complex. Operators in this world, from Fred Trump to Anar Mammadov, couldn't function without such things as public investment in construction, planning and zoning laws, and the power of public bodies compulsorily to purchase private property.

A crucial feature of this version of the free market is that it is not really free. Government does not melt away. It becomes an enabler, a booster, a helping hand to the invisible hand. Opportunities are rife for the trading of influence and worse. Power generates money and money buys power. But, given that no developed country has found how to grow and build without public intervention, it's a fantasy to wish it away. So the challenge is rather to understand how private property works, how it tends to favour accumulation and defend advantages, and how its characteristics interact with those of government.

These tales of iniquity do not establish that everything that comes under the heading of private property is rotten, nor that every kind of real estate development is corrupt and destructive. What they do show is that there is a particular kind of power, pervasive and growing, that exploits human instincts for shelter and territory, along with the apparatus of law and politics that frames those instincts.

Ismet Hezer, the man in Ayvansaray who drank the pesticide, survived. His neighbours heard his groans and got medical help. But he then faced a demand that he make renovations that he could not afford, or be evicted. Not everyone is so unlucky, nor is every property-related story so dramatic, but he stands for citizens all over the world who have encountered the force of property. Others include the losers in the 2007 sub-prime mortgage crisis in the United States, or the many Englishmen and -women denied any prospect of their metaphorical castle by their country's house prices, or farmers pushed off their land to make way for construction in the new cities of India, or the dupes of mis-selling by unscrupulous developers anywhere.

Even if you are more fortunate, you will still have felt the unprecedented influence of the property business. Its peculiar values have come to be accepted as normal. Its effect is not only in the shaping of homes and cities but also in culture, politics and everyday life. It is present in the high value given to private home ownership in most advanced economies, for example, sometimes at the expense of a wider idea of society.

The ability of developers to shape cities according to their own rules (albeit with significant help from government) can be seen with particular force in India, thirty kilometres south-west from the centre of the capital New Delhi. Here is a city that has grown and prospered at exceptional speed, whose residents often express satisfaction and pride with the results, which is simultaneously deficient in those shared facilities – infrastructure, public space – generally thought fundamental to urban life. It takes the logic of private property about as far as it can go.

6

CITY OF MONADS

'My daughters', said the owner of an apartment in Gurgaon, India, 'are certainly in private property when they go from their bedroom to their school.'

> Leave their bedroom, go out of their door, catch the lift downstairs . . . and the school gate opens out onto our complex. So they don't have to cross any roads or anything like that. That was initially one of the important reasons why we chose to live here. From the bedroom to their school is about a five-minute walk.

He and his family live in one of the city's many privately developed enclaves, high-rise communities of hundreds or thousands of homes that offer their residents an array of comforts, luxuries and amenities. You don't just get 'swanky apartments', to quote the publicity material for one, 'designed to complement the fine lifestyle that you have always dreamt about'. You also get modular kitchens, air conditioning, a health club, swimming pool, high-end bath fittings, jogging tracks, skating rink, amphitheatre and meditation court, on-site school, electrical generators and water cisterns, 'three-tier security' and certified compliance with the traditional Hindu architectural science of Vastu Shastra – all of which is 'nestled in a green and serene backdrop'. Your life will probably be eased by domestic servants, who in many cases will be subject to 'security protocols' run by your development's management and will reach your flat by a separate system of lifts and circulation from that of the residents.

These enclaves are mostly the work of a few large property companies – DLF, Ansal, Unitech. You will be protected, within their boundaries, by private security guards and by private fire services. If you live in one of the developments created and managed by DLF, you will benefit from its Quick Response Team, whose black-clad personnel roam the estates in SUVs, and on motorbike and horse. You might spend your leisure time in one of the city's many malls, shopping for Chanel or Louis Vuitton or Mercedes, or on one of Gurgaon's golf courses, and work in one of its corporate parks. You will probably travel between home and work and play in a private car, or in some cases in a vehicle owned by your employer.

'Entering a private colony is like crossing an international border,' a Gurgaon resident told the *Guardian*. 'Firstly, the checks you go through at the gate with the private security guards. And when you do eventually cross the gate, it's like you're in America . . . with perfectly manicured lawns, and sprinklers and picket fences.'

You can live, if you wish, in a series of bubbles – home, mall, office, car – within which you are secure and safe, your pleasures and needs and health and self-esteem well serviced. What all these environments have in common, golf courses included, is that they are fenced and managed, such that unpredictable and undesirable elements can be excluded. You will, however, find it hard completely to ignore what goes on in the spaces between the enclaves, outside the protection of the walls.

Here the order and comfort inside the private enclaves turns, in many places, into its opposite. Sewage overflows into undeveloped sites. Inadequate roads are blocked with traffic jams caused by development that is dependent on cars, or they flood in monsoons. Streets end at property boundaries, causing disconnection between one part of the city and another. Supplies of electricity

and water are prone to failure. The responses of the private developments to these shortcomings add to the problems: private boreholes lower the water table; diesel fumes from private generators pollute the air. The lush landscapes of the golf courses compare with the poverty of green space available to the general public. The architect and urban theorist Suptendu Biswas has written how one of Gurgaon's waterways was 'reduced to a filthy drain full of sewage and solid waste' while surrounding land became 'a derelict place for open defecation and a pasture for pigs'. In the same neighbourhood, 'barrack-type' housing has been built for migrant workers, living at densities several times higher than previously in this location, with impacts on infrastructure that are largely unaddressed.

The city's fragmentation is expressed in its architecture. Here the aim is differentiation, not cohesion. Office buildings are pointy, twisty, curvy, swoopy, stepping, leaning, hanging, floating, crystalline, cantilevered, mirror-glassed, peacock-coloured. Some offer portals to the sky. They compete for attention, claiming to be futuristic, iconic, seeking to sell themselves as the 'most unique'.

Apartment blocks are breathtakingly vast and repetitive, long walls of real estate that can be thirty or more storeys high. They don't try too hard to conceal the fact that their principal aim is the accumulation of units. They look, almost, like the mass housing of communist regimes – the prefabricated *Plattenbau* slabs of East Berlin, for example – except that their developers make such modest gestures to individuality as might help to market their products. They add arches, pinnacles, pediments and decorative screens, or arrange the balconies in striking patterns. They import the inventories of accessories – swimming pools, spas, en-suite bathrooms – that earn the adjective 'luxury'.

Private villas might be Spanish-style, or Mughal, or modernist. Blocks for what is called the 'Economically Weaker Section'

– publicly built affordable homes for people on relatively low incomes – are plain and functional. There's the odd hostel or school whose sensitive and environmentally friendly adaptation of traditional brick construction might get it into the international architecture publications. Gurgaon is a city of multiple architectural characters, which don't seem to have much to say to each other.

Although the big developers all offer fundamentally similar products, they strive to assert their difference, dressing fundamental sameness in superficial diversity. Then, at the property boundaries, at the points where private office and residential developments interact with the shared and public spaces of the city, indifference takes over. You might find a blunt fence, or some basic paving and planting, or an abrupt transition to a multi-lane highway. The latter will be publicly financed, but the vehicles that use it will mostly be private capsules of space, as they travel between the also-private places of home, work and leisure.

Gurgaon is an urban diagram of private luxury and public squalor. It has become a place, over the last twenty or more years, where the public authorities responsible for basic amenities have failed to keep up with private property companies' pace of development, which generates chaos, to which the private sector responds by making their projects still more inward-looking and self-sufficient. It has achieved notoriety, even celebrity, for its extremes and contrasts, becoming the subject of media reports and academic studies.

It is, according to Biswas, 'a city where the state has shrugged off its responsibility in all possible ways. It is a city of the private, by the private and for the private.'

The New York architect Nathan Rich has called Gurgaon 'an archipelago of private zones, with little public fabric holding them together. Glassy skyscrapers grow from dirt roads. Private companies provide basic services like water and electricity. Militarized fences and gates protect favoured users from poorer outsiders.' And so a child's walk to school, which in other cities might involve contact with other worlds than her own, which might contain the possibility of exploration and discovery, here becomes a trip down the lift and across the lobby, perfectly sheltered from external risk and with it external stimulation.

Yet for all this, Gurgaon is admired, celebrated and envied. A well-watched YouTube video proclaims that Golf Course Road, a six-lane tower-lined highway that is one of the city's main arteries, is 'one of the most beautiful in the National Capital Region', an area that includes the historic marvels of the city of Delhi. Gurgaon is the fastest-growing city in India and its third wealthiest, one that has grown to the size of Philadelphia in twenty years, on what was a mesh of agricultural smallholdings. Kushal Pal Singh, the former cavalry officer and billionaire developer who pushed the growth of Gurgaon more than anyone else, has called it a 'pacesetter in urban development', a 'gigantic dream city' of 'glittering' malls, skyscrapers, multinational corporations and 'exciting nightlife'. Pramod Bhasin, former CEO of Genpact, found it 'young, energetic and enterprising', a 'complete marvel' as well as a 'complete mess'.

————

Fifty years ago there was little sign that any of this could happen. Gurgaon was a small town where the flatlands to the south of Delhi start to rise into the Aravali range of hills. It was surrounded by farmland, poorly irrigated and none too productive, owned in plots of six acres or less, generally by families who had held them for generations. It was a 'poor district', said an official report in 1983, populated by 'peasant proprietors owning small holdings'. It was within the National Capital Region, an area around Delhi which had been designated for planned development, and where public agencies were charged with encouraging and managing growth. One, the Haryana Urban Development Authority (HUDA), had the power to acquire land and extract contributions for developers to pay for such things as roads and housing for the Economically Weaker Section. There were plans and policies for growth. But Gurgaon and its district did not seem to have any particular promise.

It existed in an environment of centralised planning created in post-independence India, whereby government would direct growth under ambitious master plans, while also restricting what it considered undesirable development. Thickets of laws aimed to protect agricultural land from building and prevent urban sprawl. The Land Ceiling Act of 1976 limited the size of holdings that any one owner could assemble, in order to prevent the concentration of too much land in too few hands. One colonial-era law, the Punjab Pre-Emption Act of 1913, gave a right to relatives of a vendor to challenge a sale of land years after it had taken place. 'No development, leave alone a gigantic endeavor to build a city,' said K. P. Singh, 'would ever have been possible with such archaic laws in force.'

But the same laws could allow exceptions and manipulations and empowered local or state government to authorise such changes. It was possible, for example, to declare 'controlled areas' close to existing towns and along roads where building would be permitted. There was a 'power of relaxation' whereby farmland might be redesignated for development if such a change were 'in the public interest'. In the state of Haryana, where Gurgaon/Gurugram is located, 'competent authorities' could allow developers to assemble parcels of land larger than the official limit.

Gurgaon was considered too small and insignificant to have

a local government empowered to make planning decisions – which, in terms of promoting property development, turned out to be an asset. Planning – those relaxations and special designations, for example – was determined higher up the chain of authority, by the chief minister of Haryana, who could be lobbied by property companies to make decisions more expeditiously and advantageously for them. Gurgaon's relative lack of government enabled it to be a zone of exemption. It gave it competitive advantage. Clearings could be made in those thickets of laws, making possible what was obstructed elsewhere. Planners had seen the nearby city of Faridabad as a more promising candidate for growth, but it turned out to be slowed down by the greater planning powers of its city government. Gurgaon outstripped it.

The 'controlled areas' where development could happen expanded over time until they encompassed the whole past and future city. Official plans were drawn up, only to be distorted beyond recognition by the demands of developers. The effect of planning was not to create sustainable growth, where the interests of private profit and public benefit were balanced, and where investment in infrastructure and parks and public facilities could keep pace with the sprouting apartment blocks and offices, but its opposite. Planning became a device for unleashing property values. The 'controlled areas' were in effect uncontrolled, Klondike zones for the maximisation of individual profit.

The money-making potential of planning designations and relaxations was colossal: they could transform impoverished farmland into sites ripe for development. The farmers who owned such land could be vastly enriched, but they lacked the influence and access to the politicians and officials who could dispense these golden tickets. An intermediate layer of brokers and developers therefore grew up, who had the means to unlock the official permissions. The Land Ceiling Act, which was about 'bringing about an equitable distribution of land in urban agglomerations to subserve the common good', achieved through its exemptions the vast concentrations of ownership that it was supposed to prevent.

So there was an official desire for growth, and means such as HUDA were put in place to achieve it. There were laws and policies which, from a developer's point of view, were constrictive. There were ways round these constrictions which Gurgaon could exploit. There was also opportunity: Gurgaon is thirty kilometres from the heart of Delhi and seventeen kilometres from its airport, well placed to welcome residents and businesses squeezed out of the capital's crowded and expensive centre.

K. P. Singh took over from his father a declining property company, Delhi Land and Finance, or DLF, whose opportunities in the capital city had been shrunk by the government's grip on construction. He saw an opportunity to rebuild the business in the relatively free air around Gurgaon. He set about lobbying, successfully, for the repeal of the Punjab Pre-Emption Act. He also set about befriending land-owning farmers, with a view to buying their property. These, says Singh, were 'simple folk' who were 'emotionally attached to their land even if it was unproductive'. For them 'selling land just to have a better lifestyle was actually a disturbing concept'.

'I used to go and meet them early in the morning just after sunrise or after sunset when the farmers would be at home. I sat with them, discussed various topics and had endless glasses of milk, tea or buttermilk.' He went to weddings, funerals and birthday parties, and helped settle disputes and arrange school admissions and medical care. 'I was firm', says Singh, 'that we would not take the farmers for a ride. We wanted to pay them adequately . . . we never forced or arm-twisted a single farmer into selling his land.' DLF's 'basic premise' was that 'land acquisition is a transaction which should be a beneficial transaction to all concerned – the seller, the buyer, the community and the end user'.

Singh credits some of his success to the fact that, like the farmer-proprietors, he was brought up in the countryside, and that he is from the same Jat caste as many of them. Many also had family members in the army so, according to Singh, they appreciated his military background. Whatever the sources of his magic, it worked: he managed to coalesce small plots individually owned by about seven hundred families into the '3,500 acres of raw land on which a large part of the city of Gurgaon stands today'. He started building the first city's residential enclaves.

Gurgaon also received the attentions of India's most powerful family. In the 1970s Sanjay Gandhi, son of the prime minister, Indira, chose it as the location for the factory of Maruti Motors Ltd, his pet project to build a 'people's car' for middle-class Indians. With the help of the then chief minister of Haryana, Bansi Lal, agricultural land was converted into industrial, and thousands of farmers were evicted. A precedent was set that would be useful for the builders of apartments and office blocks: with the right connections and an understanding of the procedures, it could be possible to circumvent the protections on farmland.

Sanjay was killed in a plane crash in 1980, but Maruti eventually flourished, with the help of a partnership with the Japanese company Suzuki: its Gurgaon factory opened in 1983 and was producing a hundred thousand units a year by 1988. It further helped that K. P. Singh had (as he tells the story) chanced on a 'young man' stranded in the not-yet-developed wilderness with a broken-down jeep. Singh helped fix the vehicle and befriended the man, who turned out to be Sanjay's brother Rajiv, who became prime minister after Indira's assassination in 1984. Rajiv became a supporter of development in Gurgaon and, at Singh's urging, repealed legislation that the latter felt was holding back property development.

In the 1990s, following the government's deregulation and liberalisation of the economy, multinationals started outsourcing large parts of their operations to India. Gurgaon took advantage: in 1989 Singh had wooed Jack Welch, the CEO of the American company General Electric, to locate their outsourcing office in Gurgaon, which later became a separate company, Genpact. IBM, American Express, British Airways and other multinationals followed. Later came consultancies such as McKinsey, Deloitte, PwC, Ernst & Young and KPMG, and also construction and engineering businesses. Gurgaon's developers built business parks with office buildings to the international standards that these companies expected and apartment buildings to house their expanding white-collar workforces.

The character of the city and its surroundings had rapidly shifted from agricultural to industrial (with the coming of Maruti), to a centre of tech and service businesses. Its population multiplied, from 57,000 in 1971 to 229,000 in 2001, to 877,000 in 2011 to 1.2 million in 2021. At first Gurgaon had functioned largely as a satellite of Delhi, offering more affordable homes to people priced out of the capital, but it began to acquire at least some of the attributes of a big city: by 2011 it had twenty-six shopping malls and seven golf courses. Several private universities have sprung up. It has become the setting of filmic crime dramas. In 2016 the right-wing BJP, in power in the state of Haryana as in the nation as a whole, renamed it Gurugram, after the Hindu hero Guru Dronacharya, who according to legend lived where the city now stands. The move provoked scepticism, being seen as a cosmetic attempt to distract from Gurgaon/Gurugram's problems with some nationalistic branding, but it at least showed that the city was now seen as a place worth mythologising. It was no longer just a collection of functional developments.

It would be wrong to see Gurgaon as a pure untrammelled creation of the private sector. It has also been shaped by politics and government, by laws and regulations and by their relaxation and manipulation, and by public investment in, for example, roads. Political figures, such as the Gandhi brothers, have intervened. It has also been formed by the policies of its neighbours – the high level of government involvement that pushed DLF out of Delhi; the complexities of planning control in Faridabad – which enabled Gurgaon/Gurugram to profit from its comparatively low levels of regulation. Singh's 'fairy tale' is in reality a construction of dry and opaque legislation, that favours those best placed to navigate its labyrinths.

But within this state-created framework, private property companies call most of the shots. The enclaves are shaped as they want them. The fabric and pattern of the city are determined by large developments, with the territory that might be called shared and public forming a neglected infill between their protective walls. Private golf courses occupy the spaces that in other cities might be taken by public parks. Universities are private, in some cases funded by property companies. Neighbourhoods are named after them – DLF Downtown, DLF Cyber City, DLF Phase 5, Ansal Florence Super, Unitech Nirvana Country. Certainly the big property developers would prefer the public infrastructure and public realm to be better managed, but their priority is minding their own land.

The result is a city of monads, of individual and self-sufficient entities minimally connected and related to each other. 'Overall', according to one study,

> the city lacks a homogeneous experiential quality or shared identity . . . People living in different communities seek to surround themselves with people who share similar mindsets,

and there is a feeling of superiority in the people living inside the costlier gated communities. They interact less with the people outside and are well connected inside these communities.

Biswas reports 'a palpable social separation' between the city's different social groups: the prosperous residents of the enclaves, the low-paid migrant workers from other regions of India, the indigenous villagers who, depending on their luck in selling their ancestral farmland, may or may not have cash in the bank. The city's 'mixing points' are 'malls, pubs, clubs, food joints, roads', places that typically restrict entry, or require spending in order to be enjoyed, or ownership of a car. 'The culture of consumption', says Biswas, 'swamp[s] the spirit of public spaces.'

Gurgaon's villagers, whether or not they have money, are often not welcome in these places. Fights have broken out over the exclusion of those deemed undesirable from the city's malls, and there have been conflicts between different castes. There has been some hand-wringing by residents of the enclaves over their lack of connection with the villagers: 'They are patriarchal and culturally different from us,' said one of the former to the Indian English-language newspaper the *Business Standard*, 'but we, the urbanites, have made the situation worse by blocking them out.' 'We want to integrate with them,' said another, 'but they don't know how to do so with us.'

———

It is dangerous to draw definitive conclusions on a city as new and fast-changing as Gurgaon. It might yet find ways to rectify its flaws. There are some small signs that it has started to do so: activists successfully campaigned to protect Mangar Bani, a community-conserved forest on the edge of the city, from development. Citizen groups, NGOs and corporate sponsors have combined to rejuvenate polluted watercourses. In the void formed by government's neglect of the public interest, self-organising groups have started to step in.

It could also be argued that the city's defects are the necessary consequences of its commercial success, that there is no other realistic way that it could have grown so much so fast, especially in the context of India's complex governmental structures. It is hard to prove or disprove this thesis: cities are not laboratory experiments where alternative scenarios can be measured and tested. There is only one Gurgaon, and its history is what it is. Yet it is hard to believe that this is the best possible way of growing a city, even at speed.

Gurgaon offers a picture of a certain kind of city, one shaped by private property interests. The role of the public sector is not to balance, direct or regulate, but to enable and collude. It is far from being a pure creation of market forces, however – its phenomenal growth is in part the consequence of multiple policies, laws and administrative bodies, both in India as a whole and in the state of Haryana. Many of the fortunes made in Gurgaon derive from exemptions and distortions of this planning framework. They reflect neither the natural advantages of the location, nor any particular skill on the part of developers in providing better products than elsewhere, but their ability at manipulating the system and finding loopholes in it.

In some ways the gigantic enclaves of Gurgaon's big property companies resemble the informal housing that is erected in India and in cities around the world by people near the bottom of the economic pile, who have nowhere else to go. Both stand outside the intentions of official planning policy. In both cases the internal logic of the development proves stronger than the regulations that are supposed to manage them. Both in some sense break the rules. The difference is that the property companies have ways to get their rule-breaking sanctioned and legalised.

In some respects Gurgaon is not unique or aberrant or particularly new. It follows the long-established pattern of American cities such as Houston, where private enclaves are also distributed around a network of highways, and where there are stark differences in the provision of services and the quality of physical environments. Other boom towns in India – Bangalore, Hyderabad – follow similar patterns. In Vauxhall in London a clump of towers is rising which is Gurgaonian in its lack of architectural coordination and in the licence given to developers to build self-contained complexes that follow only their own rules. In Hudson Yards, New York, a vast and self-sufficient luxury development imposes a property-led monoculture on Manhattan's otherwise diverse and intricate fabric.

Both Vauxhall and Hudson Yards have their baubles. The first has an all-glass swimming pool that bridges a void between two buildings several storeys high, exclusive to the residents of expensive apartments in those blocks. Hudson Yards has the Vessel, a 46 metre-high, $200 million 'artwork' by the British designer Thomas Heatherwick, up whose multiple staircases – when they are not closed for safety reasons – the public is invited to walk. Again, fantasy and luxury fill a space where public life might be.

Vauxhall and Hudson Yards do a better job than Gurgaon of managing their waste and their supplies of water and power. Their architecture is arguably more tasteful. But they share with the Haryana boom town a tendency to create fractured cities. The Gurgaon model, in fact, is becoming the default setting for urban growth all over the world. It offers a picture of one kind of future, one that on current trajectories is highly likely, in more and more places, to arrive.

An essential characteristic is the predominance given to the interests of private property. Or, rather, of the version of private property enacted by large development companies. There is little interest in small holdings and multiple ownership, the eradication of much of which was a precondition for the city's expansion. Another essential characteristic is the involvement of government, whether at national, state or local level, in enabling and assisting the property companies. The imbalance of power between private and public is such that the latter is subservient to the former.

Which raises some questions. Will the financial power of big property always, in the end, crush that of governments and the people they are supposed to represent? Is any other arrangement possible? And under what philosophies does private property come to be so potent? What is the theoretical justification for the ideologies that lead to Gurgaon, and what might be the basis of any alternatives?

THE PHILOSOPHY
OF PROPERTY

7

PROPERTY IS HEFT

Your sheep, which are naturally mild, and easily kept in order,
may be said now to devour men.

Thomas More, *Utopia*

Capital comes [into the world] dripping from head to foot,
from every pore, with blood and dirt.

Karl Marx, *Capital*

The dominant modern idea of private property is this: land can be wholly and exclusively owned by individuals, who may do with it what they like. They can sell it, rent it out, bequeath it, use it as collateral, develop it, mine it, cultivate it, play with it, leave it to run wild, allow it to decay or to flourish. They can augment it or subdivide it. They can fence it in or leave it open. It may be subject to legal restrictions such as covenants and rights of way, and to public policies on planning and taxation, but the ideal is that land should be as free as the individuals who own it. Owning land is not in this view fundamentally different from owning a car or a watch. It is disposable and tradeable.

In societies that have adopted this idea, it is treated as natural and self-evident. It is taken for granted. Yet in many parts of the world and for much of human history, the opposite belief has been held, that land cannot belong to individuals. It has often been thought to belong to God or gods, by whose permission it might be cultivated, cleared or built on, which permission might be dispensed through hierarchies of intermediaries – monarchs, clans, priests, chiefs, nobles. Those who worked the earth might be entitled to own the produce of their labour, but not the ground itself.

Andro Linklater, in *Owning the Earth*, gives extensive and diverse examples of societies where 'earth was ultimately deemed to belong to the creator' – Islamic states from North Africa to Java, in India, China and much of Europe, the Iban people of Borneo. He identifies belief in divine ownership in the book of Leviticus and quotes a leader of the Wampanoag people in north-eastern America, for whom the land was 'our mother, nourishing all her children . . . How can one man say it belongs only to him?'

In medieval Europe, under the feudal system, possession and use of land came with customs and rights established over time. Peasants had to provide services and dues to the lords of the manor, in return for the right to cultivate and live off a piece of land, as well as such things as the use of tools and protection in the manorial courts from other peasants and from the outside world. The lords of the manor had the power to dispense justice, but were subject to written and unwritten constraints. They were expected, for example, to help the sick and needy, through gifts or reductions in rent. There was also common land, 'the poor's overcoat', which, as Guy Standing says in *Plunder of the Commons*, was available for livestock to forage or graze, and provided firewood and fuel for warmth and cooking, and materials for thatching or making fences.

All of which would be dismantled, eroded and destroyed, starting in England, and replaced by the modern idea of private property, a radical and drastic transformation that, initially, had much to do with sheep. The rising populations of the late fifteenth and early sixteenth centuries, who needed to be clothed in what was the most widespread material of the time, led to dramatic increases in the price of wool. South-east England was, for several geographic reasons, well placed both for farming sheep and trading wool. And sheep could be farmed much more effectively if small strips of open land were combined into fenced-in pastures. It meant that the animals' manure would be automatically recycled as fertiliser for the grass growing beneath their feet, and gave them some protection from the diseases to which roaming flocks were prone. It made it easier to watch and care for them.

Such changes could not happen without conflict. Those strips of land that were so logically amalgamated had been the livelihoods of the peasants who formerly grew a variety of crops on them. A compacted and enclosed pasture enriched its owner, but few others. It required less labour to tend the sheep than the cultivation of the same area of land had previously entailed. Enclosed pasture converted an economy based on the exchange of services to one based on money, in which everything had a price.

The many families who lacked written records of their tenancies – whose rights existed only through tradition and verbal agreement – might be driven from their land. Others could be pushed out by rising rents and legal pressure. Whole villages were destroyed. Homeless vagabonds wandered the roads, harassed by new laws that could have them branded with red-hot irons for the crime of having had their means of sustenance removed. 'The rich men not only by private fraud, but also by common laws,' wrote Thomas More in *Utopia* in 1516, 'do every day pluck and snatch away from the poor some part of their daily living.'

Churchmen protested, peasants revolted, and the government drafted statutes and proclamations intended to stop the conversion of ploughland into pasture, to little effect. Henry VIII's dissolution of the monasteries, from 1536 to 1541, accelerated the acquisition of property by large private landowners, who took over estates formerly run by monks and ejected their strip-farming tenants. Common land also became prone to enclosure by private landlords.

What these stories indicate is that, in its early incarnations, the modern idea of private property was an instrument of force, a weapon wielded by the powerful on the weak. It was not the benign and empowering concept described by twentieth-century advocates of the property-owning democracy, a builder of community spirit and responsible citizenship. When, in 1539, the abbot of Glastonbury resisted the acquisition of his abbey's lands by stooges of the king, he was hung, drawn and quartered for treachery.

The justification for enclosure, and of other forms of displacement of people and consolidation of land, was and is that it was productive and efficient. Linklater argues that the centuries of expulsion and enclosure corresponded with rises in population, in the face of which feudal practices would no longer have been sustainable. England's population doubled during the sixteenth century, which might have been expected to lead to food shortages, instead of which there was an improvement in general diet. 'The soil', according to a source from the 1570s, William Harrison, 'had growne to be more fruitful, and the countryman more painful [painstaking], more careful, and more skilful for recompense of gain.' The main reason for these changes, says Linklater, was enclosure.

John Locke gave intellectual formulation to such justifications in the late seventeenth century: 'He that incloses land, and has a greater plenty of the conveniencys of life from ten acres, than he could have had from an hundred left to nature, may truly be said to give ninety acres to mankind.' A rising tide lifts all boats, as it would be put in more modern times. Wealth, once created, will trickle down. In which case enclosure was not something to be resisted: the most important moral question became the compensation of the displaced.

Indeed, one should not be nostalgic for the feudal period. It was hardly a paradise of freedom. It was very much not egalitarian. For millions it meant lives of severely limited rights and prospects. Nor should one assume that common land was automatically benign and inclusive, a romantic view made attractive by the injustices of enclosures. Rights of access and exploitation could be assigned to particular communities and groups, rather than to absolutely everyone, which meant that it had the power to exclude and disadvantage those who fell outside its blessings.

It is also a crucial question whether the cruelties of enclosure were intrinsic to the idea of private property. It is after all possible to construct laws that outlaw the torturing to death of elderly abbots in the interests of private property. But those who enjoy and celebrate the benefits of the modern concept of property should give more than a passing glance at the suffering bodies on which it was built – not least because it retains its ability to divide, subjugate and brutalise.

———

In the seventeenth century the practices of enclosure were applied to the colonisation of the New World – a process in part driven by land-hungry people displaced by these same practices in the old country. There was some discussion, in the years following the arrival of the *Mayflower* in 1620, about the morality of appropriating land from the indigenous people already living there. Captain John Smith, leader of the Virginia colony, the man who according to his own account was saved from execution by Pocahontas, put it like this in 1631: 'Many good, religious, devout men have made it a great question, as a matter of conscience, by what warrant they may go and possess those countries which are none of theirs but the poor savages'.' Smith's words have a note of contempt for these bleeding-heart believers, for 'such tender consciences', as he put it.

It was decided quickly enough that such land could in fact be taken. Land was so abundant in America, in Smith's view, that there would be enough for everyone, and so it was justified to take possession of what he saw as unoccupied ground. In any case Native Americans could be bought out with laughable ease, 'for a copper knife and a few toys as beads and hatchets'. John Winthrop, one of the founders of the Massachusetts Bay Colony, developed a concept that would later be highly influential, that men could acquire 'a civil right' to land through the labour of enclosing, fertilising and cultivating it. The Native Americans, he argued, had a 'natural right' to land through long-established occupancy, but 'They inclose no land neither have they any set-tled habitation nor any tame cattle to improve the land by.' For Winthrop this meant that 'if we leave them sufficient for their use wee may lawfully take the rest, ther being more than enough for them & us'. The Reverend John Cotton, who preached a farewell sermon before Winthrop's ships left Southampton, found bib-lical passages to support Winthrop's theory. It is a 'Principle in Nature', he said, that 'in a vacant soyle, hee that taketh possession of it, and bestoweth culture and husbandry on it, his Right it is'.

These men were aware of the significance of their mission. It was Winthrop – also on the occasion of their departure from Southampton – who said that their community would be 'as a city upon a hill, the eyes of all people are upon us'. But they cannot have imagined the extent to which they were writing the script for the future colonisation of the North American contin-ent. For the idea that hard and productive work entitled you to own and enclose apparently unclaimed land, to draw lines of ownership around it that could potentially endure for ever, at the expense of people who had no concept of private property, underlay the expansion of what would be the United States.

Winthrop's and Smith's arguments make assumptions. They

suggest that native use of land was unmanaged and unregulated, that the indigenous population plucked nature's bounty when it pleased them, in an almost Edenic and childlike state, that there were no rules, rights or customs. They also imply that colonisation is a matter of enclosing land, taking it into private ownership, cultivating it and thereby 'improving it'.

Sixty years later, in his *Two Treatises of Government* of 1689, John Locke would base a philosophy of property on similar assumptions. Although he never travelled to America, he had a role in its colonisation: in 1669 he co-authored *The Fundamental Constitutions of Carolina* with his patron Lord Ashley, who was a lord proprietor of the colony. Locke's version of the continent is a fusion of fact and myth that proved convenient to his theories. On the one hand he drew on practical knowledge and ideas acquired in his work for Ashley, on the other on prevailing fantasies about the continent and its native inhabitants. These were seen as both noble savages, living in an uncorrupted state somewhat like a real-life Garden of Eden, and as hopelessly wasteful occupiers of their land, who should move aside in favour of the more efficient colonists.

Like Winthrop and Smith, Locke imagined a continent whose limitless natural riches were at the disposal of the 'wild Indian', as he called them, 'who knows no enclosure'. It was a place without the trappings of civilisation, unchanged since the times of the first humans: 'In the beginning all the world was America,' wrote Locke. It was in effect a vast commons, like common land in England, with the difference that the latter was protected by 'the law of the land'. Native Americans, thought Locke, knew no such laws. In this view their continent was an open-access universal commons. England by contrast had 'particular commons', not available to everyone to do anything, but to defined groups with defined rights.

As with commoners in England, only more so, Native Americans' use of land was (for Locke) profligate and inefficient:

> An acre of land that bears here twenty bushels of wheat, and another in America, which, with the same husbandry, would do the like, are, without doubt, of the same natural intrinsic value: but yet the benefit mankind receives from the one in a year is worth 5 pounds and from the other possibly not worth a penny, if all the profit an Indian received from it were to be valued, and sold here: at least, I may truly say, not one thousandth.

Like Winthrop and Smith, Locke believed that anyone who cultivated and enclosed unclaimed land was, through the work they put into improving it, entitled to own it. 'The labour that was mine', he said, in extracting goods such as grazing, turf or ore from the commons, 'hath fixed my property in them.' And if someone's labour made land more productive, everyone would benefit, which also gave title to such individuals: 'God gave the world to men in common; but since he gave it to them for their benefit, and the greatest conveniences of life they were capable to draw from it, it cannot be supposed he meant it should always remain common and uncultivated.' So God particularly gave land 'to the industrious and the rational'.

It was important to Locke's theories that the supply of land, especially in America, was so abundant that it would never run out. Not for him was Mark Twain's later observation that 'they're not making it anymore'. He shared Winthrop's and Smith's views there would always be enough left over for the indigenous people: 'There are still great tracts of ground to be found, which . . . lie waste, and are more than the people who dwell on it do, or can make use of, and so still lie in common.' Which meant it was acceptable to appropriate a portion of that vastness through enclosure.

Native Americans, in Locke's description, are specimens of natural humanity – the opposite of the civil society of which he was part – for whom concepts of law or ownership were impossible. It was a formulation that idealised them even as it dispossessed and disempowered them – if they couldn't own land, European colonisers could. It set an intellectual template of colonisation that, as the Canadian historian Allan Greer puts it, 'sees property as a single thing, the hallmark of civilisation and modernity'. It could therefore be imposed on peoples who lacked such a concept.

Native Americans were not, though, the unsophisticated browsers of nature's bounties described by Smith, Winthrop and Locke. As the early colonisers would have discovered (and their written accounts show that they did), some of the indigenous populations practised agriculture as well as hunting, fishing and gathering. Hunting and fishing were themselves managed and structured activities: the land and waters were 'groomed', as environmental historians put it, by such things as using fire to clear undergrowth, and the building of dams, in order to get the most out of nature.

Nor was the use of land completely unstructured and ungoverned, but included the recognition that some benefits from land might accrue to individuals, others to wider communities, and used systems of tribute whereby chieftains permitted the use of land that was in their power, in return for a share of the produce. They tended to be less preoccupied with fixed boundaries than English landowners, and more focused on its produce than its acreage – the anthropologist Kathleen Bragdon describes how Massachusetts natives would say 'I eat the land' as a way of saying that they owned it. But these different perceptions did not mean that there were no rules at all. Locke believed that government, written law and money were necessary prerequisites for rights over land; the Native Americans, as did the English commoners, demonstrated that unwritten custom could also be effective.

This ignorance of Native American cultures – which must have been at least partly wilful – was convenient. It allowed the continent to be considered as essentially blank, and its land as unencumbered, as close to other tradeable commodities as can be. Locke's theories about Native Americans, according to Greer, 'effectively disqualified them as proprietors'. His 'misdescription of colonial property formation as the enclosure of a great universal commons was anything but an innocent mistake'. It served to erase native property in land at the outset and assimilated colonial expansion with 'improvement'. 'The concept of the universal open commons', Greer writes, is 'a figment of the imperial imagination'.

Early colonisation was not in fact all a matter of enclosure and private property. Appropriation was often first achieved through the expansion of colonists' common land – that is to say, territory was claimed with herds of unfenced livestock before it was demarcated with boundaries. The eventual outcome, however, was the division of land into individual and corporate ownership – land that had never been owned in that way before. What is now the United States of America is a land largely subdivided into demarcated parcels of private property. The majority of the continent reached this state rapidly, over a period of about eighty years, from a point in the late eighteenth century where most of the land mass was still undesignated. It did so using a formula that turned Lockean theories into geographic fact.

In a series of ordinances following the conclusion of the American Revolutionary War in 1783, the new country's government set out how land in newly settled territories would be distributed. They were motivated partly by ideals, by the founding fathers' beliefs about property rights, for example that the 'one great obj[ect] of Gov[ernment] is the personal protection and security of property' (Alexander Hamilton) or that 'government is instituted to protect property of every sort' (James Madison), or John Adams's belief that 'the moment the idea is admitted into society that property is not as sacred as the laws of God, and that there is not a force of law and public justice to protect it, anarchy and tyranny commence'.

They were driven in part by Thomas Jefferson's vision of a nation of yeoman farmers, based on his belief that 'cultivators of the earth are the most valuable citizens. They are the most vigorous, the most independent, the most virtuous, and they are tied to their country and wedded to its liberty and interests by the most lasting bonds.' Each American, in Jefferson's view, should have enough land on which to live and prosper through hard work.

The ordinances were also driven by urgent needs. The government was indebted by war and had to raise cash. It had to work out what to do with the Northwest Territory, an area comprising all or part of what are now the states of Ohio, Indiana, Illinois, Michigan, Wisconsin and Minnesota. These were still largely unsettled by and unknown to Europeans, but they had nonetheless been declared – using colonisers' common indifference to native land rights – the property of the British Crown. As such, they were now considered to belong to the new nation.

It was decided that settlers could buy land from government, within a framework that also provided for the building of schools, the incorporation of cities and, when the population grew big enough, the creation of new states. Certain laws applied to these territories: slavery, for example, was not permitted.

In order to be sold, this land had to be surveyed and measured in such a way that both sellers and buyers knew what was changing hands. The traditional English way of defining boundaries through 'metes and bounds' – that is, through geographical features such as streams, paths, walls and trees – required a long-standing familiarity with terrain that was not available to the settlers of what was for them unknown territory. So a radical and potent instrument, called the Public Land Survey System, was set up to address this challenge. Starting in 1785 from a point in East Liverpool, Ohio, this would demarcate the land with a pattern along north–south and east–west lines, designating parcels that could then be sold. It was an approach that presupposed nothingness, that previous customs and claims on the land had no value, that sites could be cut up and traded like pieces of cloth. It was the logical outcome of the theory that America had been a universal open commons.

The grid turned from abstract conception into physical reality, as fences and roads formed along its lines. In due course the method was applied to larger territories further west and south, until, in the 1850s, it reached the Pacific Ocean. The consequences can be seen from outer space or on a map, from a plane or on the ground, in the gridded fields and straight-lined perspectives of middle America. The grid is felt in cities as well as landscape, where blocks follow the same geometry and dimensions. It is the largest piece of landscape design in the world. It is America's geographic DNA.

In this project, as in the early period of colonisation, reference was sometimes made to the rights of the Native Americans who already possessed the land in question. 'The utmost good faith shall always be observed towards the Indians,' said the 1787 Northwest Ordinance; 'their lands and property shall never be taken from them without their consent; and, in their property, rights, and liberty, they shall never be invaded or disturbed, unless in just and lawful wars authorized by Congress.'

As had been the case for the early colonists, title could be

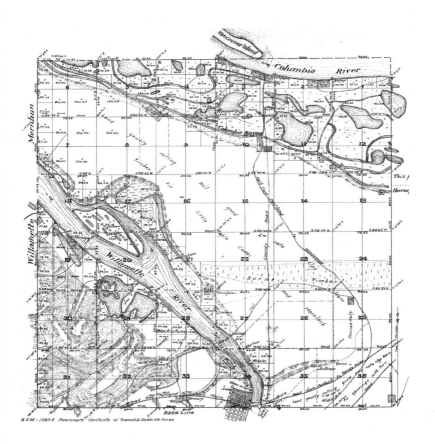

earned by work and enclosure, subject to somewhat vague assurances about the claims of the land's original inhabitants. Which vagueness, of course, led to their displacement from most of the continent. The 1787 ordinance's concept of a 'just and lawful' war proved to be broad in its application. Such a campaign, starting with the Northwest Indian War of 1786–95, could be conducted against any native nation or confederation that opposed the US government's decisions on the distribution of land. Winthrop's proviso that 'we leave them sufficient for their use', rephrased many times over the centuries, eventually turned out to mean the reservations to which they would often be forcibly removed.

The conflicts between the native populations of America and the colonisers were conducted through incompatible concepts of land: on the one hand the belief that use could be managed through custom and unwritten agreement, on the other the idea that property could be measured, drawn and legally inscribed and documented. Native Americans were obliged to play a game whose rules were not their own, and which they were bound to lose.

The ideas of enclosure and private property, having demonstrated their superpowers in what became the United States of America, were then redeployed by Britain in other colonising projects. The occupation of Australia, from the later eighteenth century onwards, was based on the idea that it was *terra nullius*, land belonging to no one. As in America, the practices and customs of indigenous populations – evidence that the land did in fact belong to them – were ignored. As in America, early appropriation took place partly through expanding the colonial commons of unfenced livestock. Ultimately the concept of *terra nullius* allowed the continent to be treated as a blank space onto which straight lines of surveying and ownership could be projected.

So there is a narrative of the colonisation of America (and, later, Australia) that it was based on the enclosure of untamed wilderness. 'When the English took possession of lands over-seas,' wrote the American historians Peter Linebaugh and Marcus Rediker in *The Many-Headed Hydra*, 'they did so by building fences and hedges, the markers of enclosure and private property.' Enclosure and dispossession fuelled colonisation with the export not only of an idea, but also of people. Many of those Europeans who endured the extreme hardships and dangers of pioneer col-onies were themselves displaced. They crossed the Atlantic out of desperation, or were forcibly transported there as punishment for vagabondage or crime. Colonisation, in this telling, can be seen as the continuous expansion of enclosures, from their origin in green English counties such as Warwickshire and Essex to forests, prairies and outback, until they covered swathes of the planet.

———

In theory enclosure need not require force. If it brings greater productivity to land and thereby increases wealth, there should be enough to compensate those displaced. Again and again the colonisers of America told themselves that there would be enough land to go around for everyone, including its native inhabitants. In practice the attractions of that wealth overcame notions of fairness, with violent consequences.

As I'll describe later, a feature of theories of property is often that rights of ownership are similar to your rights over your own body. A threat to one is a threat to the other. To take someone else's land is akin to removing a limb. But the reverse, although this philosophy is less often articulated, was seemingly also considered true: if someone had no rights over property, their rights over their own body were also diminished. Or, if a sec-tion of society gives itself power over the land of others, it also gives itself power over the bodies of others. How else might you explain how property-owning societies, in some cases immersed in philosophies of individual liberty, could support slavery, dispossession and murder?

In *Caliban and the Witch* the political theorist Silvia Federici argues that the practice of mass witch hunts, sometimes seen as inexplicable outbreaks of superstition, was in fact part of a deliberate war against women in the interests of private property. Women, she says, were particularly badly hit by the transition from a feudal economy to one based on money and property. In a system based on mutual obligations and the exchange of services there was comparatively little difference between a woman's work and a man's – everything from raising crops to raising children contributed to the well-being of a community. In the new economy it was found necessary to set the financial value of women's work at zero. It suited elites, argues Federici, if the huge and essential work of 'reproduction of the work-force' could be done for free. Women's rights to own property were restricted. Women's customs, knowledge and networks of support – for example around childbirth and folk healing – where they conflicted with the new order, had to be disrupted.

If women resisted, as they did, their resistance had to be broken, by witch hunts, trials and burnings. Persecution was not the result of sudden crazes among the general populace, but was directed from above, by the 1532 legal code of the Holy Roman Emperor Charles V, which imposed the death penalty for witchcraft, and by English Acts of Parliament of 1542, 1563 and 1604. A witch hunt required organisation, administration and indoctrination by public authorities, for example by travelling from village to village to warn of the dangers of witches and the ways to recognise them.

The phenomenon was at its peak in the sixteenth and seventeenth centuries, when common land was being enclosed and the idea of private property was developing, not in the supposedly more barbaric Middle Ages. Federici notes that women accused of witchcraft were often also accused of crimes against newly enclosed property, and that regions where witch trials were most common, such as the English county of Essex and the Scottish Lowlands, tended to be those where most land had been enclosed. And witch hunts didn't stop because their practitioners saw the error of their ways but because they were successful. According to Federici they 'expropriated women from their bodies', which were thus better able 'to function as machines for the production of labour'.

Notoriously, the founding fathers who so concerned themselves with liberty simultaneously engaged in philosophical contortions to justify the deprivation of freedom of the sixth of the population of the United States who were enslaved. Slaves were both human beings and – in the minds of their owners – private property. They could not therefore be freed without threatening the property rights that were so essential to the young republic. 'Actual property has lawfully been vested in that form,' an elderly Jefferson would write of slavery in 1824, 'and who can lawfully take it from the possessors?'

The idea that slaves, like land, could be private property replaced a traditional European concept, carried over into the early American colonies, that people might be enslaved if they fell into debt, or were captured in a just war – principles that at least contained the possibility that they might earn freedom once they had paid off their debt or expiated their military failure. From the later seventeenth century, however, laws in the American colonies started to assert that slaves absolutely belonged to their owners for the rest of their lives, and that their children would also be slaves. It was decided in Virginia that an owner who killed a slave could not be convicted of murder, on the basis that 'it cannot be presumed that premeditated malice (which alone makes murder a felony) should induce any man to destroy his own estate'. It could not be a crime to attack your own property.

Later codes would develop these themes. That of Louisiana in 1834 ruled that a master could sell a slave, and thus 'dispose of his person, his industry, and his labour', whereas a slave 'can do nothing, possess nothing, nor acquire anything, but must belong to his master'. In practice such laws meant that an owner could do almost anything to a slave, including beating, maiming and killing, with impunity. As a North Carolina judge put it in 1830, in acquitting an owner who had shot and wounded a slave girl, 'The power of the master must be absolute, to render the submission of the slave perfect.'

At the time that the United States constitution was formed it was argued that the minority who owned slaves had to be protected, as James Madison would later put it, from the 'injustice' that might be inflicted by the majority 'who have no interest in this species of property'. From such considerations arose the compromise, at the 1787 Constitutional Convention, that slaves would be counted for three-fifths of a free person, when assessing the tax paid by each state and the number of representatives to which they were entitled. 'To the framers of the Constitution,' as Andro Linklater puts it, 'a slave-owning society might be shameful, but it was possible. A society without property was inconceivable.'

The history of slavery demonstrates with grotesque force how property is an instrument of power. It is also a continuation of the logic of private property as realised in enclosure and colonisation: if rights over your body require the protection of rights over your property, then the removal of one can lead to removal of the other. Property, in these histories, is heft.

Yet the ideas of property that contributed to these brutalities also grew from desires for emancipation and freedom, for protecting individuals from over-mighty power. They were rooted in beliefs in a good God, and interpretations of his wishes for humanity. They sought explanation and justification in (always with an upper-case N) Nature. They tried to base ownership in what was 'natural' and just. Not that Nature and justice necessarily led to private property – there were significant theories that proposed the opposite – but the idea that private property is necessarily benign and liberating and natural became one of the most powerful of modern Western society.

8

A CONVENIENT FICTION

The big ideas of property that have shaped nations and redrawn continents, that assisted the industrial, American and French revolutions, that now affect the daily lives of billions, can be found in the words and deeds of pamphleteers, activists and troublemakers of seventeenth-century England. These awkward and rapidly suppressed outsiders captured an opposition which, always unresolved, accounts for the uses and abuses of property today. Is individual property ownership a natural right, was the question, like life or freedom? And if so, why would Nature want it to belong to some and not others, to the point that this inequality could curtail those other rights – life and freedom – thought to belong to everyone?

On Sunday 1 April 1649 a group of men, who would be described as 'labourers' in an ensuing court case, gathered on St George's Hill in the English county of Surrey, a little to the south-west of London. There they started to dig and cultivate some wasteland, inviting others to join them, with the promise of 'meat, drink and clothes'. These were followers of the Diggers, a loosely formed radical group opposed to what they saw as the slavery of property. They were taking their chance in a brief chaotic moment after the conclusion of the English Civil War and the execution of King Charles I in which almost anything seemed intellectually and politically possible.

The leader of the occupation, Gerrard Winstanley, thought that thousands would join their band, and their experiment in communism was indeed imitated in other parts of England, but it didn't last long, as landowners alarmed by its implications had them ejected with violence. Winstanley's beliefs, expressed in pamphlets before and after the occupations, had more lasting significance. The Earth, he said, should be 'a common treasury of livelihood to whole mankind, without respect of persons'. Private ownership was a corruption that came with the fall from the Garden of Eden, a sin against the will of God, who had created the world to be enjoyed by all. As 'a man had better have no body than to have no food for it', and as food came from land, 'true freedom lies in the free enjoyment of the earth'. 'The poorest man', said Winstanley, 'hath as true a title and just right to the land as the richest man.' He proposed as a starting point that land confiscated from Church and Crown should be handed over to communal use.

The Diggers' ideas drew on concepts of common access to land that went back to the Middle Ages, but the turmoil of their times and the availability of printing gave them a new prominence. They were not the only group to be challenging the status quo on ownership: there were also the Levellers, a movement that grew up during the Civil War and drew support both from the army that was fighting the king and from the populace of London. (The Diggers liked to call themselves the True Levellers: to avoid confusion I'll call the two groups 'Diggers' and 'Levellers'.)

Both sought to uphold the rights of the common people against the established powers of aristocracy, Church and monarchy. 'It must be the poor, the simple and mean things of this earth,' said the leading Leveller Richard Overton, 'that must confound the mighty and strong.' The Levellers, radically for the time, wanted every man to have a vote. They differed, though, in a crucial respect: whereas the Diggers believed that ownership was inconsistent with justice, and that land should be communally owned, the Levellers championed individual property. The latter 'never had it in our thoughts to level men's estates', said a Leveller manifesto published two weeks after the occupation of St George's Hill, 'it being the utmost of our aim that . . . every man with as much security as may be enjoy his property'.

For Richard Overton property was natural, personal, almost bodily. He all but erased the boundary between one meaning of 'property' – the things you own – and another: your personal attributes. Your being and your belongings were inseparable. He said: 'To every Individuall in nature, is given an individuall property by nature, not to be invaded or usurped by any: for every one as he is himselfe, so he hath a selfe propriety, else could he not be himself.'

From this he argued that 'No man hath power over my rights and liberties, and I over no mans . . . For by naturall birth, all men are equally and alike borne to like propriety, liberty and freedome, and as we are delivered of God by the hand of nature into this world.'

From the point of view of those in power the Diggers and the Levellers were almost equally troublesome. They were 'a despicable and contemptible generation of men', said Oliver Cromwell, after the victory of his parliamentarian side in the Civil War: 'persons differing little from beasts . . . Did not the levelling principle tend to reducing all to an equality . . . to make the tenant as liberal a fortune as the landlord? . . . A pleasing voice to all poor men, and truly not unwelcome to all bad men.' Cromwell's government crushed and marginalised both groups. 'You have no other way to deal with these men,' as he put it, 'but to break them in pieces.'

But in the subsequent history of politics and philosophy their ideas had different fortunes. They became, simply put, the two opposing big ideas of the following centuries: communism versus liberalism, collective versus private property. A central question

was that of what was 'natural': was individual ownership a gift of nature (Overton), or its corruption (Winstanley)?

In Britain, roughly speaking, the Levellers won. Their position – that private property is natural and inalienable – became mainstream, albeit with their concern for the poor reduced. A version of it became the ruling philosophy of Great Britain, then of the United States of America, then of much of the modern world. There are echoes of it in the French revolutionary Declaration of the Rights of Man and of the Citizen, of 1789 and 1793, and in twentieth-century attempts to define human rights by, for example, the United Nations.

Forty years after the occupation of St George's Hill, in *An Essay Concerning the True Original, Extent and End of Civil Government*, John Locke declared that 'every man has a property in his person'. Here he sounds much like Overton: property is almost bodily, an extension of the self, and injury to property resembles injury to a person. He based this view on an argument from nature, imagining an ideal primitive state before the existence of boundaries and laws. He described a man, someone a bit like Adam in the Garden of Eden, wandering the landscape looking for food. Suppose, he said, such a person picks apples and eats them. At some point they are clearly his 'property' in the sense that they become part of his body, to which no one has any right but himself. 'I ask then,' continued Locke, 'when did they begin to be his? when he digested? or when he eat? or when he boiled? or when he brought them home? or when he picked them up?'

The answer was clear. This hypothetical man made what had formerly been common into his personal property by the act of gathering it – his 'labour', the 'work of his hands' which, 'we may say, are properly his'. He didn't have to ask everyone else's permission, 'otherwise everyone would starve'. He should not, however, take more than he needed and hoard food so that it rotted away.

This Adam's apple, unlike the one in the book of Genesis, did not lead to a Fall. It was what 'natural reason', or God, intended. An abundant world was created for humanity to enjoy. 'Men, being once born, have a right to their preservation, and consequently to meat and drink, and such other things as nature affords for their subsistence.' They were also given the ability to improve themselves and their surroundings with their labour, through which they could acquire property, which means not only the produce necessary for survival but also the land that yields it. Labour makes land more productive than if it is left wild – tenfold or a hundredfold, said Locke. So, to use the argument that early colonists like John Winthrop had earlier found so congenial, whoever does this benefits humanity as a whole and should be rewarded.

Things get more complicated when societies become more sophisticated and when populations grow to the point where there is competition for land. Money is invented, a way of converting useful but perishable products into enduring but less useful objects whose value is established by consent. Money allows accumulation and surplus, and helps to sustain the inequalities that originate in the differing abilities of individuals to be industrious and productive. Locke is happy with this, seeing it as part of the natural order, the permanence of gold and silver having absolved his objection to the wasteful hoarding of things that decay.

Locke starts from a similar position to the Diggers, that everyone has a right to life and to the means to support life, and that in a hypothetical original state the world was given to everyone equally. His stress on the rights acquired by labour causes him to diverge, albeit braked by his ban on surplus. His theory of money then takes the brake off. Anyone may own as much as they can, and it is God's will that they do – he gave the world 'to the use of the industrious and rational (and labour was to be his title to it), not to the fancy or covetousness of the quarrelsome and contentious'.

America was for Locke a vast abundant wilderness, an almost-Eden where the 'Indians' could like Adam hunt and gather at will. There's an unexamined contradiction in Locke's belief that these same people should move aside for the more industrious colonisers: on the one hand Native Americans were 'natural' people very like Locke's imaginary apple-picker; on the other they had to give way to the ramifications of the 'natural' idea of property. But never mind: he took the continent's existence as evidence that there was plenty of world left for man to inhabit and cultivate, and that therefore there should be no worry that the conversion of common into private property would deprive anyone of the means to live.

Locke's apple was as influential in his field as Isaac Newton's, at almost the same time, was in his. It is not a stretch to say that the industrial revolution would not have happened in the same way without the practical application of Locke's philosophy of industriousness and ownership. These ideas, of which he was at least a mouthpiece, and in many ways an initiator, are fundamental to the development of Western society since.

Nearly a century later, when founding fathers such as Hamilton and Madison spoke of the protection and security of private property, and of the importance of government in upholding it, when the constitution that they helped to write also protected property, and when the Public Land Survey put 'the increase of lands' into practice, they were at least partly following Locke. There is a direct line between the thoughts of this bookish English philosopher and the bloody conflicts over land that would eventually be glorified in cowboy films, an unbroken thread between *An Essay Concerning the True Original, Extent and End of Civil*

Government and John Wayne. Thus America, the land whose part-mythical incarnation was such an inspiration to Locke, became the greatest fulfilment of his theories.

The privileging of property has endured, for example in the requirement that only property owners could vote, which in Britain lasted into the twentieth century. The philosopher's lean figure stands behind (for example) the words of an English lord chief justice called Baron Ellenborough, who in 1803 condemned to death a group of conspirators for, among other things, opposing the 'natural and inevitable as well as desirable inequalities of property'; also the French politician and eventual president Adolphe Thiers, who in 1848 called property the 'natural instinct of man, child and animal, single goal and indispensable reward of labour'. Locke is present in the twentieth-century theory of a 'property-owning democracy', espoused by Conservatives from the 1920s MP Noel Skelton to Margaret Thatcher. Locke is the inspiration – often acknowledged by name – for the continued commitment of American politicians to private property.

The question of the naturalness of property partly reflects the preoccupations of seventeenth-century philosophy, for which the question of what is and is not 'natural' was a burning one, but it still has consequences today, for it lends weight and authority to the concept – if something is 'natural' it is treated as unarguable. It is lifted out of the cut and thrust of human concerns and devices. It has a kind of sanctity.

If property is also heft, its supposed naturalness gives its owners advantages. Not only can I use this thing to subjugate or repel you, they can say, but any opposition or resistance on your part constitutes an act against nature. And if the heft of property tends to favour those who have more over those who have less, the idea that it is part of the natural order of things again amplifies its strength. I or my ancestors may have acquired all this by force or deception or sheer chance, but my rights to it are now as immovable as mountains and as inevitable and preordained as the cycles of the years. I'm sorry, the rich man in his castle might say, but don't blame me for inequality. It's what God wants.

These, too, might have been the thoughts of the oligarch Oleg Deripaska, former owner of Hamstone House, an art deco mansion at St George's Hill in Surrey. For, by a quirk of history, the site of the Diggers' stand is now a well-defended 964-acre gated estate built around what the cognoscenti call a 'superb' golf course. At the time of the Russian invasion of Ukraine a quarter of its 430 luxury homes belonged to owners from Russia or former Soviet states. Deripaska – who emerged from the aluminium wars of the 1990s as Russia's richest man – was perhaps the best-known individual to buy there.

At this point what might have been obvious all along needs to be said. To the statement that 'property is natural', the only sane response is 'No, it's not.' There is nothing natural about demarcating fixed lines in the ground, recording them in maps and plans, and documenting them and protecting them by laws. Private property in the modern sense only appeared late in the development of human beings, and only in certain societies. Concepts such as possession and territory may be known to almost all humans and even to animals, but they can take many other forms than the codified and bounded systems of private property.

And if you look now at the world that Locke's theories helped make – at *Selling Sunset*, or the Trump Organization, or Las Vegas, or Gurgaon – you would be hard pressed to describe it as 'natural'. Nor could you say that God's will has been done, if it were as Locke said to keep property away from 'the fancy or covetousness of the quarrelsome and contentious'. Donald Trump, and the other Hieronymus Bosch creatures who rustle across the modern property universe, owe much to a philosopher who would have hated them.

As successful as Locke's theories were in the vast extent of their practical application, their conceptual basis proved flawed. Whatever private property is, it is something other than a work of nature. Which point – although it might seem abstruse – has powerful and often damaging effects.

———

Consider half-foot. Consider aoghairean. Consider crofting. It's possible that you don't very much, and in truth you may not need to know what each of them is. They are all different ways of occupying and using land in Scotland, with each characterised by a different relationship of rights and responsibilities.

Or you could contemplate the facts that in Europe land title can be allodial or inalienable, held as life estate, in fee simple or fee tail. Again, never mind the meanings of these words – the point is that they are multiple. In different times and places human societies have developed countless ways of occupying and using land, usually in response to contrasting physical and human situations. These terms and practices challenge the belief that property is a natural right. If it takes multiple forms, and different ones in different situations, how can it be universal?

Land might be private, public, common or open-access. It is rented in many different ways. It can be subject to share-cropping, liens and easements. In some parts of the world rights are dependent on stewardship, on a responsibility to keep it productive – use it or lose it, you might say. In Latin America there are informal and illegal settlements, sometimes growing to the size of towns and cities, where prolonged occupation leads to the acquisition of *de facto* and *de jure* rights and the autonomous growth of civic structures. In China, the recent explosion in private home ownership notwithstanding, the ultimate owner of land is still the state.

There are the customs of aboriginal Australians, based on patterns of movement and use rather than boundaries, so attractive to Western romantics for their distance from Western models, but specific to places where land is vast and often barely fertile, and people are few. Comparable customs grew up in other desert regions, with no knowledge of each other, such as the Arctic territories of Europe and North America. Nomadic peoples and hunter-gatherers have less need for fixed boundaries than agricultural societies, who want fences to protect their crops and control their livestock. The English attitudes to enclosure, later developed into divinely approved philosophy, had much to do with the management of sheep. Forms of tenure, far from being universal and God-given, are practical responses to specific conditions. They are products of geography rather than theology.

There is another problem with giving the right of property the same status as life and liberty, which is that it never belongs to all. Everyone living by definition has life, and everyone in theory can be free, but there is unlikely to be a world in which everyone owns land. At best there will be such disparities in what people own that the right to property will mean something very different to some than others.

Attempts to define human rights tend to fluctuate when it comes to property, at least partly as a result of the difficulties in deciding its status. For Locke the three natural rights were life, liberty and estate (by which he meant property), a formulation that was repeated in the Declarations and Resolves of the First Continental Congress, held in Philadelphia in 1774. 'The inhabitants of the English colonies in North-America, by the immutable laws of Nature,' said the document, '. . . are entitled to life, liberty and property.' In the Declaration of Independence of 1776 'property' was replaced by 'the pursuit of happiness'. The Declaration of the Rights of Man and of the Citizen, adopted by France's National Constituent Assembly in August 1789, and its 1793 revision, reinstated the essential role of property.

The United Nations Universal Declaration of Human Rights of 1948 states that 'everyone has the right to own property' and should not be 'arbitrarily deprived' of it, but does not give this right the same status as its French predecessors did. The right to property is not part of some supreme group of three or four, but appears in Article 17, which means it has roughly equal significance to (for example) the rights to travel, to education or to the free choice of employment. That is to say, it is important, but it is not part of the fundamental basis from which other rights follow.

The further statements and covenants on human rights that followed the UN's declaration have, thanks to its impurity, struggled to agree about the right to property. Some recognise it, others do not. The American Declaration of the Rights and Duties of Man, adopted by the Ninth International Conference of American States in Bogotá in 1948, attempts a middle way: it permits 'every person' the right to own private property, but only such as 'meets the essential needs of decent living and helps to maintain the dignity of the individual and of the home'. A protocol added in 1952 to the 1950 European Convention on Human Rights recognises a right of 'legal enjoyment of possessions', but qualifies it: 'except in the public interest and subject to the conditions provided for by law'. The Canadian Bill of Rights of 1960 declares 'the right of the individual to life, liberty, security of the person and enjoyment of property', but in the Canadian Charter of Rights and Freedoms of 1982 property disappears. 'Everyone', it states, 'has the right to life, liberty and security of the person.'

While there's widespread agreement about life and liberty, in other words, these grand statements can't make up their collective mind about property rights. This confusion – together with the world's multiplicities of tenures – suggests that they are not so fundamental and universal after all. They are still important, and none of these declarations would support arbitrary or illegal confiscation, but they are contested and negotiable.

The idea of the natural right of property also tends to come with a debatable belief in the nature of the individual – the view that someone's identity can be established within the boundaries of her or his body, and that the social aspect of humanity is correspondingly less significant. Locke's apple-picking man is notably solitary. The Peruvian economist Hernando de Soto Polar made such arguments with particular clarity in 2016 when he wrote that property is

> the source of life, where all living systems – whether created by God or organized by man – originate and operate only in encapsulated spaces. Cells, molecules, body organs, computers or social groups – each and every one – is contained and constrained within a boundary, whether it is a membrane, an epidermis, a wall, or a legal property right.

So in this view property is natural, divine even, not only because of its origins in the actions of an imaginary natural man, but also due to the demarcated boundaries that are fundamental to its operation. Such boundaries, de Soto argues, are essential aspects of all existence.

The examples he gives invite challenge. When he says that computers are 'contained and constrained' you wonder if he has heard of networks. In nature there are waves and forces as well as particles and cells. It is surely also easy to think of 'social groups' whose edges are fluid and indistinct, which merge and overlap with other groups freely and often. Nor do individuals exist solely within the confines of their skin – their existence and identities come into being through interactions with others.

Similarly with land and buildings. Ownership of land and buildings implies relationships with other people – neighbours, public authorities, providers of utilities, those who might impinge on your daylight (in a city) or water supply (in the country), or on your rights of access, also with those on whom you might impinge. Such things as wind, wild creatures, seeds, fire and pollution readily cross property boundaries. Land tends to have history, and with it rights and customs. An 'isolated individual', as Karl Marx put it, 'could no more have property in land and soil than he could speak'.

This observation now has greater truth than he could have imagined, as the effects of climate change are indifferent to property lines. Holding title gives limited protection against drought and flood. The actions of a landowner in one place – the extraction and consumption of fossil fuels, the generation of pollution – will change the lives of others in other places, whether or not they are landowners. The atmosphere is held in common across the whole world, and no modern version of the Public Land Survey has been devised to subdivide it into rectangular plots. If 'Nature' has a stake in questions of property it's this: it has to be sustained and protected in ways that are beyond the means and motivations of private ownership.

———

If private property, then, is not a natural right, what else might it be? And if it is based on an incomplete, over-individualistic view of human nature, what part could it play in societies where the social aspects of existence are more fully acknowledged?

Property is a legal construction, a concept with a large and specialised body of law attached to it. It is a fiction, if a convenient one – that is to say, it is a set of invented ideas, practices and laws that seek to manage fundamental questions of territory, shelter and survival. Often, it performs this role well. It is a tool or an instrument that can be useful, effective and beneficial for individuals and societies. It is one such tool among several, with different characteristics and applications in different geographical and social situations.

It can be a weapon, both defensive and offensive. It can be, as Overton wanted, a protection for individuals against arbitrary power. It can also be, as it was in the colonisation of America and Australia, a means for dispossessing peoples with different customs for occupying land. It is something connected to what might be considered a fundamental human right – the freedom from removal of your means of sustenance or shelter, or of the products of your work – but not a unique and intrinsic way of upholding that right. For, if it is agreed that people should be protected in this way, then private property does little to help those who don't have it.

Here it is important to note a significant difference between contemporary discussions of land and property, and those of the seventeenth and eighteenth centuries. For Overton or Locke or Jefferson the primary purpose of land was agricultural, and ideas for protecting possession of it came from the desire to protect the livelihood that came from it. It was a matter of life and death: without access to land, you could starve. Now, of course, land continues to remain vital as a source of sustenance, but many people's lives are sufficiently far removed from food production that its ownership doesn't seem to be a pressing concern to them. Urban land ownership has become relatively more significant, an arena in which physically constructed spaces are governed by legally constructed concepts. Yet 'natural' ideas of land, rooted in growing and harvesting crops, are transferred unquestioned into the artificial landscapes of cities.

The idea of private property in land, treated as natural and self-evident by those many societies that have adopted it, has strange and perverse characteristics.

This idea is at odds with the nature of land. Land is immovable, but private property aspires to treat it in the same way as a mobile good. Its supply is largely finite – it can be improved but not created, with some exceptions such as reclamation from the sea – which again sets it apart from almost every other good.

Property is social, while it is described as private. This contradiction carries the potential for conflict between the freedoms of the owner and the rights and claims of other interested parties. The desire to trade and sell tends to prefer property to be simple and unencumbered; the implicated and enmeshed nature of land tends to complicate it.

Legal and political devices have grown up to handle such tensions: covenants, contracts, planning policies, building regulations, party wall agreements, easements, rights of way and rights of light. The social–private nature of property can be positive and collaborative. It can lead neighbours and communities to discover what their common interests are, and act accordingly.

At the same time the duality of property has the potential for violence. There is profit to be had, since trade wants simplicity, in purging encumbrances, in nullifying the claims and enjoyment of others. Inequality of power and the size of potential profit are both multiplying factors of such violence – which is a simple description of what happened with enclosures in England and in the American colonies.

It is not the tenure in itself that is a force for good or ill, but the way it is used. Nor is private property the only form that appropriation can take. History offers plenty of examples of invasion and seizure without the assistance of Lockean philosophy. Private property, then, is not as its greatest enthusiasts would claim a sufficient guarantee of freedom in itself, but neither is it uniquely exploitative and brutal.

What might be surmised is that this weapon tends to end up in the hands of those with more rather than less power and wealth, absent a concerted attempt by government and society to push in the opposite direction, whether through distributing the blessings of ownership more widely, or through other forms of protection and empowerment, such as public housing. James Madison, for example, although a champion of private property, envisaged that 'equalising laws' would counteract concentrations of ownership and balance the interests of the landed and the un-landed.

What does this history mean for those of us who live in the world made possible partly by enclosures and appropriation, who enjoy the benefits of its great cities and efficient agriculture? It means, firstly, to know its capacity for violence and dispossession, to mistrust claims for its natural benevolence. And it poses a challenge: if so much of the history of private property is that it was acquired through enclosure and colonisation, what does the concept become if it does not entail the forcible exclusion of others? Is it even possible that property can be held not at someone else's expense? Given that Locke's theory of infinite land – that there would always be somewhere else for displaced people to go – has been disproved, what happens to his philosophy, that depended so much on it?

9

POSSESSION AND DOMAIN

'We hold these truths to be self-evident,' says the United States Declaration of Independence of 1776, 'that all men are created equal, that they are endowed by their Creator with certain unalienable Rights, that among these are Life, Liberty and the pursuit of Happiness.'

As we have seen, this famous statement departed from previous attempts to define the rights of the embryonic nation by substituting 'property' with 'the pursuit of happiness'. It was not a trivial or an accidental change, but reflected the views of the declaration's primary author Thomas Jefferson, for whom it was 'a moot question whether the origin of any kind of property is derived from nature at all'. Happiness, unlike property, could in principle belong to everyone. In Jefferson's usage, which drew on ancient Greek and Roman philosophy, it included public virtues of courage, moderation and justice, as well as private fulfilment.

The declaration's choice of words very much did not mean that property was considered unimportant. But the substitution embodied a philosophical conflict that would continue to embroil American and European politics. Where private property supports the pursuit of happiness, then all is well and good. But in circumstances where it demonstrably has the opposite effect, which takes precedence? And on what basis is one considered more important than the other? Common sense suggests that happiness is more important than ownership, but it is hard to define. You can draw lines around a piece of land and write contracts to define it, but how can law and policy uphold a state of mind?

Property, wrote the American political economist Henry George about a century later,

> robs the shivering of warmth; the hungry, of food; the sick, of medicine; the anxious, of peace. It debases, and embrutes, and embitters. It crowds families of eight and ten into a single squalid room; it herds like swine agricultural gangs of boys and girls; it fills the gin palace and groggery with those who have no comfort in their homes; it makes lads who might be useful men candidates for prisons and penitentiaries; it fills brothels with girls who might have known the pure joy of motherhood; it sends greed and all evil passions prowling through society as a hard winter drives the wolves to the abodes of men.

In his *Progress and Poverty* of 1879, George condemned property as 'robbery', as 'an usurpation, a creation of force and fraud', as the parasitic means for diverting wealth generated by productive work and investment into the hands of owners, a process that confounded 'what are really the profits of monopoly with the legitimate earnings of capital'. He distinguished 'capital' – which he saw as a beneficial ally of labour in generating wealth and progress – from privately owned land, which was a means of extracting profit from society. Money paid in rent, he argued, necessarily reduced the amount left to reward labour and capital. 'With material progress,' what is more, 'rent everywhere advances': there being a 'fixed quantity' of land, on which there were increasing demands, owners could charge ever more for its use. There was no corresponding advance in wages and interest.

George saw how, in California, land values went up in expectation of railways being built: in other words that owners benefited who had contributed no risk or effort to their construction, and that those same raised prices forestalled the rush of immigrants to the newly connected areas that might otherwise have been expected. Rent, he said, 'does not arise spontaneously from land; it is due to nothing that the land owners have done. It represents a value created by the whole community.' Yet 'the increased production of wealth goes ultimately to the owners of land in increased rent'. He quoted as illustration an English translation of an old Indian land grant: 'To whomsoever the soil at any time belongs, to him belong the fruits of it. White parasols, and elephants mad with pride are the flowers of a grant of land.'

For George this process of extraction explained a phenomenon of the mid-nineteenth century, which was that the riches created by the industrial revolution visibly failed to improve the lives of the workers on whom it depended. The 'association of poverty with progress', as he put it, 'is the great enigma of our times'. 'It is the universal fact', he also wrote,

> that where the value of land is highest, civilization exhibits the greatest luxury side by side with the most piteous destitution. To see human beings in the most abject, the most helpless and hopeless condition, you must go, not to the unfenced prairies and the log cabins of new clearings in the backwoods, where man single-handed is commencing the struggle with nature, and land is yet worth nothing, but to the great cities, where the ownership of a little patch of ground is a fortune.

George attacked the view, widespread in his time as now, that poverty and misery were the necessary results of increasing population. Famines in Ireland and India were not caused by overpopulation but by 'an absentee and alien landlord' – who in both cases though in different forms happened to be British. The linking of poverty to population served 'to justify existing inequality by shifting the responsibility for it from human institutions to the laws of the Creator'. It deflected attention from the fact that private property in land 'always has, and always must, as development proceeds, lead to the enslavement of the laboring class'.

The solution could only be to abolish the source of the injustice: 'Nothing short of making land common property can permanently relieve poverty and check the tendency of wages to the starvation point.' George proposed a tax on land values, one that he believed would yield so much revenue that all other taxes could be abolished. It would mean that owners could keep their title to their property, but would have to hand over all their unearned proceeds from it. 'We may safely leave them the shell, if we take the kernel,' wrote George. 'It is not necessary to confiscate land; it is only necessary to confiscate rent.'

George was influential and widely read in his time. *Progress and Poverty*, for a while, outsold every book except the Bible. His land value tax continues to be an attractive proposition to political parties, though rarely those with real prospects of power. His ideas were a force, for example, behind the movement to build 'garden cities' – communities that among other things shared the uplift of the value of land from investment – that started in Britain in the late nineteenth century.

It is also striking that he was writing nearly a century after the ordinances of the young American republic put theories of private property into large-scale practice. By Henry George's time the grids of the Public Land Survey had reached the Pacific coast. George, who worked as a journalist in San Francisco, could observe what happened when the great commons of America had been enclosed, once (as he put it without much sign of sympathy for the victims) 'we drive back the Indian and exterminate the buffalo'.

The infinitely receding frontier, so important to Lockean

theories, had become finite. Property, as a consequence, was no longer a reward for honest work, George believed, but its opposite: the means for cheating labour and investment of its profit. Nor was it in any sense natural. The thing that Locke hoped wouldn't happen – that the accumulation of wealth by some would obstruct the ability of others to improve their lot – was coming to pass. George's answer was one the Diggers would have recognised, that land (or at least its benefits) should be common property.

For the ideas of the Diggers hadn't gone away. If the Levellers' view that private property is a natural right could conquer continents, the contrary belief that land should be a 'common treasury', and therefore cannot be owned by individuals, has also been powerful. Thus the French philosopher, politician and self-proclaimed anarchist Pierre-Joseph Proudhon, in *What Is Property?* of 1840, attacked the idea – expressed in the 1793 reworking of the Declaration of the Rights of Man and of the Citizen – that property is a 'natural and inalienable right', alongside liberty, equality and security. He wrote: 'If we compare these three or four rights with each other, we find that property bears no resemblance at all to the others; that for the majority of citizens it exists only potentially and as a dormant faculty without application.'

Since many people don't own property, in other words, it is a less essential right to them than liberty, equality and security. Proudhon denounced as a 'shameful equivocation' the association of different meanings of 'property' – as personal attributes and as the things that you own – to be found in the writings of Overton and Locke. His 'ten propositions' declared that 'property is impossible' (among other things) because it is the 'mother of tyranny' and 'the negation of equality'. He said it is 'chimerical' and 'the suicide of society'. 'Property', he famously said, nearly forty years before George called it robbery, 'is theft.'

Proudhon made a distinction between 'possession' and 'domain'. Possession here meant the ability to put land to beneficial use, in contrast with the legal right to control it for whatever purpose an owner chose. What mattered, he argued, was that all people should have possession of land sufficient to their needs and to the shared benefits of society. The key was to suppress property while maintaining possession. And, while the individual passes away, society never dies, which means that it should hold land in trust for future generations.

Karl Marx and Friedrich Engels, in *The Communist Manifesto* of 1848, were likewise scathing about the natural and liberating qualities attributed to property by liberal philosophers. Rather it was for them an essential mechanism in the systems of accumulation of capital that they would overthrow. 'Modern bourgeois private property', they said, 'is the final and most complete expression of the system of producing and appropriating products, that is based on class antagonisms, on the exploitation of the many by the few.' They described capital as 'that kind of property which exploits wage labour, and which cannot increase except upon condition of begetting a new supply of wage labour for fresh exploitation. Property, in its present form, is based on the antagonism of capital and wage labour.' Like Proudhon they pointed out its non-availability to much of the population: 'The necessary condition for [its] existence', they said, 'is the non-existence of any property for the immense majority of society.'

Marx and Engels proposed that 'capital is converted into common property, into the property of all members of society'. They called for the 'abolition of property in land and application of all rents of land to public purposes'. So powerful and oppressive was private property, and so emancipating its removal, that it would be at the centre of their revolution. 'The theory of the Communists', they said, 'may be summed up in the single sentence:

Abolition of private property.' Their revolution would be 'the most radical rupture with traditional property relations'.

Jefferson, George, Proudhon, and Marx and Engels were far from being kindred spirits, but they shared the belief that property, rather than rewarding honest labour, enabled the profits of workers' efforts to enrich owners who might do little or nothing for their wealth, other than control the spaces in which production took place. It created a class of more or less idle rentiers. There was nothing natural about it. Nor was it an inalienable right.

They also agreed that the value of land was never a purely private concern, but that it was made by collective actions and should serve collective interests, as in Marx's observation that isolated individuals could not own property in land. 'Rent,' as George put it, 'the creation of the whole community, necessarily belongs to the whole community.'

All offered different responses to the inequalities of private property. George had his land value tax, a self-contained if large public intervention in what would otherwise be a free-market economy. Proudhon proposed that all property 'becomes collective and undivided', that the 'right of occupation' should be 'equal for all'. Marx and Engels demanded that the state take control of property on behalf of the proletariat.

We are still waiting for any of these grand plans to achieve unequivocal success. George underestimated the difficulties of identifying and taxing that element of the value of property that could be attributed to the actions of the community, while leaving untaxed that part that was particular to the owner. He also overestimated the size of the revenue his land value tax might earn. Proudhon's egalitarian allocation of land encounters difficulties: how is it decided what makes two portions equal, given that land is not a uniform product? And by which authority?

How is equality maintained under the pressures of shifting populations, and with varying rates of birth, death and migration? More than a century after the creation of the world's first communist state, the Soviet Union, there has yet to be an example of one that fulfils Marx and Engels's hopes for a liberating, egalitarian and prosperous society, while there have been many that achieved the opposite.

But their insights remain. It is plainly true that property can be used to extract wealth and deny opportunity and growth. It is also the case that the value of property does not exist in a vacuum, but depends on actions beyond its boundaries, such as law, infrastructure and investment by others than its owners. It is social as well as individual.

For these reasons Proudhon's distinction between possession and domain has force. It can be agreed that people should have rights to security, to shelter and to their ability to benefit from their own work. But these rights do not necessitate absolute and total ownership of land. This distinction returns to land's fundamental purpose of sustaining human life and dignity. It has implications: it is the basis on which the profits on land might be shared between its titular owners and the society of which they are part, or on which people who are not owners might have rights of access or enjoyment. It has the potential to redress the extreme inequalities that arise from private ownership.

It is not an extreme position, to believe that ownership is social as well as individual – some of the founding fathers of the United States, in particular Jefferson, thought so. 'The earth belongs in usufruct to the living,' he wrote, which meant that people might have rights to the benefits of land in their lifetime but not absolute ownership. Jefferson's 'usufruct', developed in the 1780s, sounds a little like Proudhon's concept of 'possession', as published in 1840. He based his views, as would Proudhon and George in the following century, on the observation that the concentration of ownership could exclude non-owners from the possibility of improving their lives or, in some cases, of livelihood. 'It is clear that the laws of property have been so far extended', he said, 'as to violate natural right.'

He hoped to put his idea of usufruct into practice on the land west of the Appalachians that the United States had taken over from the British. He proposed that this land should be permanently owned by the government, who would lease it to individual citizens for terms of nineteen years. In this way the Jeffersonian idea of democracy would be achieved and sustained, in which 'the small landholders are the most precious part of the state'.

As chairman of the committee charged with drawing up a plan for this territory, Jefferson had some prospect of making his ideas reality. His idea of leasehold, however, gave way to that of fee simple, whereby ownership was held in perpetuity, with unlimited power to sell or give away. We can only guess what would have happened if Jefferson's dream had come to pass, that of a balanced society based on usufruct.

———

The essential aim that lies behind rival theories of property is the nurturing of human freedom and happiness. Whatever grotesqueries might flourish around both private and public ownership should not conceal this principle. It matters more what property does than what it is – it is the means to an end, whatever form it takes, whether individual, collective or owned by the state.

The idea of possession returns to fundamentals. In principle, it protects survival. It states the basic necessity for shelter sufficient to sustain life and dignity, without which all other liberties and rights are worthless. It emphasises benefit and enjoyment over abstract accumulation. It recognises the value of shared space. No good life, after all, is exclusively led in segregated monadist cubicles. Possession is the foundation on which a renewed concept of property could be built.

The embrace of this concept need not entail, as it did for Proudhon, the abolition of the useful and productive tool of legal ownership, or of the prosperity and security it brings. Much of the time, possession and ownership give each other strength. They are, usually, on the same side in the cause of emancipation. But when accumulation leads to corruption they come into conflict. At present, in most developed countries, the exceptional importance granted to property as a natural right overrules rights of possession. It becomes a legal weapon against the human values it was intended to defend.

The concept of possession could help you, too. If you are an owner it could help you to see the boundary where property stops assisting fulfilment, and starts to obstruct. If you aspire to own, or if you happily rent, it could help you to know why. If you have no home, or if you unhappily rent, it might guide your anger and frustration to their best targets.

You might also consider the space outside your door – the fact that a home is made not only by property boundaries but also by interactions with neighbours and strangers, by a locality as well as a house. The fever of ownership, in seeking 100 per cent satisfaction from a private enclosure, tends to push the value of shared spaces towards zero.

There's enough philosophy, religion and folklore to tell us that you can live a good life without owning much, that material things do not truly make us free. We've heard that money is the root of all evil, that we should lay not up for ourselves treasures upon earth where moth and rust doth corrupt, that we should consider the lilies of the field, that money can't buy you love. In our minds or souls there's a background murmur that property is one of the false realities of an impermanent world and that attachment to it is an obstacle to enlightenment.

Most of us know what this murmur is saying. Possessiveness of material things can indeed come at the expense of human relationships. It can be an unconvincing hedge against mortality, a palliative for loss, a fortification against others, a drug which, the more it is consumed, the more dependent it makes its users.

It is equally true that the protection of private property rights has, especially in Western society, brought prosperity and freedom. To preach self-denial is all very well, but it should be a choice for individuals, not imposed by external agency – to give it all up is only meaningful if you have something to give up in the first place. Among the freedoms of property, what's more, is that of accumulation – the right, whether or not it makes someone happy, to pile up acquisitions of land and buildings.

There is nothing to be gained from denying this right, except where accumulation leads to corruption. Then it creates concentrations of power and wealth that overwhelm the legal protection fundamental to the liberal concept of property. It has to be countered by a return to founding principles.

It is time to reclaim the promises of property. If its philosophy is rooted in ideas of emancipation, those roots have to be recovered. With this recovery goes the recognition that property is a right to shelter, home and the means of dignified existence – possession – before it is a right to accumulate and exploit.

WHAT ELSE COULD THERE BE?

10

LIFE IN COMMON

If land and buildings are not privately owned, how else might they be held?

One answer is: in common.

Common land is not a strange or exotic concept. For many societies in the history of the world it was or is the only way of occupying land. In others it is an essential part of a mixed economy of possession and use.

There is, for example, the role of common land in the feudal systems of medieval Europe. This could be accessed by people who did not own it for the necessities of survival: food, fuel, the materials to build shelters. It was, and is, also more than that. Common land is, says Guy Standing, in *Plunder of the Commons*, 'what defines a community'. It is a communal resource that not only provides the means of subsistence but also requires maintenance and preservation, such that it can continue to provide in the future. It is an activity as well as a place – the act of 'commoning', to use a verb that has fallen from use, which Standing defines as 'participative, communal activity'.

Common land was protected by the English Charter of the Forest of 1217, which survived for 754 years, until it was replaced with the Wild Creatures and Forest Laws Act of 1971 (the 'forest' of the title did not only mean a large expanse of trees, but rather unenclosed countryside in general.) This document, which has been called the Charter of the Common Man, is less famous than Magna Carta signed two years earlier, but also of huge significance. It defended common land against usurpation by the king and nobility. It set out rights to agistment, piscary and pawnage, that is to say to graze cattle, catch fish and let pigs feed on nuts. It set up local courts run by locally elected officials to protect animals and their habitat and to prevent excessive destruction of trees and wildlife.

Despite these protections, common land in England was progressively shrunk by waves of enclosure in the sixteenth, seventeenth and eighteenth centuries, which for the most part converted it into private property. Five per cent of land in Britain is now common, compared with about half in the Middle Ages. Much of what remains – such as rural and urban parks – serves the purposes of recreation and conservation of nature more than livelihood.

The commons endured, though, as an ideal. Campaigners at the time of the English Civil War, in particular the Diggers, were motivated by the shrinking of the commons. *Light Shining in Buckinghamshire*, a Digger pamphlet of 1648, attacked enclosures as 'the Beast's mark' and 'unfruitfull works of darknesse'. Also:

> Man following his own sensualitie became a devourer of the creatures, and an incloser, not content that another should enjoy the same priviledge as himself, but incloseth all from his Brother; so that all the Land, Trees, Beasts; Fish, Fowle, &c. are inclosed into a few mercinary hands; and all the rest deprived and made their slaves.

Rather, said the anonymous author, there should be 'a just portion for each man to live, that so none need to begge or steale for want, but everyone may live comfortably'.

The argument against the commons, made throughout the centuries of enclosure and up to the present, is that they were and are inefficient: whatever regrettable deprivations might be suffered by victims of enclosure would be more than counterbalanced by the more general benefits of greater productivity – which, in times of rising population, might be a matter of survival. And if some landowners became rich in the process, that was an incidental or even welcome detail.

In more modern times this theory has been formulated as the 'tragedy of the commons', articulated by the American ecologist Garrett Hardin in 1968. Drawing on a nineteenth-century British economist called William Forster Lloyd, he argued that, where there is open access to a resource, the short-term interests of individuals will overwhelm those of the collective: each herdsman (for example) will bring more cattle to graze until a grassland becomes a desert through overuse, at which point both individual and collective interests are destroyed. Hardin saw private property as one method of averting the tragedy of the commons, albeit an imperfect one. In the special but important case of pollution, where the actions of private landowners might contaminate 'the air and waters surrounding us' – that is to say, common resources that 'cannot readily be fenced' – 'coercive laws or taxing devices' might be needed to stop individual owners making these resources into a 'cesspool'.

Hardin's view has been challenged, most notably by the Nobel Prize-winning economist Elinor Ostrom, whose 1990 book *Governing the Commons* set out examples where 'common pool resources' are successfully managed without recourse to either private property or state control. She cited cases of self-organisation, such as fisheries in Turkey and irrigation systems in the Philippines, where contracts are made cooperatively and not enforced by external agency. She noted that many law firms, where partners pool their assets to pay for joint resources and develop internal governance, follow similar principles.

The tragedy of the commons is not, Ostrom demonstrated, inevitable. This conclusion did not lead her to the conclusion that common access or ownership, or 'self-governing forms of collective action', are universally practical or beneficial ways of managing shared resources. There is, she said, no single prescription. The examples she gave tended to flourish in specific circumstances, for example where populations are stable, in which case 'individuals have shared a past and expect to share a future'. Ostrom's aim was not to propose one solution but many, and to show that differences between public and private ownership are not absolute. Above all, she wanted to emphasise the ability of communities to manage themselves from the bottom up.

So common or shared access to land and resources – what we might call 'the commons' – is not inherently catastrophic, nor is it a universal panacea. Sometimes it works, sometimes it doesn't. It almost always requires some form of governance and organisation – completely unrestricted, unmanaged resources are rare. It tends to serve some groups more than others. Some consequences follow. One is that the commons takes many forms, with structures and principles specific to particular times, places and societies.

Allan Greer, the historian who questions the Lockean idea of a universal open commons, makes a distinction between 'inner' and 'outer' commons. The first might be a communal pasture for the inhabitants of a specific village, the second peripheral areas or moor or forest more widely available for such things as grazing, fuel and construction materials. Both types were subject to rules and customs about access.

It follows that the commons can exclude as well as include, that they can be used by those who benefit from them to the detriment of those who don't. Greer argues that, in the case of the colonisation of North America – and, later, Australia – native populations were not only displaced by enclosure and private property. The appropriation of their territory came, as well as through the building of fences, through the expansion of what Greer calls the colonial commons – unenclosed land where livestock could roam – at the expense of the native commons. Herds of cattle could push out the deer off which native populations lived, and pigs could destroy the ecology of their lands.

Common ownership and access, in other words, are not inherently good or bad. Rather, like private ownership, they are instruments or tools and sometimes weapons, that can be used to liberate and enrich or to oppress and impoverish. But common ownership becomes more attractive in circumstances where other mechanisms are failing. And, given that most discussions of the commons revolve around the role of land in providing food more than shelter, how do its principles translate to places of inhabitation, to cities and towns and the complex constructions in which people live?

————

During the Cold War, when Berlin was the nucleus of potential global nuclear conflict, this fissile city was split by opposing views on property. The East was governed by an ideology which saw property ownership as 'capitalist egotism' and private residences as 'remnants of past worldviews', whose inhabitants had no understanding of 'the foundations of socialist communal living'. West Berlin offered a version of liberal capitalist society, in which the right to private property was fundamental.

Within this opposition there were variations and contradictions. Socialism, said the lawyer Inga Markovits in her writing on East German law, was 'fixated on property, in ways that remind me of Christianity's preoccupation with sin', and as with Christianity and sin it had to accommodate rather than abolish the object of its fascination. The East German government was obliged to follow the Soviet precedent, which admitted limited forms of ownership, such as 'weekend houses' and gardens. Private possessions such as these were 'tiny enclaves of self-determination', as Markovits also said, 'in an otherwise tight and regimented world'.

In both West and East Berlin there was also squatting, the occupation and setting up of communes in properties left vacant by the inefficiencies of the respective systems. Squats were both practical responses to the need for housing and political statements – opportunities to create alternative models of shared ownership and shared responsibility. The fall of the Wall multiplied the opportunities for squats in vacant buildings in the former East. They became emblems of Berlin, incubators and symbols of its creative culture and – wearing the spray paint, layered posters and crumbling plaster that is the uniform of anti-uniformity – tourist attractions.

Both before and after 1989 Berlin's squats were, from some anarchist viewpoints, what they called Temporary Autonomous Zones – utopian places where humanity could recover an imagined pre-agricultural condition of ordering itself in 'bands' of about sixty people. Other squatters would be more pragmatic, primarily seeking places to settle that suited their way of life. There was a divide between 'negotiators' – those who would do deals with government or property owners to keep their squats going – and the non-negotiators, who would not.

A squat could be amiable or sinister. It could be a place where music, art and vegan Thai curry were offered at little or no cost, or the base from which the *Autonomen*, masked and black-clad radicals, could go out to throw Molotov cocktails at the forces of law. It could be Tacheles, the shell of a department store made into an 'art squat' where squatters could achieve 'self-realisation', a 'utopia' according to one art writer 'where art seemed to actually be about experimental lifestyles and defiant visions of social freedom'.

By the teen years of the twenty-first century rising values caused more and more squats to be reclaimed by the property business. The look of Berlin squats turned into graffiti chic, applied to cafes and hot-desking workspaces for start-up tech companies. Tacheles was closed in 2012 and its premises later bought by a New York financial services firm. In 2015 the artistically aware but not-anarchist practice of Herzog & de Meuron produced plans to make it into a mixed-use development of apartments, hotel, shops, offices and cultural space. The project's developers promised it would be 'an extraordinary place and space . . . for the very highest standards in residential living . . . for stunning cosmopolitan architecture . . . for international class and that famous Berlin lifestyle'. Very much not, then, a radical alternative to property ownership and conventional social order.

The moral of these stories might seem to be that sooner or later everything reverts to real estate. Havens of anarchist freedom fade away, and their sites are parcelled up, priced, marketed and sold. In a microcosm of events elsewhere, the fall of communism removed the gap between it and capitalism, a gap in which alternative and esoteric ways of living had been able to thrive, and one that the property market would eventually fill and close. But in the decades in which Berlin acted as an experimental zone, those alternative and esoteric models lived long enough and with enough impact to show that there are, in fact, multiple ways to view the relation of ownership and inhabitation.

Sometimes, moreover, their spirit and principles endure and prosper, even after the squats and communes have disappeared. Take modern Vienna, which owes much to the desperation and enterprise of the 'wild settlers' who, driven by the economic collapse that followed Austria's defeat in the First World War,

occupied land on the city's outskirts. These groups of what were essentially squatters started a process that, a century later, still shapes the city's social and physical fabric.

By 1921 thirty thousand families, unable to find or afford homes, and feeding themselves only with difficulty, had moved into sheds and cabins on what were originally allotments, created to help feed the city during the war. They farmed and gardened. They built new structures and adapted what they found. They set up cooperative forms of self-government that were championed by the political economist Otto Neurath. 'It is not the individual house that is the object of design,' he said; 'the individual house is a brick in a building.' For Neurath the settlements were a way towards the collective happiness which, he believed, was the aim of economics.

Austria's Social Democratic Party, at first suspicious of the settlers' entrepreneurship, was persuaded with the help of Neurath's advocacy to support them. Later in the 1920s, in control of Vienna and with a tax base to support them, the party addressed housing need at much greater scale, with 'superblocks' of a thousand homes or more. These were in some ways the opposite of the informal settlements – they were in the city rather than outside; they were large, planned and often monumental in their architecture. They can indeed be seen as a way of taming the dangerously anarchic spirit of the settlements, but they continued from the latter the spirit of community. Central to their concept were shared courtyard gardens, laundries, libraries, cinemas, kindergartens and theatres.

The most famous of these developments, the kilometre-long Karl-Marx-Hof, celebrates the working people it houses with a series of triumphal arches. Red-painted expressionist compositions of towers and balconies, each bearing a flagpole, march like robots across the elevations. When civil war broke out in

1934 it became a citadel for socialists against the fascists who would eventually win the conflict, its balconies used as gun emplacements. It is still there now, its gardens and shared facilities generating an atmosphere of communal peacefulness that is at odds with its violent history.

What also survived, despite the intervention of Nazi rule and world war, was the principle that municipal government should support such housing. In the 1990s, when Britain and other countries were selling off their social housing, Vienna continued to build it. Sixty per cent of the city's population now lives in homes built and run by the city, or by not-for-profit cooperatives that it helps to support. It makes for a metropolis where people of different incomes can share the same neighbourhoods, and where homes are close to places of work and leisure. As other cities become zoned and polarised these are prized qualities. Vienna wouldn't have them without the chain of events that the wild settlers started.

Like the Tacheles squat, or Scottish crofting, or legalised favelas – or speculative residential developments in Shenzhen or New York – neither the wild settlements of Vienna nor the Karl-Marx-Hof provide universal solutions. They were specific responses to specific circumstances that were also subject to evolution, as new pressures and opportunities emerged. But they are evidence that the inhabitation of land is not a matter for individuals alone, and that private ownership is not necessarily the best or only way to achieve it.

11

COMMUNITY AND COOPERATION

'I often have to explain to people when they're driving past Co-op City what it is,' says Diane Patrick, who has lived in this colossal development in the Bronx, New York City, since 1970, 'and I just say it's the world's largest housing cooperative, and it's great, and I'm sorry you don't live here.' 'I wouldn't change it for the world,' says Bernie Cylich, also resident since 1970. 'A friend of mine who lived on the Upper East Side came to see my apartment and was amazed, because my living room could hold her living room and kitchen all together,' says Alena Powell, who moved in in 1973. 'And that's just one room. I like the fact that I'm not on top of other people as if I was living in Manhattan. You're not really going to find a situation like this in other parts of New York City.' Patrick praises the spaciousness and light of her 'beautiful apartment'. 'When I come home I can hear my footsteps,' she says. 'I can hear the birds . . . Sometimes I'll see a racoon or a skunk. I hear there's deer now. I might see Bambi soon. It's very quiet . . . I just enjoy coming home to Co-op City. I really do.'

These residents were speaking to the film-maker Adam Tanaka for his 2018 documentary *City in a City*. Their enthusiasm is remarkable for the fact that they live in a place which, according to almost all urban theorists for the last sixty years, cannot and should not work. It is, architecturally speaking, an unusually faithful realisation of the visions that the Swiss–French architect Le Corbusier developed in the 1920s: Co-op City has ranks of concrete towers of up to thirty-three storeys in height, uniform and repetitive, set in expansive parklands, served by broad, sweeping roads. Drawings that Le Corbusier made to shock and provoke his Parisian audiences here take on monumental reality, right down to the crisply diagonal fall of shadows on the cruciform towers. Such buildings, goes the theory, are alienating and dehumanising. 'The high cost of hideousness' was how one report branded Co-op City when it was new. 'The spirits of the tenants', predicted the American Institute of Architects, 'would be dampened and deadened by the paucity of their environment.'

But then these residents are not primarily concerned with form and aesthetics. They are more interested in the fact that they have affordable, secure and sufficient housing, achieved through Co-op City's structure as a limited-equity cooperative governed by its residents. This means that residents can buy for a fraction of market prices, plus a monthly maintenance charge. If they sell, they have to do so for the price they originally paid, plus interest. So they forgo the chance to make a profit on their property. On the other hand, says Tanaka, 'In a city whose median home price recently surpassed $800,000, two-bedroom apartments in Co-op City go for just $20,000 down to income-qualified applicants.'

Surplus value belongs to the cooperative, which is run by a board elected by residents. It can be invested in common benefits, such as maintaining the 80 per cent of the development that is open space. 'If we have extra cash it's there, it's ours, it belongs to all of us,' says Cylich. 'Every tree is your tree, every bench is your bench.' 'You don't own in the same sense,' says a former director of the United Housing Foundation, which is the not-for-profit organisation that sponsored and built Co-op City, 'but you have control. It makes for a better building, makes for a better block, makes for a better city.'

This shared ownership and management helps explain the success of Co-op City's common areas. A frequent failure of

Corbusian town planning comes from the neglect of the parks and the communal facilities that lie between the towers, often as a result of the underfunding and disinterest of the local authorities or public agencies that run them. In stereotypical examples crime and vandalism take over the open spaces, and residents have to take inconvenient bus rides to access basic services such as shops and doctors' surgeries.

In Co-op City, where everyone has a stake in the well-being of the whole, planting is tended, streets are maintained and local facilities are sustained. 'Just name a service and we probably have it,' says Alena Powell, 'whether it's our own police force, seniors' programmes, programmes for youth, just about every denomination of churches are here, there are stores. If you don't want to leave Co-op City you don't have to.'

Residents celebrate what one calls the 'mixture of all kinds of cultures. We have teachers, we have nurses, doctors, blue-collar workers, municipal employees, federal employees. It's a very unique place. It's large but then it's small at the same time.' Its diversity is also ethnic. Ever since it opened in 1968 it has housed Jewish, Irish, Italian, African American and Latino residents, in shifting proportions. It was 'in sharp contrast', as Tanaka puts it, 'to the segregation that marked most new suburban communities'.

Co-op City was the culmination of a cooperative housing movement going back to the early twentieth century, whereby labour unions provided affordable and decent housing for their members. It was intermediate housing, for the benefit of a 'forgotten middle' of working families who couldn't afford what the private market offered, but weren't poor enough to qualify for public housing. Tens of thousands of homes were built across New York City in this way.

This movement was driven above all by Abraham Kazan, president of the credit union of the Amalgamated Clothing Workers of America, who argued that apartments should be 'valued for their ongoing use as habitation rather than their potential speculative value as a commodity'. Among the organisations that he helped to set up were the United Housing Federation, the largest of all cooperative housing builders, which created Co-op City.

Cooperative housing was created with the help of government initiatives, at city, state and federal level. In 1955 the Mitchell– Lama housing programme was set up in New York state, which enabled developers to acquire land for affordable housing through eminent domain, and to benefit from tax abatements, low-income mortgages and guaranteed returns on investment. Politicians both Democrat and Republican – John F. Kennedy, the New York governor Nelson Rockefeller – supported it. Such projects demonstrated, said the president, 'what labour with good, effective, progressive leadership, and the city and the state and private groups and the federal government, together and in cooperation, can do for this city and this country'.

Co-op City would be a particularly large and spectacular beneficiary of the programme, built on marshy ground near the north-east edge of the city, on the site of a failed amusement park themed on American history called Freedomland USA. If the word 'cooperative' suggests something bottom-up and community-led, this was also a product of the grand and sometimes grandiose thinking which, under the leadership of the city official Robert Moses, had bestowed expressways, bridges and giant housing projects on the city.

With fifteen thousand homes in thirty-five buildings on a 320-acre site, it would be the largest cooperative housing scheme in New York, possibly the world. It was the largest architectural project, in terms of square footage, ever built in the city. The $250.9 million mortgage that financed it would be the biggest in history – enough to build, it was pointed out, several Empire

State Buildings. It had schools, community centres and auditoria, shopping centres, its own power plant.

This was the era of 'white flight', when the white middle classes were leaving cities for suburbs where people of colour were effectively barred from living. Co-op City was an attempt to counter this tendency, by offering the benefits of suburbs inside the city limits. Much was made of the comforts of the new homes – eat-in kitchens, indoor bathrooms, cross-ventilation and central air conditioning – and, if the big towers didn't look much like the little detached houses you might get in a Levittown, the abundant greenery and road space of Co-op City did have something of the suburbs.

The intention was always to house a diverse population. Cooperative housing in New York had a reputation of being mainly for the benefit of Jewish communities, and when it first opened Co-op City's population was 75 per cent Jewish. Twenty per cent were African American, a proportion that would increase over the years, with the help of conscious efforts of the residents' advisory committee, including pioneering forms of affirmative action.

Co-op City, it seemed, was remarkably effective at achieving the ambitious and desirable goals it had set itself. But then problems hit. Construction faults led to high maintenance costs, which led to hikes in the monthly charges. There were complaints about incomplete facilities. In 1975 the complex defaulted on its mortgage. In the same year the residents started a thirteen-month rent strike, which was only ended by a compromise brokered by the governments of the Bronx and New York City.

There were recurring accusations of corruption. 'The idea of Co-op City is wonderful,' a resident, a hospital secretary called Lillian Ryer, would tell the *New York Times* in 1986. 'Unfortunately, the practice isn't. There are too many fingers in the pie, and there always have been. Co-op City was put together with spit, glue, and graft. Not enough spit and glue. But plenty of graft.' Financial crises would continue into the twenty-first century, driven by the high cost of repairs, with accompanying demands to restructure loans. A further enormous refinancing, of $621.5 million, was required in 2012.

At the time of its fiftieth anniversary, in 2018, Co-op City was – in the eyes of the residents who talked to Tanaka – fulfilling its dreams of affordable cooperative living. It was possibly as settled and secure as it had ever been. Now, though, it faced a challenge from a new direction, which was the temptation to go the way of some other cooperative developments in New York, whose resident-shareholders had opted out of their restrictions on affordability. The appeal was great – apartment owners could now sell their homes at market values that were many times what they paid for them – but the cost would be the destruction of the ideals on which Co-op City was built and in which so much financial and human capital has been invested.

At the time of writing Co-op City remains cooperative and affordable. It stands as the greatest monument to the cooperative housing movement, but also as a memorial. Nothing remotely like it has since been attempted in New York City. The conditions for its creation, including the availability of huge empty sites that might be acquired by public authorities through eminent domain, would be hard to replicate.

Since Co-op City's well-publicised problems coincided with the debt crisis that hit New York in the 1970s, it came to be seen as a work of an obsolete and discredited attitude, a 'progressive overreach' that favoured grandiose and extravagant ways of distributing public money. From now on urban renewal was to be driven by private-sector developers, albeit with support from public authorities, the approach that would bring Donald Trump's Commodore hotel deal. The long march towards gigantic chunks of city like Hudson Yards, where developers make rules and shape buildings, had begun.

Apart from its cost and maintenance issues, there are other complications to Co-op City's approach. The ever-widening gap between the price of a home there and in New York's private housing market makes it increasingly difficult for residents – who don't have the equity built up by private home owners – to move from one to the other. 'You've got the cardboard box, the homeless shelter, the park bench,' was how one described her options, 'or there's Co-op City.' 'Many shareholders', wrote Tanaka, 'have chosen to stay put for decades, limiting turnover and, in some cases, occupying apartments much larger than they need.' So Co-op City's ageing population, with no prospect of finding comparable homes elsewhere, remains in homes that might beneficially go to their equivalents in the next generation or two.

But that same gap in prices makes more essential than ever the affordable homes that developments like these provide. There are also clear advantages to the stability of its population – the spirit of community, the networks of friendship and support. An obvious response to the problems of turnover would be to build more places like this, not fewer: if there were a larger stock of cooperative housing, there would be greater prospects of mobility within it.

The central attractions of the Co-op City idea are the removal of profit and speculative value from the price of land and construction, such that homes can be more affordable, combined with residents' ability to have a say in their own homes and neighbourhoods. Other benefits potentially come too. Socially, it encourages interaction between residents and shared responsibility for the city as a whole. Financially it makes it possible (for example) for municipal governments to support such developments with loans, or through making land available, rather than by spending taxes on grants and subsidy. In theory and sometimes in practice, such developments can sustain themselves.

It's an appealing prospect – affordability *and* community spirit, social benefit *and* a business-like proposition. It's hardly surprising, then, that versions of this idea go back more than a century and a half, and that New York is far from the only city to have had a try at realising them. But it also has to be acknowledged that, in this long time, they have not swept the world. Some cooperative housing projects fail to achieve their stated aims, some achieve housing in quantity at the expense of their participatory ideals. Some are successful at a small scale, without expanding beyond the niche they have carved for themselves.

Some work well for residents who have the social heft and energy to navigate the complexities of establishing cooperatives, less so for those less empowered and privileged. Many of the most successful cooperative developments, perhaps most of them, require significant support from city, regional or national governments, as Co-op City does. In these cases the co-op idea becomes a variant of other forms of subsidised social housing, one that might have significant advantages, but is not a radical alternative to them.

Cooperative housing can take different forms – in some projects residents own their homes, in others they rent, in some it's effectively a combination of the two. There are also related but not identical ideas, such as co-housing, where residents typically share communal facilities while owning individual homes in a conventional way, or community land trusts, where land is owned and developed by community-based non-profit organisations.

The broad idea of collective living is not bound to any one economic model or political ideology. Some collective housing is physically indistinguishable from other types; some seek new forms and layouts to serve new ways of life. It can reflect different motivations: sometimes a practical wish to share facilities such as gardens, saunas and communal dining rooms, sometimes an ideal about communal society, or a desire to provide an alternative to the cellular units of traditional family life. Often an aim of collective housing is to encourage inter-generational living: providing homes and facilities for people at every age enables people to stay together in the same location from cradle to grave.

The category of collective living includes Narkomfin, a housing project built in the early years of the Soviet Union on the site of a demolished monastery in Moscow. Here high-ranking finance ministry staff were housed in a block of radical constructivist design, where cooking, laundry and childcare were communally organised, while individual flats were built without kitchens. The concept also includes the Collective, a creation of the heated property market in twenty-first-century London, developments where tiny living quarters are complemented by shared dining rooms and workplaces, a cinema, library, roof terrace and gym.

The theory behind Narkomfin was to disrupt bourgeois family life with a more socialist way of living, one that would liberate women from domestic drudgery. The Collective's business model was to attract young professionals who, despite being relatively well paid, might struggle to buy a home in the London market. Here they could pay for a small number of square feet, with their limited private space being augmented by the shared facilities. These two projects embody extremes of communism and capitalism, but both come under the heading of collective living.

One could also look at the *kollektivhus*, a type of co-housing developed in 1930s Sweden, which aimed to free middle-class women from domestic labour by centralising tasks and performing them more efficiently, a project that was given added impetus by a shortage of domestic workers at the time. Or, also

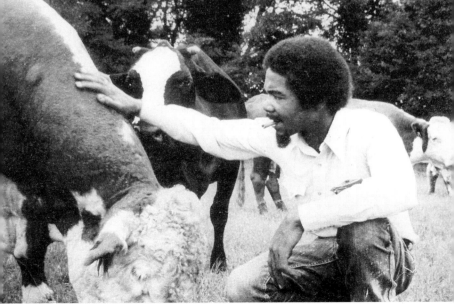

in Sweden, at the Stacken community in a suburb of Gothenburg. Here a partly vacant residential tower was made into a collective of thirty-five apartments that has been running successfully for over forty years. Tenants share craft workshops as well as the more usual laundry, kitchen and play facilities, and take decisions together on the running and maintenance of the building. Or one could look at a hugely ambitious project in the American South, which sought to hold both homes and farmland in a trust, for the shared benefit of all. It failed, but the model that it pioneered flourished elsewhere.

———

In January 1970 a group of lawyers and others working on behalf of a community organisation called New Communities Inc. walked into a bank in Albany, in the US state of Georgia, to certify cheques necessary for concluding the purchase of 4,800 acres of farmland and woodland. Their journey had not been easy – a faulty door had almost led to the cancellation of the last available flight from New York, where the cheques had been drawn. 'The fate of the New Communities experiment', says one account, was 'virtually hanging on the rope the passengers used to hold the door shut during the flight.' Nor did the day go smoothly. The sellers of the land, made reluctant by hostility to the deal from the local white population, started to walk out of the room, just as the deadline for closing it approached.

The reason for the hostility was that the intended beneficiaries of the transaction were black. New Communities Inc. was an organisation that had grown out of the civil rights movement. Arguing that access to land gave power, and that black people were consistently obstructed from ownership, it proposed a new model, the community land trust. Here land would be owned by a trust from which residents could hold secure long-term leases. It was hoped to build a new town for local poor people, especially black sharecroppers, who could work and live off the agricultural land.

A 1972 book on the New Communities project, which called itself 'a guide to a new model for land tenure in America', described the community land trust as 'a legal entity, a quasi-public body, chartered to hold land in stewardship for all mankind present and future while protecting the legitimate use-rights of its residents'. It held land 'in perpetuity – probably never to be sold. Thus, the problems of exchange value are virtually eliminated.' It was removed, in other words, from the vicissitudes and inequities of the speculative property market.

The leases secured use-rights of residents, leaving them 'free to control and build their own community through co-operative organisations or individual homesteads'. The trust 'distinguishe[d] between land with its natural resources and the human improvements thereon'. While the land would always be held in trust, anything created by the residents, such as 'homes, stores, and industrial enterprises', would belong to them, either cooperatively or individually. In these ways, it was hoped, the community land trust would address 'the contradiction between the private ownership of land and its inherently limited nature in the face of multiplying population pressures'.

The underlying philosophy came from a Native American belief that, as the book put it, 'land belongs to god'. The book quoted the Shawnee chief Tecumseh, who resisted the early expansion of the United States into his people's lands: 'Sell the country . . . why not sell the air, the clouds, the great sea?' The concept also owed something to the theories of Henry George's distinction between the 'legitimate' earnings of investment and productive work and the 'robbery' of private ownership and rent. It followed George's insistence that land should be not be private property, although with a different structure: the community land trust model enacted 'ownership for the common good' rather than the 'common ownership' that George proposed.

The practical form of the trust drew on the garden city of the English town planner Ebenezer Howard, who, heavily influenced by George, proposed a structure whereby 'unearned increment' – the uplift in the value of land – would be reinvested in facilities for the good of the whole community. The 1972 book cites several other inspirations, including practices in Mexico, Tanzania and India, whereby individuals might have rights to use land, but could not own it, and where villages and communities would manage it for the common good. A particularly influential model was the *moshav shitufi* type of cooperative settlement in Israel, which 'provides small plots for individual farming as well as encourages cooperative farming'. A study trip to Israel was arranged, so that the organisers of New Communities Inc. could see them in practice.

Back in the Albany bank the deal for the farmland was finally done: it was now the largest black-owned tract of land in the nation. This, sadly, was not the end of the project's struggles. The concept proved unequal to the brutal realities of farming and building in this territory. Interest on the loans with which the trust bought the land was high, and blights and heavy rains in the first year of operation meant that it earned less than half the amount needed to service the debt. Hostility from white neighbours continued. The segregationist governor of Georgia, Lester Maddox, a man who had once handed axe handles to white customers in his Atlanta restaurant, to use on any black people who were thinking of dining there, called the organisation's founders 'communists'. Federal loans and aid that were available to white farmers were withheld from New Communities Inc., or at best delayed.

Idealistic college students came down from the north to offer volunteer labour. Many, defeated by the harsh realities of working these fields, then rapidly went home. Three or four villages had been planned of two hundred families each, with a hospital and industrial, cultural and education centres. As it turned out, there were never more than a dozen families living full time at New Communities. In the end a series of droughts in the 1980s finished the project off. Again denied aid that was given to white farmers, it declared bankruptcy, and the farm was turned into subdivision lots. The US Department of Agriculture eventually admitted systematic discrimination against black farmers, but it was too late. Although New Communities Inc. continues to advocate for social justice, the original dream was not realised.

But the idea of the community land trust survived. The most successful American example would be one created in Burlington, Vermont, under the mayoralty of the future presidential candidate Bernie Sanders. Here, in the years following Ronald Reagan's election as US president in 1980, access to housing was hit by a reduction in national government funding, high mortgage interest rates, rising house prices and limited legal protections for tenants. Neighbourhoods in the city's downtown suffered from both deteriorating housing stock and decreasing affordability. Advocates of community land trusts proposed creating one as a response to all these problems.

Sanders initially had some doubts, but was won over to the cause. The Burlington Community Land Trust was set up, supported by city and federal funding. It would hold land in perpetuity, while selling homes on it at affordable prices to low-income households, on condition that resale could only be to similar buyers on similar terms. The ideal was to achieve 'permanent affordability', described by its supporters as 'the only socially equitable and fiscally prudent way to achieve affordable housing'.

The trust had other attractions. It would have a democratic

structure. It would be eligible for funding and tax breaks unavailable to the city government, be independent of political fluctuations in said city government and gather support across party divides. It would be easier to sell this unfamiliar concept if it came from a charity, which would reduce accusations that it was a dangerously socialist project. The trust was likely to be a better steward of the homes in its care than government officials, with better relationships with residents. The trust, as its chief executive would later write, prevents absentee owning, deferred maintenance and predatory lending, while enabling intervention to prevent foreclosures.

The community land trust still attracted opposition. Some local property developers hated it. A group was formed called HALT (Homeowners against the Land Trust); they organised pickets of city hall, where protestors adapted the lyrics of 'Home on the Range'. 'Oh give me a home on land that I own,' they sang, substituting the buffalo and antelope of the original with a less romantic statement about tenure. Financial institutions were dubious about the security of properties jointly owned by the trust and by residents, until they found that the foreclosure rate on community land trust homes was exceptionally low. Sanders worried that the scheme would create second-class home ownership for working people, until he was persuaded that it would offer a better deal than renting.

In 1985 the trust helped its first resident, an assistant librarian and single mother of two called Kathy Neilson, to acquire her own house. It would help people like Bob Robbins who, despite being unemployed at the time, found a home for his family through the trust in 1995. 'We don't understand why housing isn't done this way everywhere,' he told *Slate* magazine twenty years later. The cheaper mortgage, he said, allowed his family to save money for college and retirement. 'It's just such a logical thing to have land owned by a community and the house be your private property to do with as you wish. We've just had a terrific life here so far because of it.'

By 2019 the trust had a portfolio of six hundred shared-ownership homes and owned another 2,400 rental apartments. The properties in their care included six cooperatives. It expanded into the county in which Burlington stands, then into two more, and eventually merged with the Lake Champlain Housing Development Corporation, a non-profit provider of affordable rental housing, to become the Champlain Housing Trust.

By offering a range of different tenures, it could help people with different levels of income and enable them to move from one to the other – for example, from renting to shared ownership – as their needs changed. It could offer financial education and counselling. It also started enabling community projects that were not residential: a pocket park, a community centre, office space, the conversion of a bus garage into commercial spaces.

What the trust did not do was break the mould of housing provision in America. As a broadly sympathetic *Slate* article noted in 2016, the community land trust 'remains a niche model', at the time providing twenty-five thousand rental units and thirty thousand home-ownership units across the United States. These numbers are 'dwarfed' by those provided by traditional public housing.

Community land trusts play a similar role in the United Kingdom. They provide affordable, well-run and equitable communities whose residents report high levels of satisfaction, but in small numbers and sometimes with considerable difficulty. One of the best known, the community land trust at the converted St Clement's Hospital in East London, benefited from the support of the London mayor and the impetus of the 2012 Olympics, which was held nearby, but even with these advantages it took eight years of effort to achieve its first twenty-three affordable homes. Another celebrated trust, Granby Four Streets in Liverpool, where residential and communal spaces were beautifully formed out of derelict Victorian houses by the young architectural collective Assemble, created eleven homes.

Tom Chance, chief executive of the National CLT Network, says that community land trusts in Britain create 'one or two hundred' homes per year. This, he acknowledges, is 'minute', when set against a national annual housing need estimated at three hundred thousand. His ambition is that CLTs could grow, to deliver 'tens of thousands a year', but he doesn't see them supplanting the local authorities and housing associations that provide most of the county's affordable housing. The strength of the concept, for him, is not so much that it is a more effective way of achieving affordable housing than others but that it creates 'participatory democratic organisations' where communities get to have a say in the design and running of their neighbourhoods.

Projects for collaborative living, such as community land trusts, cooperative housing and co-housing, do not magically transform the economics of property. If they promise the two benefits of affordability and community spirit, they don't always achieve both at the same time. Sometimes they pursue the latter more than the former – the dream of a shared existence takes precedence over accessibility to people on low incomes.

Nor are they for everyone. It takes effort to set up, build and run collective living projects. Plenty of people, especially the time-poor, have other uses for their evenings and weekends than going to meetings. You may not want to work at being your own developer and landlord, any more than you necessarily want to bake your own bread. A lot of people, a lot of the time, just want to buy their loaves from a shop. They also want professionals to look after their housing needs.

Community land trusts are sometimes criticised for serving

those on moderate incomes better than those in greatest need. Not everyone can access the family homes for sale that they typically offer, although the Champlain Housing Trust's portfolio does include apartments for the chronically homeless. Collective housing in general can also raise the question of what exactly a 'community' is: who is out and who is in? And if you're a local resident who is not a lucky recipient of its blessings, what does it do for you?

Collaborative living remains an appealing idea that could beneficially be more widespread. It doesn't seem likely to be transformative or universal, but rather one potentially desirable option among several. Importantly, it almost always requires public subsidy if it is also to be affordable, in which case one should pay attention to a type of property that has created vast quantities of homes across the world: that owned and built by local and national governments, or by agencies supported by governments. Council housing, as it is sometimes called in Britain, or social housing or public housing, as it is also called there and elsewhere. One should also look at the power of the state to build at scale – whole towns and cities – in ways of which the private sector, acting alone, is incapable.

12

THE VISIBLE HAND

In the county of Buckinghamshire, in southern England, a long straight road aims at the point on the horizon where, at the summer solstice, the sun rises. A shopping centre, shining and elegant, runs for 750 metres along one side. There are abundant trees, a park at one end, and leafy residential districts a little further away. This is Midsummer Boulevard, the central axis of Milton Keynes, a city both druidical and Californian in inspiration. It is a success, one of the fastest-growing cities in Britain, consistently rated highly by its inhabitants when they are asked about their quality of life.

They say things like:

There's no beginning and there's no end. It's all about open skies, opportunities and keeping moving.

Milton Keynes is so much more democratic and open-minded than a lot of places because people are still moving here. Because it's an easier city to live in, people are less stressed.

I think the future of England is here in Milton Keynes; and there's a lot of young people and the city can only get better because of it will grow . . . It's difficult for me to find a negative thing about Milton Keynes because I love the place so much.

Oh wow! Yes, this is home! This is home! From schools, again everything goes back to my children, from schools to safety, to an environment where children have so much to do, there is so much for families! In fact, you have so much choice here.

They've made friends here, their roots are here! Absolutely! This is our home.

In the 1960s the area it occupies was mostly farmland, with a scattering of villages. It is now home to 280,000 people. It is notoriously difficult to create towns and cities out of almost nothing – unintended consequences intervene, they lack older settlements' centuries of organic growth and of learning through trial and error, they are said to lack soul and identity – but Milton Keynes has done it.

It owes its existence not to the unalloyed magic of private property, nor to community action, but to the intervention of the state. It was brought into being by a government order in 1967. It was planned and run by publicly appointed agencies. It was achieved through purchase of land by government, compulsorily if necessary but with compensation paid. It was financed by harnessing the uplift of value that came with investment in roads and pipes and parks and other beneficial services and through the conversion of agricultural land into homes, and into places of work and leisure, a process helped with low-interest government loans. This was done so effectively that it ultimately cost the British taxpayer little or nothing to build.

As the New Communities project in Georgia tried to do, Milton Keynes puts into practice the arguments of Henry George, that the value of land is a social more than a private creation, and therefore that it should be put to social benefit. George advocated a tax on the value of land, which he thought would be so effective that it could replace all other taxes. The capture of value that enabled Milton Keynes was not technically a tax, but it achieved a similar effect.

Milton Keynes was the last and largest of the thirty-two new towns created by the British government after the Second World

War, a programme which delivered homes where 2.8 million now live. It was driven by one of the most influential ideas in the history of town planning, that of the garden city, proposed by Ebenezer Howard in his 1898 book *To-Morrow: A Peaceful Path to Real Reform*, republished in 1902 as *Garden Cities of To-Morrow*.

Howard, a London-born son of a baker, had tried his hand as a farmer in Nebraska and a reporter in Chicago before returning to his native city to take on the somewhat dusty job of a parliamentary clerk. Bald, bespectacled and solemnly moustached, he was both visionary and pedantic. He was an unobtrusive man who had read Walt Whitman and Ralph Waldo Emerson, and who from witnessing the reconstruction of Chicago after the fire of 1871 knew that great works were possible. His combination of the romantic and punctilious would, when it came to being a transformative figure in the making of towns, be effective.

He proposed the creation of 'garden cities', well-planned settlements of thirty-two thousand people each, where town life, industry and agriculture could all take place in close proximity. If they started to grow beyond their ideal size, new settlements could be built close by, but with a belt of countryside in between. The cities would have parks and tree-lined boulevards. A circular 'crystal palace' would ring the centre, combining the more enjoyable forms of shopping with a winter garden, free of commerce, for strolling and sociability. Factories and warehouses would be placed in an outer ring. Electricity would supply clean energy; railways would efficiently connect the parts of the city and its neighbours. Farms might be a combination of large and small, capitalist and cooperative, with individual smallholdings and allotments. Houses would be 'excellently built' and the cities would be dotted with philanthropic and charitable institutions.

There would be practical advantages to this arrangement, such as putting the production of food and products close to both to workforce and consumers. It would also create a 'healthy, natural and economic combination of town and country life' that would 'raise the standard of health and comfort of all true workers of whatever grade'. The 'old, crowded, chaotic slum-towns of the past' would give way to 'the new towns, bright and fair, wholesome and beautiful'.

The cumulative effect of the clusters would enable inhabitants of relatively small towns to enjoy 'all the advantages of a most great and beautiful city; and yet all the fresh delights of the country – field, hedgerow and woodland – . . . would be within a very few minutes' walk or ride'. The idea would solve what were seen as twin evils of the time: the overcrowding of cities and the depopulation of the countryside.

Fundamental to the concept of the garden city were the ways in which it would be financed, and Howard devoted the best part of his books to detailed descriptions of their funding. Garden cities would be held in trust, administered by responsible individuals, and profits from the land would be returned to the benefit of their citizens. This would be, thought Howard, self-evidently superior to the systems of rentier capitalism in a city like London, whose residents were 'in pawn to the owners of its soil, who kindly permit them to live upon it at enormous rents'. In Garden Cities, '*because the people in their collective capacity own the land* on which this beautiful group of cities is built, the public buildings, the churches, the schools and universities, the libraries, picture galleries, theatres, would be on a scale of magnificence which no city in the world whose land is in pawn to private individuals can afford'.

Howard's concept was anti-capitalist but not communist. 'Though Communism is an excellent principle,' he wrote, 'Individualism is no less excellent.' He sought to combine the virtues of both. He hoped that the garden city would succeed in a competitive market economy through its practical and social strengths. He did not want to impose any particular kind of economic behaviour on its citizens. 'It is not the area of rights that is contracted,' he said, 'but the area of choice that is enlarged.'

After the publication of his books, Howard was involved in attempts to build real-life functioning garden cities, at Letchworth and Welwyn, north of London. These achieved, as he had hoped, pleasant living environments where homes are close to nature and orderly combinations of industrial and residential areas. They were developed and run by companies that returned surpluses earned on land to be spent on the common good. They were admired around the world and inspired versions of the garden city idea in countries including Australia, Finland, Germany and the United States.

They also inspired a campaign, in the 1930s, to encourage the planned creation of new communities and the dispersal of populations from big cities. Wartime bombing, and the desire and need for reconstruction, would give additional impetus. Ideas derived from Howard – the building of new towns on garden city principles, the managed depopulation of major cities, the creation of green belts around towns and cities – became official policy. In 1946, under the post-war Labour government, a New Towns Act was passed. In the following years the first towns – Stevenage, Harlow and others around London; Peterlee and Newton Aycliffe in the north of England – started to appear. Several more New Town Acts, generating more towns, would be enacted under both Labour and Conservative governments from then until 1969.

Howard's principle that increases in value would finance public benefits remained at the centre of the idea. There was, though, a key difference: this distribution in value would now be in the hands of development corporations established by the state, rather than private companies. They were able to draw on long-term government loans and to purchase land compulsorily at values current at the time, and so exploit the uplift that would come thanks to public investment and changes of use. It was the ingredient that would enable garden cities to be built in unprecedented numbers.

Milton Keynes, coming at the end of the programme, was bold and confident. It would be a city for the post-industrial era, shaped by knowledge, information and leisure. It put new ideas to the test, in particular those of the American urban theorist Melvin Webber. The settlements of the future, he said, would be made up of dispersed and decentralised communities linked by webs of communications, what he called 'non-place urban realm'. There would, he said, be 'community without propinquity'.

The new city would accordingly be laid out on a grid of roads, inspired by those of American cities, straight and rectangular in the centre but with a rustic wobble, out of respect for English landscape traditions, in the residential areas. Here roads had gentle and irregular curves, making what was called a 'lazy grid'. Milton Keynes would be Los Angeles, but picturesque. Residential neighbourhoods would be placed inside the approximate, wobbly-edged squares of the grid. Places of work, rather than being concentrated in the centre, would be distributed across the city. It was also hoped to disperse shopping, though the creation of a large central shopping centre worked against that idea.

At the intersections of roads there would be traffic roundabouts, the very first example of which had been built in the first garden city, Letchworth, in the early twentieth century. Milton Keynes is now famous for its abundance of these devices. Residential areas would be shielded from the roads with generous planting – the result is that you can drive from one side of the city to another and hardly see a house, hardly know you've been there. Promotional imagery shows the place of innovation and relaxation that its makers were imagining: the draftsman Helmut Jacoby drew a helicopter-eye view of central Milton Keynes, its buildings looking as crisp and engineered as can be. The

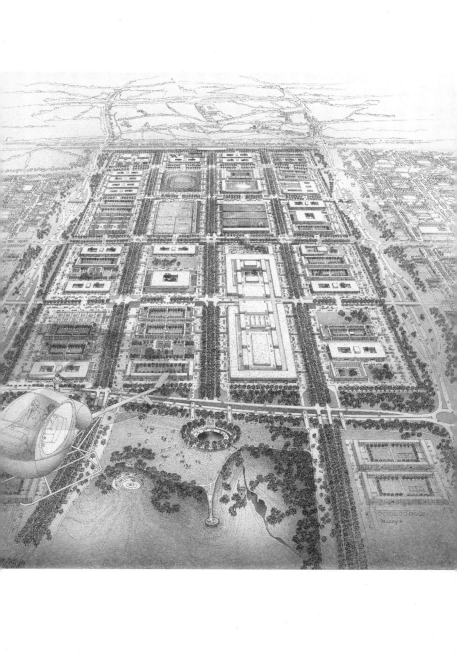

illustrator Philip Castle, using a bright colourful style developed for album covers and film posters, created an aerial image of a city of sport and leisure – water slides, concerts, palm-fringed pools, a glider – erupting with modern force from the plodding old English countryside. City Club, a leisure centre including a souk, rodeo and wave pool, was proposed but not built.

Young planners and architects and designers, excited by the idea of creating a new city, came to work there. They infused practicality and modernism with a faint aroma of new age mysticism. One solstice, the *Guardian* has recounted, they 'lit an all-night bonfire, and some marijuana, and played Pink Floyd' on the fields 'they would soon pave with a paradise of parking lots, roundabouts and concrete cows'. The city's designers also saw the chance to align Midsummer Boulevard (whose echo of Sunset Boulevard was all part of the LA love) with the summer solstice sunrise, and consulted the Greenwich Observatory to make sure they got it right. In Campbell Park, the city's main green space, they formed mysterious earthworks.

More prosaically but effectively, they created an 'infrastructure pack', which aimed to achieve high-quality design for the seating, lighting and other elements of the city's public spaces. They separated pedestrians and cyclists from cars to the extent that you can cycle or walk from one side of the city to the other without encountering a road. A parks trust, endowed with property and money, funds the upkeep of green space for the foreseeable future. Thus these planners realised much of Ebenezer Howard's dream city – leafy boulevards, a big park, homes close to nature – in updated form. His 'crystal palace' of spacious shopping arcades and winter gardens took shape as a long low rectangular form in the style of the German-American architect Mies van der Rohe, only glossed up with mirror glass and white-painted steel. The shopping centre is now one of Milton Keynes's defining icons.

It was opened in September 1979 by Margaret Thatcher, less than five months after she became prime minister. 'It shows what the private sector can do,' said her husband Denis, apparently oblivious to the fact that that it was an initiative led by public bodies. Her government would later wind up the new town development corporations, appropriating their assets to the national treasury, thereby bringing to an end their experiment with funding derived from Henry George's theories.

New towns were not universally popular. They were seen as Soviet-style interventions by the state. One, Stevenage, was nicknamed 'Silkingrad' after Lewis Silkin, the minister responsible for them. They were derided for their drabness, their lack of traditional rural charms, their sometimes naive aspirations to modernity. If you visit them now, flaws are apparent: the passion for green open space tends to make them overly dispersed, with isolated neighbourhoods reliant on private cars for transport and sometimes desolate no-man's-lands in between. Their centres, based on what are now outdated retail models, look tired. The idea of depopulating existing cities, meanwhile, has long gone out of fashion: it's now widely recognised that density of inhabitation can help them to thrive.

Nor did new towns perfectly achieve Howard's ideals, in particular the happy interrelationship of town and surrounding farmland. If you buy a cabbage in Milton Keynes, it will most likely not have been harvested and delivered locally, and will have reached you by the same networks of distribution that supermarkets use all over the country. New towns did not fundamentally change society or the national economy, in the way that Henry George would have wanted.

Their successes were more prosaic – good quality-of-life score and economic growth in some, the simple fact of housing (across the total new towns programme) 2.8 million people, the provision of basic public goods such as parks and efficient roads, the creation of affordable housing. Towns like Milton Keynes are often called 'utopian', but they became places where ordinary people lead ordinary lives much as in others – jobs in the offices and distribution centres, trips to the mall or the multiplex or the parks, concerts at the open-air bowl in Campbell Park, a team in the third tier of English football.

Residents of new towns sometimes talk of such things as the 'youthful energy, enthusiasm, and social sharing' of their early days. 'I guess the Great Dream was still alive and thriving,' says one of Harlow in about 1970. More often, especially in Milton Keynes, they say that – thanks in large part to the abundance of green space – they are good places to raise children.

This remarkable feat of town-building would not have happened without the active role of government and a method of funding that captured increases in land value for the public benefit. It's a similar idea to the one that drove the New Communities land trust in Georgia, with the difference that Milton Keynes and the British new towns were driven and assisted by the state. Given the relative success of the latter and the eventual failure of the former, one could guess that the muscle of government was a decisive factor.

Britain, the country that had done so much to develop the modern idea of private property, played a leading role in developing a profound modification. It's not an alternative – the capturing of land value still relies on the legal apparatus of ownership, of buying and selling and establishing prices – but its essential instrument is compulsory purchase, what in the United States is called eminent domain. This is a powerful tool, potentially brutal or abusive, as the citizens of Kinloch, Missouri, found when their land was acquired for the benefit of St Louis Lambert International Airport. It relies on due process and adequate compensation. But it has the potential to unlock wealth for the public benefit, and is based on the principle that property is never entirely private.

———

The new towns programme was not Britain's only challenge to the principles of private property. Another was the development of state-built housing for the benefit of families and individuals on low incomes. In the nineteenth century the idea was radical. By 1950 it was a central instrument of government policy, with politicians of both left and right competing with each other to build more. In the 1940s and 1950s more homes were built by the public sector than by the private. It was, as the social historian John Boughton writes in his history of council housing, *Municipal Dreams*, a staggering achievement. Driven by what Boughton calls the 'aspiration to treat all its citizens equitably and decently', the British council housebuilding programme, from the 1890s on, 'improved the lives of many millions of our citizens'.

Meanwhile other countries developed comparable programmes, such as the ambitious projects of Red Vienna between the wars. In the United States the 1937 Housing Act 'provided financial assistance . . . for the provision of decent, safe and sanitary dwellings for families of low income'. State-built housing, usually but not always for the poorer members of society, is now virtually universal in developed countries. Although, in the history of property, it is a relatively recent invention, it is impossible to imagine a world without it.

The first council homes in Britain, as Boughton and others recount, were two tenement blocks containing 146 units, built in Ashfield Street in Vauxhall, Liverpool, in 1869. They were called St Martin's Cottages, even though there was nothing very cottage-like about these bleak brick four-storey structures. They followed at least thirty years of public anguish about the appalling conditions of slum housing in big cities – overcrowding, disease and what one report on Liverpool called 'the most abominable state of filth' – that had led to the Labouring Classes Dwelling Act of 1866, which allowed local authorities to buy properties and build or improve homes.

It would take another generation, and further legislation, before the concept really took off, despite continued laments about 'pestilential human rookeries', horrors that were compared to those of slave ships, the thousands of deaths from 'remediable causes' and the 'vice and sensuality', including incest, that were considered the 'natural outcome of conditions like these'. But the 1888 Local Government Act created a newly empowered and well-financed type of local authority, the county council. In 1890 the Housing of the Working Classes Act gave the newly formed London County Council the authority to build homes where old ones had been destroyed in the name of slum clearance. This authority was extended in 1900 to other councils.

Local government now had the power and organisation to build housing. An early outcome was the building of the Boundary Estate in Shoreditch, East London, a development of 1,069 homes in mostly five-storey blocks, together with shops, workshops, a laundry and new schools overseen by an idealistic twenty-something architect on the London County Council's staff called Owen Fleming. It replaced the Old Nichol, the most feared of all London's slum districts, described in 1863 as 'one painful and monotonous round of vice, filth and poverty', where one child in four died before their first birthday. With patterned brickwork and terracotta, picturesque gables, bay windows and generous windows, and a tree-filled circular space in its centre, the Boundary Estate was considerably more attractive than St

Martin's Cottages. It was said to set 'new aesthetic standards for housing the working classes'.

Early council housing shared some of the ideals that animated the garden city movement at about the same time. Inspired by the writings of John Ruskin and William Morris, both reacted to the dehumanising effects of capitalist industry with a wholesome arts-and-crafts architecture of daylight, fresh air and simple but well-made detail that sought to maximise contact with nature. The Boundary Estate, within the constraints of what is a dense urban development, achieves these qualities. Council-built 'cottage suburbs' like the Old Oak Estate in Hammersmith, West London, would further play out the connection between garden city thinking and the design of council housing.

The aftermath of the First World War, with the political demand to build 'homes fit for heroes', brought council housing in Britain to another level of scale and ambition. Before 1914 the London County Council built about ten thousand homes in total; a single development project after the First World War, the Becontree Estate in outer East London, would from 1921 to 1935 realise twenty-six thousand homes, inhabited by a hundred thousand people. Becontree was particularly big, indeed it was the largest public housing estate in the world, but it was one of many built in a range of sizes all over Britain.

The Second World War, during which two million homes in Britain were destroyed by bombing, brought a need to rebuild, an idealistic desire to create a better society and a capacity for mass mobilisation of resources which, in principle, could be applied to peaceful as well as military purposes. Plans and projects were drawn up during the conflict and earnestly discussed – British prisoners of war in Stalag Luft III camp in Germany, the one that would be made famous by the film *The Great Escape*, had their own 'town planning group'.

Plans became policies became physical reality. The 1944 Greater London Plan, often called the Abercrombie Plan after its principal author Patrick Abercrombie, aimed to foster balanced and coherent communities, affordable and humane houses, ample open space for recreation, and the creation of a green belt of protected countryside around the city, with an outer ring of new towns to relieve population pressure on the centre. The Labour government that won a landslide victory in the 1945 general election enacted a series of laws with the aim of achieving well-planned development and state-built housing: the 1946 Housing (Financial and Miscellaneous Provisions) Act, the 1946 New Towns Act, the 1947 Town and Country Planning Act, the 1949 Housing Act.

The aim was, as the Labour politician Nye Bevan put it, 'to solve, first, the housing difficulties of lower income groups', in part because private builders and private finance had, before the war, 'roughly solved' the 'problem of the higher income groups in the matter of housing'. In a significant joining of responsibilities, Bevan was minister of both health and housing: good housing was seen as a matter of good health, something to be available to everyone, just as the National Health Service (whose creation he also led) made medical treatment free to access to all.

Housing, for Bevan, was a matter of quality as well as quantity: 'We shall be judged in a year or two by the number of houses we build,' he said, 'but in ten years' time we will be judged on the type of houses we build.' Importantly, his attention to the needs of the poor notwithstanding, he was adamant that residents of new housing estates should be from multiple backgrounds, what he called the 'living tapestry of a mixed community', with different levels of income: 'If we are to enable citizens to lead a full life, if they are each to be aware of the problems of their neighbours, then they should all be drawn from different sections of the community.' Segregation, he believed, was 'a wholly evil thing'.

The means to his government's ends were extensive and robust, going on draconian. The wartime practice of requisitioning empty properties continued into peacetime, in order to house people in need. Local authorities and government agencies had the power of compulsory purchase, in order to improve or rebuild properties. Public subsidies and low-interest loans were made available. Local authorities were required to ensure that a maximum of 20 per cent of new homes were built by the private sector – a strikingly low figure. The 1947 Town and Country Planning Act introduced a 'development charge' whereby developers had to pay the whole of the increase in land value following planning permission and development. This was as close as Britain had ever got to implementing Henry George's idea of a land value tax.

These policies were effective – more than eight hundred thousand council homes were built under the Labour government from 1945 to 1951, even though this was a time of post-war shortages and austerity. They also changed political attitudes for a generation. The Conservative Party, usually dedicated to private enterprise and the small state, won the 1951 election with the help of a promise to outdo Labour in building council homes. 'Housing is not a question of Conservatism or Socialism,' declared their housing minister and future prime minister Harold Macmillan; 'it is a question of humanity.' He launched a 'Great Housing Crusade' which, partly through reducing the size and quality of the council homes built under Labour, managed to achieve 229,000 of them in 1953, the most ever built in a single year. In 1968 more homes of all tenures were built in England than in any other year before or since, an achievement only made possible by the contribution of the public sector. For the next three decades the building of council housing would be a central part of all governments' policies. The social and physical landscape of the country would be transformed.

Council housing could take multiple forms. Becontree follows the garden city model in reduced version: two-storey homes with ample green space, but without much by way of a crystal palace, or the rich mixture of uses envisaged by Ebenezer Howard. Between the wars the London County Council built numerous mansion blocks to a roughly standardised design: brick, five storeys or so high, in a hybrid Georgian–modern style, with sash windows and horizontal access balconies for reaching individual flats. Some developments, like the colossal Quarry Hill Estate in Leeds, were explicitly based on the Viennese methods seen at Karl-Marx-Hof.

The broad category of 'council housing' could also include those built by Loddon Rural District Council in south Norfolk. In this area the homes of agricultural workers suffered from overcrowding, a lack of indoor heating or water supply and inadequate sanitation. In 1950, only 7 per cent of the district's homes were connected to sewers. The council responded by commissioning the local architects Herbert Tayler and David Green (who discreetly lived together as a gay couple at a time when homosexuality was illegal) to design what ended up being nearly seven hundred homes. These were simple but thoughtful, their siting in the landscape carefully considered, animated by colour and pattern, with attention paid to the specific requirements of rural workers: space for the tools with which they cultivated their own food, provision for taking off muddy boots before entering the house.

The dominant type of council housing, especially in the imaginations of the public and the media, became estates of towers and slabs, made mostly of concrete, whose height was intended to free up the ground for open space for recreation and sport.

An early example, the Alton Estate in Roehampton in South-West London, set carefully proportioned buildings amid mature trees and rolling greenswards; other versions of the type would not always be as pleasant or considered. Later, in an attempt to encourage community life that mechanistic designs were felt to deny, the concept of 'streets in the sky' was introduced, the idea of broad access balconies where neighbours might chat and children might play. Later again architects started to lose faith with their big blocks, and returned to more cottage-like, pitched-roofed, 'vernacular' styles.

Labour governments tended to increase the size and specifications of council homes. Conservatives reduced them, in the interests of achieving more units, more economically. The Conservatives also worked with construction companies to promote methods of building that they hoped would be faster, more efficient and more cost-effective than traditional means, in particular construction with factory-made prefabricated panels, known as 'system building'.

Attitudes to residents and their lives went through shifts and reversals. The Boundary Estate had come with a human cost: its flats were available to better-off workers, with more stable and secure lives; the residents of the demolished slums formerly on the site had to find new and not necessarily better homes elsewhere. Later council housing included the poorest members of society, while also aspiring to Bevan's vision of socially mixed communities. Later again, this vision faded. Faced with pressing demands, councils tended to assign homes to those most in need. Their reasons were understandable, but their actions led to the segregation that Bevan had abhorred. The concept of the 'sink estate', a place subject to downward spirals of decline, inhabited only by the desperate, came into common currency. Council homes became 'housing of last resort'.

The original dreams of council housing went sour, in ways that have been much chronicled, and often exaggerated and over-simplified, but often real. A familiar narrative was reported over and over, of working-class tenants initially grateful for a decent home with an indoor toilet and a bath, rapidly disillusioned by the inhospitable architecture of 'concrete monstrosities', poor maintenance and the anti-social behaviour of neighbours. Lifts would become broken and urine-scented and 'streets in the sky' havens for vandals and muggers. Those advanced prefabricated building techniques would develop exotic defects. Tower blocks were blamed for isolation and alienation. Council tenants, at the mercy of local authority policies and officers, were trapped, unable to improve their lot.

'To anyone who doesn't live on one (and to some who do), the term "council estate" means hell on earth,' wrote Lynsey Hanley in her 2007 book *Estates: An Intimate History*. They are 'a physical reminder that we live in a society that divides people up according to how much money we have to spend on shelter. My heart sags every time it senses the approach of those flat, numbing boxes that prickle the edges of every British town.' Hanley grew up in Chelmsley Wood, a 1960s estate of nearly sixty thousand homes on the edge of Birmingham, so she knows what she's writing about.

When Margaret Thatcher came to power in 1979, council housing was – socially, politically, aesthetically – an easy target. As we've seen, she introduced the right to buy, whereby local authority tenants could purchase their homes at a discount. She stopped councils from building new housing, although some subsidised social housing continued to be built by not-for-profit companies called housing associations. She boosted the private housing market by encouraging financial institutions to lend more in mortgages. In 1979, 42 per cent of the population lived in council homes, a figure that would fall to 12 per cent by 2008. Meanwhile the built fabric of council estates has been subjected to comprehensive makeovers and demolitions. A familiar spectacle of the 1990s was the destruction of tower blocks with explosives. Whole huge estates, such as Hulme in Manchester and Heygate in South London, have been demolished.

Council housebuilding in Britain cannot, then, be presented as an unmitigated triumph, but its achievements have been extensive and enduring. Millions of people live securely in homes they could not otherwise afford, built to space standards that are often better than those of private-sector developments. Some are well designed and built, some less so, but the overall effect was transformative. 'When cities were still filled with slums at the dawn of the white-hot technological era,' writes Hanley, 'when children were still playing on wartime bombsites twenty years after VE Day, in town centres that resembled innards, something had to be done.' That something was done.

It's also clear that perfect forms of ownership, whether private, communal or by the state, don't exist. The faults of publicly funded housing can include inflexibility and lack of responsiveness to residents' needs. A recurring complaint about council estates, whether they took the form of roads of semi-detached pitched-roof houses before the war or concrete slabs after it, was their drabness and uniformity. From the earliest years of the century-and-a-half history of council housing, fears have also been expressed that it would create dependency culture – that, as a Victorian Conservative minister said, 'it would inevitably tend to make that class depend, not on themselves, but upon what was done for them elsewhere'. Yet, somehow, very many council tenants have found the motivation to get up and go to jobs, and to raise and look after families,

And then again, private ownership created slums. The private market continues to fall short in providing homes of the numbers, type and affordability that are needed in cities such as London, New York and San Francisco. There is not much sign that the market is able to resolve the problems it causes by itself, or has been in the past. Issues such as monotonous and faulty design, or poor construction and maintenance, are also known in the private sector. As for individual choice, and the freedom to move from one place to another, in practice this can be severely limited by both affordability and the vicissitudes of the market. Choice doesn't mean much if high prices put any kind of home out of your range. If the value of your home drops, or it develops defects that make it unsellable, you can get stuck there.

No one system of tenure and ownership is, in other words, flawless. All have their triumphs and disasters. But the ideal of publicly owned housing is a powerful one. In post-war Britain, as Hanley puts it, it was the 'dream of holding a fair and equitable stake in the collective wealth of the nation – of which good housing formed a part'. Ownership, she says, 'didn't matter: what did matter was that you had succeeded in persuading those in power that you deserved better than to live in a slum'. This dream

> barely had time to bear fruit before it was punctured, without ceremony, by the idea that the only way to feel fully anchored to society, and therefore to be fully a citizen, was to own the property you lived in. Council homes were never intended to be holding cages for the poor and disenfranchised, but somehow, that's how they ended up.

But does this fate have to be inevitable? Or can the visible hand of the state go where private property cannot, and build homes and communities that people want and need?

13

IMAGINE A COUNTRY

Imagine a country where everyone could live in a decent home, securely and for life. So long as you respect your neighbours and your physical surroundings, and pay in rent or mortgage what is in your means to pay, you would not have to fear homelessness through bad luck or old age.

'Decent' means, at a minimum, warm, dry, clean, with room enough for your ordinary needs, good daylight and access to outdoor space, and with well-functioning heating, electrics and plumbing. Also the scope to make it your own, through adaptation and decoration.

A decent home gives you privacy and peace but does not exist in isolation. It is part of a block, a street, a village or an area of countryside that helps you enjoy as much connection with people around you as you might wish (or as little – this is not a place of compulsory communality). You have access to transport, schools, health, open space, contact with nature, places of work, shops, sport, entertainment. Buildings and public spaces are well made and well maintained, sustainably planned and built, and offer such simple pleasures as trees and places to linger. External appearance is not uniform, and offers choice: modern, traditional, plain, decorated and multiple variants in between.

You have mobility. If your life changes – you move for love or work, your relationships flourish or fail, you start a family, your children move out, you find yourself alone – you can find a new home that suits your new needs. If you make some money and want to spend it on a house that is bigger or better or more fulfilling of your dreams, you can.

You can buy or rent. Your home might be provided by a property company, by local or national government, by a cooperative, a housing association, a trust or other private individuals. One tenure is roughly as good as another – different choices will suit different circumstances. Ownership will not put you in a different class, financially and socially, from renters. If you live in public housing you will not be marked out as inferior.

To find a home in this country will not be a punt or a gamble, a play in speculative markets which, if it goes wrong, might have devastating effects on your life. The place where you live will be your home above all. If it also functions as an investment, that aspect will be secondary. This country will not be without struggle or inequality, because such a place has never existed. Nor will it perfectly achieve all its aims, not least because some are potentially in conflict, for example mobility and security. But it will be a considerable improvement on the current arrangements of property and housing in much of the developed world.

This, surely, is a basic description of a good society, at least of those aspects of it that relate to the places where people live. It is unlikely ever to be achieved solely through the agency of private property. Instead it relies on the principle stated by Henry George, that value in land is socially created, and that it therefore can and should be turned to social benefits.

For, in this same country, there are colossal reservoirs of untapped wealth. This is the value created when land designated for one use, such as agriculture, is given permission for another more profitable use, such as housing. The price of such land, simply through the magic of changing its designation, can go up by a factor of thirty. There is also land whose value is increased by public investment, for example in roads or railways or schools.

Unless directed otherwise, this wealth would go solely to the lucky owners of such land, a bonanza they might spend on holiday homes and pension plans and extra cars. Instead it supports public housing and open spaces and transport and other essential elements of the good society that this country achieves.

————

This imaginary place could be any of many countries. The one I have in mind when describing it is Britain, a nation which has contributed more than most both to modern ideas of private property, and to their alternatives and modifications. It is a place currently shaped by the project known as the 'property-owning democracy', which is now more than forty years old.

The place that I describe is very much not the Britain that currently exists. It is one that it could be. The means to achieve a good society are there, put in place by previous generations who witnessed the failures of private property as well as its successes. These means include laws and policies that helped create new towns and affordable public housing – the use of planning to capture public benefits from increases in value, government loans, compulsory purchase. While it is battered and partly dismantled, this framework still exists.

Britain, in particular England, is a country with powerful national myths about domestic life, the one where the Englishman's home is his castle, whose houses were admired and studied, a century or so ago, by a German diplomat and a Danish architect and other influential figures. In this nation, it is often said, there are powerful cultural attachments both to home ownership and to living in individual houses with gardens, rather than in blocks of flats. These theories of national character are only partly true – in the early twentieth century only 15 per cent of

British households were owner occupied, while the abundance of mansion blocks and multiple other types of apartment buildings in British cities shows that living in flats was not alien – but they have force nonetheless.

It is also a country with powerful feelings about its countryside. Despite the fact that it once led the world in industrialisation and urbanisation, it retains large expanses of often beautiful landscape. These feelings help to shape planning policies designed to protect the countryside, in particular the 'green belts' that restrict development around cities.

Yet there are many millions who have no chance of attaining these dreams of owning individual houses and living close to nature, or even more modest goals of a secure home sufficient for their and their family's needs. As I described in Chapter 2, high house prices have created generational, social and regional divisions, between those who have done well out of property ownership, and those without the opportunity to do so. They have had huge impacts on individual lives, on relationships, mobility and the raising of families.

The very power of myths about homeowning and the countryside has contributed to this situation. Finding land for new homes is made harder by policies to protect green space. Margaret Thatcher's promotion of a 'property-owning democracy' started an addiction to house price inflation that has pushed values to a level that now excludes younger and newer arrivals to the market. At the same time the average sizes of homes are among the smallest in Europe.

None of which is news. Commentators have, for over a decade, been diagnosing a housing crisis. They have identified classes of people who are particularly hard hit, including young professionals wishing to start a family. Except that, with time, these classes are getting older. Many are now in their forties, and face the prospect of living in expensive and insecure rented accommodation for their entire adult lives.

'Will x Solve the Housing Crisis?' has become a perennial headline, where x might be a more efficient construction method, or an ingenious way of making new homes even smaller than they are already, or a relaxation of the planning system to allow more homes to be built. The truthful answer to the question is invariably no, x won't solve the housing crisis, because the factors are multiple and complex and no one instrument can fix it by itself. Most of them, though, can contribute to improving the situation, so it's worth describing what they are.

Perhaps the most popular argument, especially among right-wing commentators, is to see the problem as one of supply and demand. If only restraints on supply could be relaxed, they argue, then the laws of economics would inevitably lead to both greater availability and lower prices. This means, above all, removing planning restrictions: those that limit building on agricultural land and those which require permission to convert an office or a shop into a home.

It's not wrong, to the extent that the creation of new homes would indeed be helpful. But it is a fantasy to think that the markets in property and homes will ever act as freely as those in (say) canned tomatoes, and that the law of supply and demand will move smoothly into action. For it is impossible to imagine that construction will never be subject to planning and therefore to restriction: building usually has effects on other people – for example in its impacts on traffic, or views, or school places, or sewage disposal, or daylight – who have reasonable claims to have a say about them.

Planning is especially necessary in a densely populated country like England, where almost every piece of land is already useful or significant to someone, whether or not they own it – they like to walk their dog on it, or they go to a pub that a developer might want to sweep away. It is also hard to imagine land whose value is not shaped by external factors such as investment in a new road or a nearby hospital. The idea of a purely free market in property, in other words, is a figment.

Nor would the private sector, if left to its own devices, build homes of all the types that are needed and at the rates that are required. It will naturally want to sell its products at the full market price, which, when values are high, will be unaffordable and inaccessible to large sections of the population. They will not build so many that prices will start to go down – rather they will slow construction. In the housebuilding business there is a concept called 'absorption', which describes the rate at which developers build without flooding their own market. For all these reasons the private sector has over decades consistently built at a rate below what is considered the national need, despite inducements to speed up. It has required public housebuilding programmes to make significant differences to the overall figures.

Another type of 'solution' proposes greater efficiencies in construction or the use of space. What if homes were mass-produced in factories, it is asked, like cars, except that their scale would require them to be made in large components, which would then be assembled on site? Some successful examples have been realised, both in Britain and elsewhere, but most of the industry still relies on workers and machines pouring concrete and laying bricks on muddy sites in the open air.

There are also periodic proposals, under catchy names such as 'microflats', for making homes even smaller than they already are, and compensating for the lack of space with clever and stylish design. There are still others for providing homes without the usual fit-out, for example without kitchens, leaving the residents to finish the job as and when they can, perhaps saving money by doing the work themselves.

These ideas have their uses, but they founder on a critical issue. The price of a home is largely determined not by the cost of its construction, but by whatever figure its seller can get in the market. Cheaper or more efficient techniques therefore benefit the builder more than the end user. Ultimately they benefit land-owners: if homes sell for amounts at a certain level but cost less to build, the value of land goes up. If homes continue to shrink, and are completed to lower specifications, the ultimate outcome is likely to be poorer products that cost much the same as before.

A further area of 'solutions' falls into the category of fiscal and financial incentives. Easy credit, deregulated finance and low interest rates put prices up, and their removal slows them down. British governments have at different times tried to play with these factors to stimulate the market: under Margaret Thatcher it was made easier to obtain a mortgage than previously, which in the short term made ownership more accessible, but in the long run put prices up. Following the 2008 crash, in which too-easy borrowing in homes played a leading part, banks made it harder to raise loans. The British government responded with its 'help to buy' scheme, whereby it lent part of the capital that buyers couldn't get from banks.

Taxation is generally favourable to private property owner-ship. There is no capital gains tax on profit made on your own home, which encourages owners to put as much available money as possible into it. In times of crisis the reflex of the Treasury is to protect house prices and boost the market. During the COVID-19 pandemic there was a temporary removal of stamp duty, the tax paid by buyers of new homes, for transactions below £500,000. There is a mortal fear of property values falling, partly for good reason: those worst hit would be recent arrivals on the property escalator, who have yet to benefit from inflation, who have stretched themselves to get where they are, and have the least margin to protect them from shocks.

The apparent aim of these incentives, of help to buy and deregulation and tax breaks, is to help citizens fulfil the powerful and widespread desire to own their home. Which is laudable. But the principal beneficiaries tend not to be aspirant buyers but those who already own. Incentives to buyers translate into increased demand and increased ability to pay, which leads to higher prices, which leaves prospective buyers no better off than they were before, while making owners richer.

A consequence of help to buy was thus that large housebuilding companies recorded huge profits and paid their directors and shareholders colossal dividends. The COVID-19 stamp duty holiday helped keep prices rising at a time when they might have been expected to slow or fall. The absence of capital gains tax means that individuals contribute no public benefit out of the profits they have made on their own homes, which, thanks to house price inflation over decades, might be a third or a quarter of their total lifetime earnings. Once again a division is made between those who have the good luck to make these profits and benefit from the tax breaks, and those who have no chance of benefiting from them. Owners are also incentivised into putting as much available money as they can into homes that are as big and desirable as can be, and then holding on to them for as long as possible. Which, when residential space is in short supply, is unhelpful.

Again and again, in other words, attempts to 'solve the housing crisis' hit the same problem, which is that efficiencies and incentives benefit existing owners more than buyers. This is because the market in property is not completely free, fluid and competitive. It cannot be, when government intervenes so actively to sustain demand – it's not much of a free market if prices are not allowed to fall. Stallholders selling fruit can't hold on to their stock indefinitely if prices threaten to drop, but have to dispose of it for whatever they can get. Housebuilders, however, can hang on to their land for as long as they like, until the prices suit them.

From this some conclusions might be drawn. Firstly, if the market is to some degree dysfunctional – if it is unable to meet the clear and pressing needs of significant sections of the population – then some other agent needs to intervene, which almost certainly means the state. Secondly, if the government is already in the game, wielding its powers of taxation and borrowing to assist the property business, as well as acting on its unavoidable responsibilities for planning and infrastructure, why might it not engage more proactively in the provision of homes? If it is prepared to write off billions in tax breaks and incentives, and tie up more billions in borrowing and lending, why might it not direct these resources to building homes that people need?

———

If, then, there is no single way to 'solve the housing crisis', and if the magic of private property is never going to address by itself the problems it helps to create, through what multiple means might the good society outlined above be achieved? What would it look like? Where would it be built? How would it be built? How would it be paid for, and by whom?

Let's start with supply. Which, more than anything, is a question of the supply of land. Britain, it is often said, is 'an overcrowded island', and with some reason, given that it is one of the more densely populated countries in Europe. Fears are often expressed about 'concreting over' its 'green and pleasant land'. Here too there is some basis in observed reality.

But, as urbanised as Britain is, only 6 per cent of its land area is built on, a figure that includes parks, gardens and other green spaces within towns and cities. Buildings themselves occupy 1.4 per cent of the land area, which is one-seventh of that taken up by peat bogs. Golf courses, by some reckonings, take up almost as much space as housing. The considerable benefits of achieving decent housing for millions should, in principle, be achievable without catastrophic loss of natural environments. The problem comes with the where. Most of the country is spoken for – it is already owned, used and loved. Precisely which fields, then, would have to be given over to building? Whose views of nature would be replaced by houses, whose country walks interrupted?

It is futile to imagine that significant construction can happen without any kind of disruption and loss. On the other hand, it is in principle possible to distribute its benefits in such a way as to compensate those most affected. We are, after all, talking about homes and neighbourhoods, creations that should add to the sum of human happiness. We are also talking about the billions in potential wealth that are released when land is converted into residential use.

This is where planning comes in. In 2014 a design company called URBED won the Wolfson Economics Prize, in which the sum of £250,000 was offered to whoever could best answer the question 'How would you deliver a new garden city which is visionary, economically viable, and popular?' They imagined a historic city called Uxcester, somewhat resembling Oxford, which would be doubled in population from 200,000 to 400,000. 'Three substantial urban extensions' would be grafted onto the 'strong root stock' of the old city.

They would be built on the city's green belt, on 'farmland around the city [that] is currently not accessible to the public and of little ecological value'. There would be a trade-off: green space would be built on, but there would be plenty left, with much more benefit to the public than previously. 'For every hectare of development,' proposed URBED, 'another will be given back to the city as accessible public space, forests, lakes, country parks etc.' There would be an exemplary public transport system connecting the new neighbourhoods to the old city. Well-designed new housing would be incentivised. The 'satellite extensions' would be 'planned to minimise their visual impact, to create a green grid of accessible open space and to generate investment in new transport infrastructure and city centre facilities to benefit the whole of the community'.

The expanded Uxcester would be financed using Ebenezer Howard's concept of the 'unearned increment', but with multiples generated by modern property prices that he could not have imagined. It would rely on the fact that land values in green belts are suppressed by the difficulty of building in them, but vastly increased if planning permission is obtained. URBED imagined that Uxcester would be delivered by a Garden City Trust that would buy land 'at twenty times its current agricultural value but only 15 per cent of its value as housing land'. The original owners of the land would do well, but there would also be wide margins to fund the new developments' splendid parks and buses.

URBED's vision relies on the tools created by Britain's post-war Labour government, based on the principle that the rights to develop land belong to the public. These rights may then be released to private landowners through granting planning permission, but some of the increase in value that follows may be returned to the public in the form of shared benefits.

Thus green belts were created, which restrict private landowners' rights and their potential wealth in the interests of a perceived public benefit – the preservation of green space around cities. Under the Uxcester proposals other public benefits are identified – sustainable new neighbourhoods and parks that are more accessible and ecologically diverse than the farmland they replace. The value locked up in the green belt land is released to make these happen. One public benefit is transformed into another, with due respect paid to private property rights.

The Uxcester idea also requires active government, local and national, to push it forward. It needs considerable public trust that the promised benefits would indeed materialise from building on part of the green belt. It involves instruments like compulsory purchase whereby landowners are obliged to sell, but are properly compensated – tough and often unpopular but commonly used for what is seen as vital infrastructure, such as roads and railways. Given that housing is also urgent and essential, there is no fundamental reason why compulsory purchase should not be used to help achieve it.

There being no one way to 'solve the housing crisis', the URBED proposal for building garden cities on green belts is one of many possibilities. Another is to build on 'brown field' ex-industrial sites, which has been promoted by architects and some politicians, enthusiastically and with some success, since the early years of Tony Blair's government.

Another option became apparent during the rise in working from home during the COVID-19 pandemic: if workers only have to go into their big-city offices two or three days out of five, they can live proportionately further away without increasing their total weekly commuting time. Britain is a country with wildly varying property values – a three-bedroom house might cost £1 million or more in London, whereas a very similar one, two hours' travel time away, might cost a quarter of that – which means that the wider commuting orbit allowed by working from home makes cheaper housing accessible to metropolitan workers. An attraction of this shift is that it eases pressure without the environmental impact of building new homes. It also responds to an important aspect of property and housing, which is that pressures and opportunities vary from region to region.

Increasing supply is not, meanwhile, just a question of changing planning designations, for example from agricultural to residential use. It involves design: in order to achieve the desirable places of the kind envisaged by URBED, and their equivalents on urban sites, the interrelationship of buildings and green space, and of both to transport, shops and schools, has to be considered and directed. If such desirable and good-looking developments are achieved, the hostility commonly directed at proposed new developments by local residents might at least diminish.

If houses are to be built at a greater rate, the current construction industry would struggle to expand its capacity to match it, which would lead to higher costs, shortages and delays. Here the idea of building homes in factories, like cars, could be helpful, as an alternative and faster way to get things done. Design plays a role in this case, too, both to ensure that the hoped-for efficiencies are indeed achieved, and to transform something that might sound unappealing – an industrial house – into a place where people would want to live, and that other people would want to look at.

Meanwhile, quite apart from the physical making and visual properties of new homes, there are abstractions of taxation and finance. Current policies encourage owners to hoard residential space. The absence of capital gains tax on your own home incentivises people to acquire as much as possible, in terms of both quality and quantity. Stamp duty, paid by buyers when a home changes hands, charged at higher rates at higher values, deters owners of expensive properties from moving to somewhere smaller – although the buyers of their home would pay the duty, they themselves would have to pay it on whatever they bought as a replacement. The practical effect is to keep ageing individuals and couples in homes for longer than they might otherwise choose to do.

A government serious about tackling housing need would address the perverse incentives of taxation. It would also see high house price inflation for what it is – something that blights lives and increases inequalities – rather than an economic sugar rush to be exploited for short-term benefits and for the illusory glow it gives to homeowning voters. Such a government might set targets, as is done with other forms of inflation, to be achieved through monetary and fiscal policies.

In order to 'solve the housing crisis', then, government and business would have to use every tool in the box: planning, design, land use, financial and fiscal policy, construction methods. They would have to respond to major regional differences across the country. All of which would still be inadequate if they believe that increasing supply alone would solve all problems of access and affordability. Because of absorption, because of developers' lack of incentive to lower the price of their products, because property is not and never will be a frictionless market, the ordinary laws of supply and demand cannot of themselves fix every problem.

Government, in other words, needs to provide affordable homes where the private market cannot. It can do this directly or indirectly. It can help not-for-profit organisations like housing associations and community land trusts and enable local authorities. It can both build new and buy existing, and offer them both for rent and for sale. It has to take these actions alongside those that increase the total numbers and quality of new homes across the whole spectrum of tenure and affordability.

State-provided housing does not have to be aimed only at those in greatest need. It does not have to be a series of ghettoes of last resort. In countries as different from each other as Singapore and Sweden, it is normal for people from many levels of income and background to rent from the state, with the amount they pay related to their ability to do so. A distinction is made, in housing policy, between subsidies aimed at the physical object that is a home, and those aimed at the human individuals who use them, but these two approaches do not have to be mutually exclusive. Governments can and do provide housing, while also trying to adapt support to the varying needs of their citizens.

Government can also build for sale as well as rent. If for many it is now more urgent to have a home at all than one of any particular tenure, the widespread desire to own is powerful and well founded and deserves respect. It is possible to offer tenants homes in such a way that they can become eligible to buy them over time – which, so long as the supply of affordable homes to rent is replenished, could constitute a more responsible version of Margaret Thatcher's right to buy.

The good society I described at the beginning of the chapter, of decent housing that is accessible and secure, of mobility and choice, where classes are not divided by their tenure of property – where it is equally desirable to rent or own and to obtain your home either privately or from the state – can, in other words, be achieved. It would never be perfect, as the significant failings of Britain's last mass programme of public housing, fifty and more years ago, make clear. One can hope that lessons would be learned from that experience, and – in the subsidised housing that has been built since then – they have been. But public agencies in control of large budgets will (just as, in their own ways, will private companies) make mistakes.

As always with public expenditure, it's reasonable to ask how such a transformation would be paid for. In the case of housing in Britain there are at least three good answers. One is the fact that spending on housing is not lost but is investment in an asset, which in principle retains or increases its value over decades. Another is the huge amount of public money (according to one estimate £23.4 billion) spent every year on housing benefit – help with rent for people on low incomes. Much of this currently goes to private landlords, who can charge the high rates of the current markets. If more housing were publicly owned, this spending would return to the public purse. The third is the capturing of land value, the turning of Ebenezer Howard's unearned increment to public benefit.

It is not outrageous socialism nor fantastical idealism to propose public intervention in such a crucial public good as the provision of homes. In Singapore, a state often praised by neoliberal commentators for its rip-roaring private enterprise, 80 per cent of the population live in state-provided housing. In Britain, as in most developed economies, a considerable amount of publicly funded homes are already in use or under construction. There are mechanisms for capturing uplift in value. The question is one of scale and intent, of using existing and tested tools more effectively, not of inventing new magic formulas.

It's not rocket science. Nye Bevan described a desirable society plainly enough, and his government provided several of the methods to achieve it. But it does require a mental adjustment, one that places the social nature of property above or equal to its private character, to make such a vision come true.

14

HOW TO SOLVE A HOUSING CRISIS

Could, after all, the dream of solving the housing crisis come true? Could the imagined country of decent homes for all, the land of joy and health and relaxation that Steen Eiler Rasmussen described so lyrically nearly a century ago, come into being? Could a philosophy that sees property as social translate into actions that would improve people's lives?

In July 2024 the Labour Party came to power in the United Kingdom. Within a month, the deputy prime minister, Angela Rayner, announced to Parliament 'a radical plan to get the homes we desperately need'. The country was facing, she said, 'the most acute housing crisis in living memory'. There were 150,000 children in temporary accommodation, nearly 1.3 million households on social housing waiting lists, total homelessness at record levels, shrinking prospects for younger people to own their own home, rent increases of 8.6 per cent in a year.

Her government, she promised, would 'raise living standards, for everyone, everywhere'. One and a half million new homes would be built within her government's expected term of four to five years, or about 300,000 per year. They would give 'the biggest boost to affordable housing for a generation'. Local authorities, driven by targets that would if necessary be imposed upon them, would give permission for more homes. Green belts around British cities would selectively be relaxed, so as to free up land for building. There would be new towns. There was talk of capturing increases in land value and turning them to the public benefit, a descendant of Ebenezer Howard's ideas for funding garden cities.

Listening to Rayner, you might – almost – imagine yourself back in the years after an earlier Labour landslide victory, in 1945, when Nye Bevan set out 'not only to put up the houses that Hitler's bombs blew down', but also to 'try and make up for the arrears of housing left by fifty years of Tory misrule'. For those of us who had been pointing out the miseries and absurdities caused by Britain's scarce and over-priced housing, it was heartening to see the new government put the issue at the top of its agenda. The scale of the problem is comparable to that of the post-war years – it requires the ministerial leadership and charisma that Bevan brought back then.

But cranking out numbers is not by itself a solution. It begs questions: what should these new homes be like, of what tenure, for whom and where? Who will build them? What difference would they make? What other ways are there of addressing need, other than the carbon-profligate practice of mass construction? Labour's announcements, unless supported by other policies, will only lead to a future of ever-increasing numbers of environmentally damaging new houses, without much change in affordability or quality of life.

A 1 per cent increase in stock, according to government research, lowers prices by 2 per cent, absent other factors. As Britain has about 30 million homes, Labour's extra 1.5 million would add 5 per cent, which in theory could lead over five years to a fall in price of 10 per cent, a welcome although not transformative change for those trying to buy their first home.

It's unlikely, though, that homes will be built in the promised numbers – or, if they were, that they would make a significant impact on affordability. Those other factors excluded by the government's calculations – rising population, changing financial markets, the effects of speculation – would intervene. A 2018 report by the former Conservative minister Oliver Letwin found that large housebuilding companies slow their rates of construction if the value of their product is in danger of falling – which, if a glut of planning permissions were handed out due to the Labour government's proposed reforms, would be highly likely to happen again. It's not obvious where the labour and materials to sustain a building boom, both of which are already in short supply, would come from, and their lack would drive construction costs up. Any price adjustment from rising numbers would be agonisingly slow – it's not much comfort to families now struggling in small and insecure flats to hear that they might be able to buy a slightly cheaper home, somewhere in the green belt, some time in the future.

A rush for sheer numbers will also endanger the quality of whatever is built. Those characteristics that make a new community successful and enjoyable – trees, neighbourly and pedestrian-friendly layouts, shared open spaces, access to shopping, learning, health and sport, thoughtful house plans that (for example) make best use of space and daylight, touches of generosity and distinctiveness, basic standards of durability and workmanship – would be squeezed. It is easy to foresee the stories that would start coming out in the years after a splurge of construction – cracks, mould, homeowners trapped in houses made unsellable by their defects, new neighbourhoods without schools and shops. Haste would make it harder to achieve the levels of sustainable design that the government would rightly say are essential.

There is, above all, the inconvenient truth that construction is a major contributor to climate change – according to one study a rate of building 300,000 homes a year until 2050 would use up 104 per cent of England's total 1.5°C carbon budget. Addressing one crisis, of housing, risks deepening another, of the environment.

An obvious and necessary way to tackle this problem is to build in ways that consume less energy and generate lower emissions than the brick boxes that are currently developers' basic products. There are rapidly evolving techniques of building in timber and stone that reduce environmental impacts. Again, though, if the only aim is to push housebuilders to pump out as many units as possible, it's unlikely that these innovative methods would be put into practice.

It would be even better not to build at all unless it's truly essential. Any plan to address housing need has to recognise that built space is a precious resource, and to favour ways of better using what is already there over building new. Whatever is newly built has to be as effective as possible in improving living standards.

According to research published by the London School of Economics, there is already 'sufficient' housing in England. Here 'sufficiency' is described moderately generously, as having a bedroom for every couple and single adult, with some sharing by younger children, plus one spare room. 'Excess', says the report, is 'widespread', by which the authors mean unused bedrooms and additional spare rooms, more than entire houses going empty. One part of the population, in other words, has abundant surplus living space, while others struggle to find enough for their basic needs. The occupiers of excess space, the report also notes, are more profligate in their consumption of domestic energy than those who fully occupy their homes.

The discovery of this surplus space in theory raises the beautiful vision of solving the housing crisis without building anything. If only the extra rooms could be matched to the people who need them, then no concrete need be poured, no brick laid, no holes dug. The hard part, as the authors acknowledge, is how to redistribute the spare space without some Soviet-style act of forced collectivisation. Less drastic ways to do this, but still politically challenging, include dismantling the apparatus of taxation that – by charging nothing on the unearned profits made on your own home – encourages the hoarding of domestic space. The LSE report proposes a levy on superfluous floor area, based on the distinction between need and luxury: everyone needs a home, goes the argument, but few need a second or third spare bedroom. You should be at perfect liberty to own such things, if you can afford them, but it's also reasonable for them to be subject to taxation. It's like food – necessities like bread are not taxed in the same way as luxury items like caviar.

Such a shift in incentives would encourage the better use of the country's existing built fabric. It would not, though, as even the report's authors acknowledge, do away with the need for building altogether. Among other demands, there would be a need to create the smaller and more accessible homes into which ageing downsizers could move.

The next best option is to repurpose the country's redundant buildings – the office blocks that emptied out during and after COVID-19, the shopping centres and department stores made redundant by online shopping, such ex-industrial buildings as are still untransformed. It would be an environmental and urban scandal to leave these buildings rotting while building new elsewhere. Here, another tax reform is crucial. At present value added tax is charged at 20 per cent on renovations of existing buildings, while none is levied on new builds, an unjustifiable incentive for demolition. As both conservation groups and construction experts have long argued, this 'perverse incentive' (as a House of Lords committee called it) should be removed by equalising the rates of tax.

Underused building types like offices and stores don't always convert easily into homes – they often, for example, have deep plans with some spaces a long way from windows. Done wrong, such conversions would repeat the mistakes that made lives so miserable for the office-block kids described in Chapter 2. While developers in Lower Manhattan have made good business by creating thousands of homes for young professionals out of old office blocks, they often come with windowless rooms.

But with generosity, imagination and some basic standards and principles they could be made into fine places to live. In the Îlot Saint-Germain development in Paris the architects François Brugel and Associates have made an old office building into airy, well-proportioned social housing formed around a communal garden. An earlier generation showed how warehouses and lofts, which often had such negative features as deep plans and low ceilings, can be made into desirable residences, and there is no fundamental reason why offices could not be similarly transformed.

Still, however creatively existing stock might be used, there is a need to build completely new homes. There is space for them, despite claims to the contrary, on a small proportion of the green belt, and on pockets of land in big cities. Russell Curtis, of the architects RCKa, has shown how new homes could be built on golf courses, while leaving space enough to play the game. He has also identified such opportunities as the spare land around rural train stations, which would come with readymade public transport. The car-dependent suburbs that ring British cities, typically made up of two-storey semi-detached houses, can be densified with apartment blocks around their transport connections. Done right, such development will improve life for both existing and new residents – if more people live in an area there will be more economic and social activity, which would make it easier to sustain buses, trains, shops, restaurants and open spaces.

There should be new towns, like the proposal for Uxcester described in Chapter 13, places where homes are created with sufficient scale and vision that they come with the essentials of shared life – open spaces, access to nature, schools, shops, places of work, leisure and health – organised within a coherent, beautiful and working overall plan. These don't have to be implausible utopian fantasies – with the development of Houlton on the edge of Rugby, a consortium of developers and investors is building a town that will eventually have 6,200 homes, laid out around a network of leafy routes for walking and cycling that connect homes with shops, social centres and well-designed schools. New towns concentrate new housing in a few locations and make places where people want to live. They can be extensions of existing settlements or wholly new creations. They may be made out of repurposed old buildings – a 'new town' could be fashioned out of an old retail centre or office quarter. They are a way of acting rather than a physical type.

Given the environmental cost of new construction, it is fundamental that it genuinely addresses the housing crisis. This means that in most cases building new private homes for sale will be the least desirable option. It's well established in the property business that homes for rent can be achieved more quickly and effectively, as it takes less time for tenants to sign up and move in than buyers, and developers will build in greater numbers at a time, with less fear of flooding their own market. Homes built for rent tend also to be of better quality, as their owners retain a long-term interest in the condition of their property. Tenants generally use their homes more effectively than owner-occupiers – if you're paying rent for a certain amount of space every month, you probably won't want to waste it.

And housing driven by public intervention, with genuinely affordable rents and prices, will meet the most pressing needs more directly than that built privately for profit. Put very simply, there has to be a programme of public housing to match that of the post-war governments. It should not be housing of last resort, but fulfil Bevan's dream of a 'living tapestry of a mixed community'. As in Singapore and Vienna, the public sector can be a landlord to people at many levels of income, charged according to ability to pay. Given the government's immense payments to private landlords through housing benefit, capital spent building such homes – where rents would return to the public purse – would be a sound investment.

Meanwhile right to buy, the policy whereby council tenants can purchase their own homes, has to be suspended. As a report by more than a hundred local authorities, published in September 2024, put it, it has had a 'devastating impact' on the stock of social housing. Right to buy is unquestionably popular among its beneficiaries, and its basic principle – of offering tenants a route to ownership – is a good one, but in circumstances where there is a severe shortage of affordable homes, it is impossible to justify the continued shrinking of these numbers that it entails.

The provision of new housing also creates the opportunity to help residents be secure in their homes, through both control of rents and protections against evictions, as proposed by tenants' groups and by increasing numbers of politicians, including the mayor of Greater Manchester, Andy Burnham. Clearly, the benefits of having a place to live can be greatly reduced if you're uncertain whether you can stay there for long, but rent controls alone, without an increase in supply, risk reducing the availability of homes to rent. Combined with an expansion of affordable homes, they can contribute to a more humane and civilised culture of housing.

Such a culture will not be achieved without active intervention from government. It has to set standards, change tax incentives, build homes and create the organisations whereby new towns can be planned. It has to perform such boring but essential tasks as enabling the long-term investment that pays for schools and trees and other public goods at the start rather than the end of a development. It must pass the legislation that enables land to be compulsorily purchased and its increases in value to be captured for the public good. Housing has to be treated as essential national infrastructure, like railways or roads, and driven with determination. Believers in small government might object, but the current domination of high-priced private ownership was itself created by public policies going back to the Thatcher years. It's just a question of changing priorities.

The prize is to make, through the places where people live, a better version of the society we have now. It includes a minimum standard of shelter for everyone, security from eviction and neighbourhoods that are sociable and supportive. It means taking the gambling and anxiety out of housing markets, and the obsession with rising and falling prices, so that everyone can get on with the rest of their lives. It would be based on an essential shift in the understanding of property, as being social as well as private. It would return the idea of a home to what it should be: not a unit of profit but the setting of your life.

CONCLUSION

My name is Rowan Moore and I am a millionaire. That is, I own assets with a value well over a million pounds sterling. This is not because my work as an architecture critic is fabulously lucrative, or because I am a financial genius, or because I inherited great wealth, but because I have lived in a particular time and place in which the ownership of a home has been a ticket to an unearned and untaxed fortune.

I am lucky. I may have made some decisions I might retrospectively consider smart, and have made some bets that paid off, and weathered some financial squalls, and worked hard, but most of all I am lucky. There are other people as smart and hard-working as me who don't have so many zeros on their capital – because they are younger, for example, or live in a different city, or for some other reason did not have the opportunity to get on the property escalator at an advantageous time.

So what do I do with my luck? Do I give everything away to others less fortunate? Mostly I do not. I hang on to my assets. I think they might be helpful for my children's security, and for their own prospects of getting a home in an overpriced market. I'd like to store up some cash to pay for my potential care needs in old age, in the knowledge that in this respect I can't hope for much help from the state. It seems a little futile unilaterally to renounce my wealth when others like me do not. And, frankly, when you have stuff it's difficult to give it up.

But I am uneasy. I don't feel that I deserve it all. I know that there are so many others who are struggling to achieve a sliver of what I have. It is impossible for me not to want to help my children, and there are philosophers who argue that impulses like mine are positively moral, but I know that such help perpetuates a property-based division of classes.

Actually, I don't just own one house. It's worse than that. I own several other properties – at the time of writing a London flat, a house in France, a half-share in a house in Sussex and one-sixth of a sixteen-acre field in the same county. I am a rentier. I can babble explanations: that these properties were acquired for personal reasons rather than greed, that I try to be a benign landlord, that the French house was my mother's and its value is mostly sentimental, and neither it nor the field-fraction are worth much, that there are other people much richer than me who don't seem too bothered by their fortune. But for the property have-nots, I am in the class of people who, as some would have it, should be rounded up, stood against a wall and shot. When the commander of the firing squad puts the blindfold on me and offers a last cigarette, I don't think my excuses will cut much ice.

I would like – I hope not only because I don't want to be shot – to be less rich. I would like my home to be worth less. I would welcome house price deflation, so long as prices fell roughly equally, and not disproportionately on my own property. It would also be important that other owners less well placed than me – people who have only recently bought, for example, and can only just afford their mortgage – don't get hammered.

I would welcome taxation of my unearned profits, but it would help if I could trust that the taxes raised from me and my like would be well spent: on addressing housing need elsewhere, for example. If I could believe that, whatever happened, I and my children could be sure of a decent place to live and adequate health and social care, I would have less desire to hoard. So please, dear government, take money from me, but spend it well. Until this new arrangement arrives, however, I will probably act much like other people who own: striving to protect my assets, aiming to get a high price when selling and a low one when buying.

———

The above is personal and specific to the exceptional (though not unique) circumstances of the city where I live. But my situation illustrates certain truths about property.

The first is that, as advertised by its many supporters among politicians, philosophers and economists, the concept of property can indeed bring prosperity, security and a kind of freedom to those who have it.

But these gifts are prone to disproportion. They reward luck and sometimes force. Property can fortify the proceeds of abuse and entrench divisions between those who have it and those who do not.

Land should belong, as Jefferson said, 'in usufruct to the living': what matters most is not the proprietorship of it, but the ability to benefit from it through possession.

Property is social as well as private. In my case it is built on public and private investment, and on all the striving of millions who make London a successful city. It is also based on the future prices to be paid – barring a huge crash in values – by younger and newer buyers. If they have to pay much more than I did for the same space, at least part of my fortune is at their expense – given which, society has a case for reclaiming something from me.

If property is not natural, a convenient fiction and a useful instrument, its ongoing existence has to be justified by its continued usefulness and convenience.

The concept of private property as recognised in most modern countries is not universal. There have been and are societies that believe that land cannot be owned, any more than air can be owned. Among those that do recognise private ownership within fixed boundaries, there are multiple variations of rights and laws. Again, its variability – the different forms it takes in response to different situations – reflects the fact that it is a thing of use rather than God-given.

Where, in practical terms, do these musings get us? To policies that allow the social wealth of property to be returned to society – that, in particular, redress the disproportion that private property rights tend to generate. I have given British examples, for example the ownership of development rights by government, with the potential to capture increases in value for public benefit. Other countries, property being everywhere different, will have others.

These policies are not exotic or radical, although they descend from ideas that once were. They are in many case decades old. If there are magic formulas in relation to the holding of land that have not been tried, I have not been genius enough to discover them. The philosophy and tools for addressing the inequalities of property exist and are tested, but are dusty and neglected. The main task is to put them to use.

The concept of possession could in practice mean that:
- if you buy a flat in Gurgaon, you want and expect a shared open space where your children would want to play, rather than a privatised route from bed to school.
- if you are an Ismet Hezer, the man in Istanbul driven to drinking pesticide by the threat of losing his home, you can appeal to a right to shelter above whatever technicalities of ownership are used to evict you.
- if you are a voter in Vienna, you support the city's policies in support of affordable housing.

- if you are a voter in Britain, you campaign for similar policies in your own country.
- if you are the mayor of New York, you direct tax breaks towards bettering the living environment of your citizens, and away from boosting development for its own sake.
- if you are an Erdoğan or an Aliyev or a Trump, you ask yourself why, exactly, you need to fortify yourself with so much property (granted, this degree of introspection is unlikely).
- if you are an aid agency, you support shared possession of land as well as private property.
- if your neighbours have a noisy bird, you realise that the shared life of a village is worth more than the perfect silence of your private realm.
- if you are gathering metaphorical apples, you choose not to take more than could be of any conceivable use to you.

Private property is a means to ends – shelter, security, freedom, prosperity, happiness. It is often effective and powerful. But it is the ends that matter most. Where property fails to do its job, it has to be challenged, reformed and where necessary replaced with more useful alternatives. The aim of this book is not to sweep it away, but to propose how its beautiful promises might be fulfilled.

NOTES

INTRODUCTION

2 *getting a larger share of the pie*: Joseph E. Stiglitz and Linda J. Bilmes, 'The 1 Per Cent's Problem', *Vanity Fair*, 31 May 2012

1. THE MIRACLE INGREDIENT

15 *We cannot be happy*: John Dickinson, *Letters from a Farmer in Pennsylvania, to the Inhabitants of the British Colonies*, 1768, Letter XII

16 *30 or more black families*: John A. Wright Sr, *Kinloch, Missouri's First Black City* (Charleston, SC: Arcadia, 2000), Chapter 1, Kindle location 67

– *The good coloured people*: Wright, *Kinloch*, Kindle location 49

– *a community where neighbours*: Wright, *Kinloch*, Kindle location 49

– *You didn't have to leave Kinloch*: Ben Westhoff, 'The City next to Ferguson Is Even More Depressing', *Vice*, 3 June 2015

18 *The General Motors of the housing industry*: Quoted in Colin Marshall, 'Levittown, the Prototypical American Suburb', *Guardian*, 28 April 2015

– *uniform environment*: Lewis Mumford, *The City in History* (1961; repr. Harmondsworth: Pelican, 1966), p. 553

– *Suburbanites were incapable*: Herbert Gans, *The Levittowners* (1967; repr. New York: Columbia, 1982), p. xxviii

20 *more family cohesion*: Gans, *The Levittowners*, p. 220

– *quiet things*: Gans, *The Levittowners*, p. 200

– *You talk about dreams*: W. D. Wetherell, *The Man Who Loved Levittown* (Pittsburgh, PA: University of Pittsburgh Press, 1985), Kindle location 103

– *There wasn't anything we wouldn't do*: Wetherell, *The Man Who Loved*, Kindle location 96

20 *Sure they were little boxes*: Wetherell, *The Man Who Loved*, Kindle location 94

21 *Pan Jingyuan*: 'China Is Trying New Ways of Skimming Housing-Market Froth', *The Economist*, 15 February 2018

– *There is no way*: 'China Is Trying', *The Economist*

– *an evolving roster of songwriters*: Matthew A. Postal, 'The Brill Building', Landmarks Preservation Commission, 23 March 2010, https://s-media.nyc.gov/agencies/lpc/lp/2387.pdf

– *squeezed into our respective cubby holes*: Simon Frith, *The Sociology of Rock* (London: Constable, 1978), quoted at https://the60sofficialsite.com/The-Brill-Building.html

22 *greatest builders in history*: Postal, 'The Brill Building'

– *slums, tenements*: Edward L. Glaeser, *Triumph of the City* (London: Macmillan, 2011), p. 141

23 *highest rate of home ownership among millennials*: BBC News, 'The Country Where 70% of Millennials Are Homeowners', 6 April 2017

– *multiply by nearly six*: according to the United Kingdom Census, 1,096,784 in 1801, 6,506,889 in 1901

– *Property must be secured or liberty cannot exist*: John Adams, *Discourses on Davila*, XIII, written 1790, published 1805

– *A nation of homeowners*: 'Homeowners Hailed in Roosevelt Note', *New York Times*, 17 November 1942

– *You cannot, in my opinion*: Milton Friedman, 'The Foundations of a Free Society', keynote address and Nobel Prize Memorial Lecture, 1988

– *No one who owns his own house*: Quoted in Richard Lacayo, 'Suburban Legend William Levitt', *Time*, 7 December 1998

– *He understands American values*: speech by George W. Bush, 20 December 2000, published on the American Presidency Project

– *In the 1950s and 1960s*: Steven Mufson, 'Happy Homeowners Living the New "Chinese Dream"', *Washington Post*, 2 June 1998

24 *the most important issue*: Yukon Huang quoted in Mufson, 'Happy Homeowners'

– *When people have legally documented property*: Hernando de Soto, 'What Pope Francis Should Really Say to Donald Trump', *Fortune*, 25 February 2016

25 *The rapturous idea*: Andro Linklater, *Owning the Earth: The Transforming History of Land Ownership* (London: Bloomsbury, 2014), p. 186

25 *The great and chief end*: John Locke, *Two Treatises of Government* (1689), ¶124

26 *brought into existence*: Linklater, *Owning the Earth*, p. 180
– *Nothing but real*: Linklater, *Owning the Earth*, p. 180

27 *Thirty to forty per cent*: Romola J. Davenport, 'Mortality, Migration and Epidemiological Change in English Cities, 1600–1870', *International Journal of Paleopathology*, vol. 34, September 2021, pp. 37–49
– *four thousand 'Inclosure Acts'*: Linklater, *Owning the Earth*, p. 176

28 *vagabonds, subject to severe punishments*: Peter Linebaugh and Marcus Rediker, *The Many-Headed Hydra* (London: Verso, 2000), p. 18

29 *apparent beacons of free enterprise*: Marshall, 'Levittown, the Prototypical American Suburb'

30 *wiped out much of the south-western quadrant*: Charlotte Allen, 'A Wreck of a Plan', *Washington Post*, 17 July 2005
– *agree not to permit*: Bruce Lambert, 'At 50, Levittown Contends with Its Legacy of Bias', *New York Times*, 28 December 1997
– *William and Daisy Myers*: Sarah Friedmann, 'Trailblazers: The Story of the Myers Family in Levittown, Pennsylvania', *Daily Beast*, 25 July 2019
– *a private haven*: Kenneth T. Jackson. *Crabgrass Frontier: The Suburbanization of the American West* (New York: Oxford University Press, 1985)

31 *a new municipality, Berkeley*: Wright, *Kinloch*, Kindle location 214
– *buying up and emptying land*: *Kinloch*, Kindle location 47
– *absolutely thriving*: Westhoff, 'The City next to Ferguson'

2. THE PROPERTY-OWNING DEMOCRACY

37 *drug dealers trade and fight*: Matt Precey, Julian Sturdy and Laurence Cauley, 'Inside Harlow's Office Block "Human Warehouse" Building', BBC News, 3 April 2019
– *two hundred thousand children live under threat*: '200,000 Children under Threat of Eviction this Winter', Shelter, 23 December 2021
– *125,000 live in temporary accommodation*: 'Still Living in Limbo: Why the Use of Temporary Accommodation Must End', Shelter, 2023
– *homes that have no windows*: Benedict Cooper, 'Windowless Permitted Development Flats Approved at Appeal', *Planning Resource*, July 2019

38 *substantial effects on fertility*: Andrew Sabisky, 'Children of When: Why Housing Is the Solution to Britain's Fertility Crisis', Adam Smith Institute, 2017

  – *German architect and diplomat*: Hermann Muthesius, *Das englische Haus* (Berlin: E. Wasmuth, 1904)

39 *the one-family house*: Steen Eiler Rasmussen, *London: The Unique City* (1934; repr. Cambridge, MA: MIT Press, 1982), p. 388

  – *children can be out of doors*: Rasmussen, *London*, p. 389

  – *exercise and relaxation*: Rasmussen, *London*, p. 391

  – *beneficent effect*: Noel Skelton, *Constructive Conservatism* (Edinburgh: Blackwood, 1924)

41 *sense of responsibility*: Skelton, *Constructive Conservatism*

  – *security and economic freedom*: Skelton, *Constructive Conservatism*

  – *stability of the State*: Skelton, *Constructive Conservatism*

  – *view of life*: Skelton, *Constructive Conservatism*

  – *co-partners in the companies*: Skelton, *Constructive Conservatism*

  – *widest practicable number*: Anthony Eden, speech to Conservative Party Conference, Blackpool 1946, quoted in James Vitali, 'How the Tories Lost their Way', UnHerd, 27 February 2023

  – *in her first conference speech*: Margaret Thatcher, speech to Conservative Party conference, Blackpool, 10 October 1975, published by Margaret Thatcher Foundation

  – *her last as prime minister*: Margaret Thatcher, speech to House of Commons, 22 November 1990, published by Margaret Thatcher Foundation

  – *crusade to enfranchise the many*: Margaret Thatcher, speech to Conservative Party conference, Bournemouth, 10 October 1986

  – *stimulates the attitudes of independence and self-reliance*: Michael Heseltine, speech to House of Commons, 15 January 1980

42 *basic unit*: Margaret Thatcher, speech at Conservative Party conference, Blackpool, 16 October 1981, published by Margaret Thatcher Foundation

  – *From 1980 to 1990*: 'Meeting Housing Demand', Built Environment Committee, UK Parliament, 10 January 2022, Chapter 3, 'Housing Types and Tenures'

  – *She was an icon to me*: Melanie Hall, Martin Evans and Andrew Hough, 'Whatever Happened to Margaret Thatcher's First Right to Buy Council House', *Daily Telegraph*, 14 April 2015

43 *Among the losers*: Hall, Evans and Hough, 'Whatever Happened'

– *trebled during her eleven-year term*: UK House Price Index, UK Land Registry Open Data

44 *hamster wheel*: Danny Dorling, *All That Is Solid* (London: Allen Lane, 2014)

– *feedback loop*: Josh Ryan-Collins, Toby Lloyd and Laurie Macfarlane, *Rethinking the Economics of Land and Housing* (London: Zed Books, 2017)

47 *awarded their chief executive Jeff Fairburn*: Rupert Neate, 'Persimmon Chair Quits over Failure to Rein in CEO's "Obscene" £100m+ Bonus', *Guardian*, 15 December 2017

– *annual profits of £1 billion*: Rupert Neate, 'Outrage as Help-to-Buy Boosts Persimmon Profits to £1bn', *Guardian*, 26 February 2019

– *prices rose by 40 per cent*: UK House Price Index, UK Land Registry Open Data

48 *By 2021 it was 9.1*: Office for National Statistics, 'Housing Affordability in England and Wales: 2021', 23 March 2022

– *this figure puts Britain*: Liam Halligan, *Home Truths* (London: Biteback, 2019), Kindle location 964

– *less chance of owning*: Halligan, *Home Truths*, Kindle location 1040

– *privately renting*: Halligan, *Home Truths*, Kindle location 154

– *approaching 30 per cent of income on average*: Halligan, *Home Truths*, Kindle location 1048

– *limiting life chances*: Halligan, *Home Truths*, Kindle location 1050

– 8 per cent of babies: Halligan, *Home Truths*, Kindle location 1054

49 *up to two hundred thousand homes per year*: John Boughton, *Municipal Dreams: The Rise and Fall of Council Housing* (London: Verso, 2018), p. 105

– *number of socially rented homes*: 'Social Rented Housing (England): Past Trends and Prospects', House of Commons Library, 12 August 2022

50 *number of households living in temporary accommodation*: Wendy Wilson and Cassie Barton, 'Households in Temporary Accommodation (England)', House of Commons Library, 30 January 2023

– *a shortage of adequate housing*: Rowan Moore, 'Driven from Their Capital', *Evening Standard*, 24 November 1999

51 *problems of homelessness*: Kate Barker, *Review of Housing Supply* (London: HMSO, 2004), p. 1

51 *ladder out of poverty*: Hugo Rifkind, 'Why We Should Fear the New Housing Bubble', *Spectator*, 17 August 2013

– *High housing costs*: 'Full Text: Theresa May's Conference Speech', *Spectator*, 5 October 2016

– *iron triangle*: Halligan, *Home Truths*, p. 147

52 *help turn generation rent*: Andrew Woodcock, 'Boris Johnson Announces 5% Mortgage Deposits for First-Time Owners to Create "Generation Buy"', *Independent*, 6 October 2020

– *smaller than at any time*: 'Are Britain's Houses Getting Smaller?', LABC Warranty, 21 September 2019

53 *reports by the right-wing think tank*: Alex Morton and Richard Ehrman, 'More Homes: Fewer Empty Buildings', Policy Exchange, March 2011

54 *really isolated*: Rowan Moore, '"It's Like an Open Prison": The Catastrophe of Converting Office Blocks to Homes', *Guardian*, 27 September 2020

– *People are actually choosing*: Moore, '"It's Like an Open Prison"'

55 *It's like an open prison*: Moore, '"It's Like an Open Prison"'

– *People treat us like we're a support service*: Moore, '"It's Like an Open Prison"'

56 *There were two instances*: Moore, '"It's Like an Open Prison"'

– *A woman with mental health issues*: Moore, '"It's Like an Open Prison"'

3. THE VALUES OF VALUE

61 *He is probably a nice guy*: 'Integration Troubles Beset Northern Town', *Life*, 2 September 1957, pp. 43–6

– *As a Jew*: Lambert, 'At 50, Levittown Contends'

– *also endorsed segregation*: 'An Apology from the National Association of Realtors', *Realtor* magazine, 19 November 2020

62 *the Levittown Betterment Committee*: Zachary Solomon, 'Remembering the Battle to Integrate Levittown', *Jewish Currents*, 28 March 2018

– *issued with a restraining order*: Martin Robinson, 'Man "Launched Campaign of Harrassment"', *Daily Mail*, 6 September 2017

63 *rallied to their support*: Friedmann, 'Trailblazers'

– *an outrageous £36,500*: Tony Woolway, 'Sold, a Live-In Cupboard for

£36,500', *Western Mail*, February 1987

63 *smaller than a SNOOKER TABLE*: 'On the Market for £200,000 . . . the London Flat that's Smaller than a SNOOKER TABLE', *Daily Mail*, 15 March 2010

 – *ex-broom cupboard*: 'Could You Live in a Micro Property', *This Is Money*, 20 March 2010

64 *These spaces really excite me*: Rob Waugh, 'Broom Cupboard Is Turned into Studio Flat in London and Is On Sale for £225,000', *Metro*, 4 October 2017

 – *A bit of wow factor*: Michael Holmes, 'How to Add Value to Your Home', *Homebuilding and Renovating*, 28 November 2022

65 *an empire*: Caryl Phillips, 'The Real Meaning of "Rachmanism"', *New York Review of Books*, 23 December 2019

66 *It was impossible to believe*: Michael Abdul Malik, *From Michael de Freitas to Michael X* (London: Andre Deutsch, 1968), quoted in 'Michael X and the Black House of Holloway Road', darkestlondon. com, 17 June 2013

 – *a ruined Eden*: Jonathan Raban, *Soft City* (London: Hamilton, 1974)

 – *The bankers have moved in*: Caroline McGhie, 'The Hill that Keeps on Rising', *Daily Telegraph*, 5 May 2004

67 *Mandelson's different but similar property*: Nicholas Watt, 'Sad Mandelson Takes a Tumble Down the Property Ladder to Pay Off Home Loan', *Guardian*, 29 January 1999

 – *Iceberg House*: Oliver Wainwright, 'Billionaires' Basements: The Luxury Bunkers Making Holes in London Streets', *Guardian*, 9 November 2012

69 *Two adjoining Chelsea town houses*: 'Chelsea Town Houses Collapse Forces Evacuations', BBC News, 3 November 2020

 – *ghost streets*: Joshi Herrmann, 'The Ghost Town of the Super-Rich: Kensington and Chelsea's "Buy-to-Leave" Phenomenon', *Evening Standard*, 21 March 2014

70 *safe deposit boxes in the sky*: Peter Wynne Rees, 'London Needs Homes, not Towers of "Safe-Deposit Boxes"', *Guardian*, 25 January 2015

71 *Grace is a university graduate*: Quotations by Grace and her family are from interviews by the author, February 2023

75 *London Rental Opportunity of the Week*: https://www.vice.com/en/ topic/london-rental-opportunity-of-the-week

4. THE REALITY OF REALTY

82 *property, like energy, is a concept*: Hernando De Soto, *The Mystery of Capital: Why Capitalism Triumphs in the West and Fails Everywhere Else* (New York: Basic Books, 2000), Kindle location 798

84 *$20 billion of such risk*: Michael Lewis, *The Big Short: Inside the Doomsday Machine*, (London: Allen Lane, 2010), p. 72

– *roughly $400 million a year*: Lewis, *The Big Short*, p. 78

86 *Las Vegas's founding deity*: Stefan Al, *The Strip: Las Vegas and the Architecture of the American Dream* (Cambridge, MA: MIT Press, 2017), pp. 29–36

89 *It's what God would have done*: David Spanier, *Welcome to the Pleasure-dome: Inside Las Vegas* (Reno: University of Nevada Press, 1992), p. 33

90 *I thought I would die in that desert*: Al, *The Strip*, p. 30

92 *Casino chic*: Francis Anderton, 'Put It on the Ceiling and Call It High Art', *New York Times*, 14 October 1999

– *Belle epoxy*: Wayne Curtis, 'Belle Epoxy', *Preservation*, May/June 2000

93 *before the government banned 'copycat behavior'*: Tim Nelson, 'China Is Banning Copycat Architecture', *Architectural Digest*, 12 May 2020

– *an Alpine Village in Guangdong province*: Bethany Bell, 'Chinese Replica of an Austrian Village Unveiled', BBC News, 5 June 2012

– *an English-styled Thames Town near Shanghai*: Ken Jennings, 'The British Ghost Town in the Middle of China', *Conde Nast Traveller*, 4 January 2016

– *Tianducheng, a wannabe Paris*: Rachel Newer, 'China's Tianducheng Is an Eerie Ghost Town Version of Paris', *Smithsonian* magazine, 20 September 2013

– *three hundred close-packed miniature French chateaux*: Jessica Cherner and Katherine McLaughlin, 'Inside a Massive Abandoned Town of Disney-esque Castles', *Conde Nast Traveller*, 20 October 2022

– *holistically designed and multisensory environments*: Al, *The Strip*, p. 219

– *technologically wired*: Al, *The Strip*, p. 219

94 *based on his business relationship with Michael Milken*: Al, *The Strip*, p. 136

– *They made me*: Al, *The Strip*, p. 139

95 *MGM Mirage stock dropped*: Al, *The Strip*, p. 217

– *the deepest crater of the recession*: Joel Stein, 'The Casino Town Bets on a Comeback', *Time*, 14 August 2009

95 *debt of gratitude to the Mafia*: Jeff German, 'The Mafia's History in Las Vegas: From Bugsy Siegel to Anthony Spilotro', *Las Vegas Review-Journal*, 9 March 2014

– *Oscar Goodman*: German, 'The Mafia's History'

96 *truthful hyperbole*: Donald J. Trump with Tony Schwartz, *Trump: The Art of the Deal* (New York: Random House, 1987), p. 58

5. DEVELOPER KINGS

101 *wilful disregard*: Human Rights Watch, 'They Took Everything From Me: Forced Evictions, Unlawful Expropriations, and House Demolitions in Azerbaijan's Capital', February 2012

102 *clear vision of a singular genius*: Dan Howarth, 'Zaha Hadid's Heydar Aliyev Center Wins Design of the Year 2014', *Dezeen*, 30 June 2014

– *ranked 157 out of 176*: Transparency International, 'Corruption Perceptions Index 2022'

– *Azerbaijan's richest person*: Luke Harding, 'WikiLeaks Cable Sticks the Knife into Azerbaijan's First Lady', *Guardian*, 12 December 2010

– *Azerbaijani Laundromat*: Organised Crime and Reporting Project, 'The Azerbaijani Laundromat', 4 September 2017

– *the awarding of UNESCO's Mozart Medal*: Luke Harding, Caelainn Barr and Dina Nagapetyants, 'UK at Centre of Secret $3bn Azerbaijani Money Laundering and Lobbying Scheme', *Guardian*, 4 September 2017

– *the legendary Palm Jumeirah island in Dubai*: Andrew Hough, 'Azerbaijan President's Son, 12, "Buys £30m Worth of Luxury Dubai Property"', *Daily Telegraph*, 5 March 2010

– *I have no comment on anything*: Hough, 'Azerbaijan President's Son'

– *the dealings around the putative Trump Tower*: Adam Davidson, 'Donald Trump's Worst Deal', *New Yorker*, 5 March 2017

103 *unwavering standard of excellence*: Harut Sassounian, 'Trump Tarnishes Image for a Fistful of Dollars in Azerbaijan', *Huffpost*, 12 August 2015

– *Leyla and Arzu Aliyeva*: Luke Harding, 'Azerbaijan Leader's Daughters Tried to Buy £60m London Home with Offshore Funds', *Guardian*, 21 December 2018

104 *a portion of which was revealed*: Miranda Patrucic, Eleanor Rose, Irene Velska and Khadija Ismayilova, 'Azerbaijan First Family's Private London Enclave', Organised Crime and Corruption Reporting Project, 10 May 2016

- *money launderers love construction projects*: Davidson, 'Donald Trump's Worst Deal'

105 *handed to the city government of New York*: Wayne Barrett, *Trump: The Greatest Show on Earth, the Deals, the Downfall, the Reinvention* (New York: Regan Arts, 1992), 2016 edition, Kindle location 2670

107 *the city's only major ongoing development deal*: Barrett, *Trump*, Kindle location 2611

109 *mortgage-servicing subsidiary*: Barrett, *Trump*, Kindle location 973ff.

110 *most appealing public gathering spaces*: Barrett, *Trump*, Kindle location 3082

- *In his home in Ayvansaray*: Alexander Christie-Miller, 'Erdogan's Grand Construction Projects Are Tearing Istanbul Apart', *Newsweek*, 31 July 2014

112 *often confused personal relationships*: David D. Kirkpatrick and Eric Lipton, 'Behind Trump's Dealings With Turkey: Sons-in-Law Married to Power', *New York Times*, 12 November 2019

- *He replaced formal relations*: Kirkpatrick and Lipton, 'Behind Trump's Dealings'

- *confounded his fellow Republicans*: Kirkpatrick and Lipton, 'Behind Trump's Dealings'

- *His friendliness to Turkey*: Kirkpatrick and Lipton, 'Behind Trump's Dealings'

113 *I have a little conflict of interest*: Donald Trump, interviewed on Breitbart News Daily, 1 December 2015, quoted by Ashley Dejean, 'Donald Trump Has a Conflict of Interest in Turkey. Just Ask Donald Trump', *Mother Jones*, 18 April 2017

6. CITY OF MONADS

119 *swanky apartments*: Online publicity material for Spaze Privy, Sector 72, Gurugram

- *nestled in a green and serene backdrop*: Online publicity material for Spaze Privy

120 *Entering a private colony*: Vidhi Doshi, 'Gurgaon: What Life Is Like in the Indian City Built by Private Companies', *Guardian*, 4 July 2016

123 *reduced to a filthy drain*: Suptendu P. Biswas, *Gurgaon to Gurugram: A Short Biography* (New Delhi: Rupa Publications, 2021), p. 95

124 *the state has shrugged off its responsibility*: Biswas, *Gurgaon to Gurugram*, p. 110

– *an archipelago of private zones*: Nathan Rich, 'Globally Integrated/ Locally Fractured: The Extraordinary Development of Gurgaon India', in Peggy Deamer (ed.), *Architecture and Capitalism: 1845 to the Present* (London: Routledge, 2013)

125 *one of the most beautiful in the National Capital Region*: 'Newway Journey, Golf Course Road – The Most Beautiful Road in Gurgaon – Indian Mega City', YouTube

– *pacesetter in urban development*: K. P. Singh, *Whatever the Odds: The Incredible Story behind DLF* (Noida: HarperCollins Publishers India, 2011), p. 158

– *gigantic dream city*: Singh, *Whatever the Odds*, p. 107

– *glittering malls . . . exciting nightlife*: Singh, *Whatever the Odds*, p. 14

– *young, energetic and enterprising*: Biswas, *Gurgaon to Gurugram*, p. 124

– *poor district . . . peasant proprietors*: Singh, *Whatever the Odds*, p. 10

126 *No development, leave alone a gigantic endeavor*: Singh, *Whatever the Odds*, p. 108

– *competent authorities*: Singh, *Whatever the Odds*, p. 19

128 *bringing about an equitable distribution*: Parliament of India, Urban Land (Ceiling and Regulation) Act

– *He set about lobbying*: Singh, *Whatever the Odds*, p. 109

– *emotionally attached to their land*: Singh, *Whatever the Odds*, p. 110

– *I used to go and meet them*: Singh, *Whatever the Odds*, p. 112

129 *3,500 acres of raw land*: Singh, *Whatever the Odds*, p. 108

– *chanced on a 'young man'*: Singh, *Whatever the Odds*, p. 14

130 *Singh had wooed Jack Welch*: Singh, *Whatever the Odds*, p. 243

– *setting of filmic crime dramas*: E.g. *Gurgaon*, 2017, dir. Shanker Raman

131 *the city lacks a homogeneous experiential quality*: Avtar Bhalla and Sayna Anand, 'A City of Happy Captives: A Study of Perceived Livability in Contemporary Urban Gurgaon, India', *Journal of Urban Design and Mental Health*, vol. 4, no. 8 (2018)

132 *a palpable social separation*: Biswas, *Gurgaon to Gurugram*, p. 110

– *The culture of consumption*: Biswas, *Gurgaon to Gurugram*, p. 111

132 *They are patriarchal*: Veenu Sandhu, 'The Great Divide', *Business Standard*, 6 February 2013

– *activists successfully campaigned*: Biswas, *Gurgaon to Gurugram*, p. 119

134 *Hudson Yards has the Vessel*: Edward Helmore, 'New York Sculpture Vessel Faces Calls for Closure after Fourth Jump Death', *Guardian*, 31 July 2021

7. PROPERTY IS HEFT

141 *Your sheep*: Thomas More, *Utopia* (1516), Kindle location 209.

– *Capital comes [into the world]*: Karl Marx, *Capital*, vol. 1 (1867), Chapter 31, Kindle p. 803

142 *earth was ultimately deemed*: Linklater, *Owning the Earth*, pp. 93ff

– *the poor's overcoat*: Guy Standing, *Plunder of the Commons: A Manifesto for Sharing Public Wealth* (London: Pelican, 2019), p. 8

– *a radical and drastic transformation*: Linklater, *Owning the Earth*, p. 14

143 *Homeless vagabonds wandered the roads*: Linklater, *Owning the Earth*, p. 18

144 *centuries of expulsion and enclosure*: Linklater, *Owning the Earth*, p. 22

– *The soil . . . had growne*: Linklater, *Owning the Earth*, p. 23

– *He that incloses land*: Locke, *Two Treatises of Government*, ¶37

145 *Many good, religious, devout men*: Captain John Smith, *Advertisements for the Inexperienced Planters of New England* (1631)

146 *a civil right*: John Winthrop, *Reasons for the Plantation in New England* (*c.* 1629)

– *They inclose no land*: Winthrop, *Reasons*

– *if we leave them sufficient*: Winthrop, *Reasons*

– *Principle in Nature*: John Cotton, *God's Promise to his Plantation* (1630)

147 *wild Indian*: Locke, *Two Treatises of Government*, ¶26

– *In the beginning all the world was America*: Locke, *Two Treatises of Government*, ¶49

148 *An acre of land*: Locke, *Two Treatises of Government*, ¶43

– *The labour that was mine*: Locke, *Two Treatises of Government*, ¶28

– *God gave the world to men in common*: Locke, *Two Treatises of Government*, ¶34

– *There are still great tracts of ground*: Locke, *Two Treatises of Government*, ¶45

149 *the hallmark of civilisation and modernity*: Allan Greer, *Property and Dispossession* (Cambridge: Cambridge University Press, 2018), p. 2
  – *the land and waters were 'groomed'*: Greer, *Property and Dispossession*, p. 40
  – *I eat the land*: Kathleen Bragdon, *Native People of Southern New England, 1500–1650* (Norman: University of Oklahoma Press, 2012), p. 138
150 *effectively disqualified them as proprietors*: Greer, *Property and Dispossession*, p. 247
  – *anything but an innocent mistake*: Greer, *Property and Dispossession*, p. 246
  – *a figment of the imperial imagination*: Greer, *Property and Dispossession*, p. 246
151 *government is instituted to protect property*: James Madison, 'On Property', *National Gazette*, 29 March 1792
  – *the moment the idea is admitted into society*: John Adams, *A Defense of the Constitutions of Government of the United States* (1787–8)
  – *cultivators of the earth are the most valuable citizens*: Thomas Jefferson, letter to John Jay, Paris, 23 August 1785
152 *metes and bounds*: Linklater, *Owning the Earth*, p. 224
  – *a radical and potent instrument*: Linklater, *Owning the Earth*, pp. 215–19
  – *it reached the Pacific Ocean*: Linklater, *Owning the Earth*, p. 232
  – *The utmost good faith*: 'An Ordinance for the Government of the Territory of the United States, North-west of the River Ohio', United States Congress, 13 July 1787, Article 3
154 *based on the idea that it was* terra nullius: Linklater, *Owning the Earth*, p. 240
155 *When the English took possession*: Linebaugh and Rediker, *The Many-Headed Hydra*
156 *reproduction of the work-force*: Silvia Federici, *Caliban and the Witch: Women, the Body and Primitive Accumulation* (New York: Autonomedia, 2004)
  – *the 1532 legal code . . . English Acts of Parliament*: Federici, *Caliban and the Witch*, p. 166
157 *county of Essex and the Scottish Lowlands*: Federici, *Caliban and the Witch*, p. 171
  – *to function as machines*: Federici, *Caliban and the Witch*, p. 144

157 *Actual property has lawfully been vested*: Thomas Jefferson to Jared
    Sparks, Monticello, 4 February 1824
  – *it cannot be presumed that premeditated malice*: Linklater, *Owning the
    Earth*, p. 263
158 *dispose of his person*: Linklater, *Owning the Earth*, p. 264
  – *The power of the master must be absolute*: Linklater, *Owning the Earth*,
    p. 265
  – *who have no interest in this species of property*: James Madison, speech
    in Virginia Convention, 2 December 1829
  – *a slave-owning society might be shameful*: Linklater, *Owning the Earth*,
    p. 192

8. A CONVENIENT FICTION

163 *On Sunday 1 April 1649*: Christopher Hill, *The World Turned Upside
    Down: Radical Ideas during the English Revolution* (1972; repr.
    Harmondsworth: Penguin, 1975), p. 110
164 *a common treasury of livelihood*: Gerrard Winstanley, address to the
    citizens of London, August 1649
  – *a man had better have no body*: Gerrard Winstanley, *The Law of
    Freedom in a Platform* (1642), Chapter 1
  – *true freedom lies in the free enjoyment*: Winstanley, *The Law of
    Freedom*, Chapter 1
  – *It must be the poor, the simple*: Richard Overton, *An Appeale from the
    Degenerate Representative Body the Commons of England Assembled at
    Westminster*, 17 July 1647
165 *never had it in our thoughts*: Lt-Col. John Lilburn et al., *A
    Manifestation*, April 1649
  – *it being the utmost of our aim*: Lilburn et al., *A Manifestation*
  – *To every Individuall in nature*: Richard Overton, *An Arrow against All
    Tyrants*, 12 October 1646
  – *No man hath power*: Overton, *An Arrow against All Tyrants*
  – *a despicable and contemptible generation*: Hill, *The World Turned
    Upside Down*, p. 122
167 *every man has a property in his person*: Locke, *Two Treatises of
    Government*, ¶27
  – *I ask then*: Locke, *Two Treatises of Government*, ¶28

168 *Men, being once born*: Locke, *Two Treatises of Government*, ¶25

‒ *the permanence of gold and silver*: Locke, *Two Treatises of Government*, ¶50

169 *to the use of the industrious and rational*: Locke, *Two Treatises of Government*, ¶34

170 *natural and inevitable*: Linebaugh and Rediker, *The Many-Headed Hydra*, p. 251

171 *a well-defended 964-acre gated estate*: Rupert Neate, 'Tensions Rise at the £3bn Gated Estate Russian Oligarchs Call Home', *Guardian*, 28 February 2022

‒ *a quarter of its 430 luxury homes*: Neate, 'Tensions Rise'

173 *The inhabitants of the English colonies in North-America*: *Declarations and Resolves of the First Continental Congress*, 14 October 1774

174 *everyone has the right to own property*: Universal Declaration of Human Rights, 1948, Article 17

‒ *meets the essential needs of decent living*: American Declaration of the Rights and Duties of Man, adopted by the Ninth International Conference of American States, Bogotá, Colombia, 1948, Article 23

‒ *legal enjoyment of possessions*: Convention for the Protection of Human Rights and Fundamental Freedoms, Council of Europe, Rome, 1950. Protocol (Paris, 1952), Article 1

‒ *the right of the individual to life*: Canadian Bill of Rights, 1960, Part I

‒ *Everyone . . . has the right to life, liberty and security of the person*: Canadian Charter of Rights and Freedoms, 1982, Part I, ¶7

175 *the source of life*: De Soto, 'What Pope Francis Should Really Say'

176 *isolated individual*: Karl Marx, *Grundrisse: Foundations of the Critique of Political Economy*, Notebook 5, trans. Martin Nicolaus (Harmondsworth: Penguin, 1973)

179 *equalising laws*: Linklater, *Owning the Earth*, p. 198

9. POSSESSION AND DOMAIN

183 *We hold these truths to be self-evident*: United States Declaration of Independence, 1776

‒ *moot question*: Thomas Jefferson to Isaac McPherson, Monticello, 13 August 1813

184 *robs the shivering of warmth*: Henry George, *Progress and Poverty*

(New York, 1879; fourth edition, Kindle, p. 273)

184 *an usurpation*: George, *Progress and Poverty*, p. 287

  – *the profits of monopoly*, George, *Progress and Poverty*, p. 8

  – *With material progress*: George, *Progress and Poverty*, p. 8

185 *does not arise spontaneously from land*: George, *Progress and Poverty*, p. 273

  – *increased production of wealth*: George, *Progress and Poverty*, p. 193

  – *To whomsoever the soil at any time belongs*: George, *Progress and Poverty*, p. 197

  – *great enigma of our times*: George, *Progress and Poverty*, p. 16

  – *most piteous destitution*: George, *Progress and Poverty*, p. 171

  – *an absentee and alien landlord*: George, *Progress and Poverty*, p. 92

186 *the enslavement of the laboring class*: George, *Progress and Poverty*, p. 9

  – *Nothing short of making*: George, *Progress and Poverty*, p. 9

  – *We may safely leave them the shell*: George, *Progress and Poverty*, p. 302

  – *drive back the Indian*: George, *Progress and Poverty*, p. 293

187 *If we compare these three or four rights*: Pierre-Joseph Proudhon, *What Is Property?* (1840), ed. and trans. Donald R. Kelley and Bonnie G. Smith (Cambridge: Cambridge University Press, 1994), p. 37

  – *shameful equivocation*: Proudhon, *What Is Property?*, p. 49

  – *property is impossible*: Proudhon, *What Is Property?*, p. 157

  – *the negation of equality*: Proudhon, *What Is Property?*, p. 168

  – *chimerical*: Proudhon, *What Is Property?*, p. 37

  – *the suicide of society*: Proudhon, *What Is Property?*, p. 215

188 *Modern bourgeois private property*: Karl Marx and Friedrich Engels, *The Communist Manifesto* (1848), Section II

  – *that kind of property*: Marx and Engels, *Communist Manifesto*, Section II

  – *the nonexistence of any property*: Marx and Engels, *Communist Manifesto*, Section II

  – *capital is converted into common property*: Marx and Engels, *Communist Manifesto*, Section II

  – *abolition of property in land*: Marx and Engels, *Communist Manifesto*, Section II

189 *Abolition of private property*: Marx and Engels, *Communist Manifesto*, Section II

  – *the most radical rupture*: Marx and Engels, *Communist Manifesto*, Section II

189 *the creation of the whole community*: George, *Progress and Poverty*, p. 273

190 *The earth belongs in usufruct*: Thomas Jefferson to James Madison, Paris, 6 September 1789

191 *the laws of property have been so far extended*: Thomas Jefferson to James Madison, Fontainebleau, 28 October 1785

– lease it to individual citizens for terms of nineteen years: Linklater, *Owning the Earth*, p. 208

10. LIFE IN COMMON

199 *what defines a community*: Standing, *Plunder of the Commons*, p. 27

– *participative, communal activity*: Standing, *Plunder of the Commons*, p. 27

– *Charter of the Forest*: Standing, *Plunder of the Commons*, Chapter 1

200 *Five per cent of land in Britain*: Standing, *Plunder of the Commons*, p. 67

– *the Beast's mark . . . unfruitfull works of darknesse*: *Light Shining in Buckinghamshire*, anonymous Digger pamphlet (1648)

– *Man following his own sensualitie*: *Light Shining in Buckinghamshire*

201 *tragedy of the commons*: Garrett Hardin, 'The Tragedy of the Commons', *Science*, 13 December 1968

– *fisheries in Turkey and irrigation systems in the Philippines*: Elinor Ostrom, *Governing the Commons: The Evolution of Institutions for Collective Action* (1990; repr. Cambridge: Cambridge University Press, 2015), pp. 143–5, 82–9

202 *a distinction between 'inner' and 'outer' commons*: Greer, *Property and Dispossession*, p. 248

203 *capitalist egotism . . . remnants of past worldviews . . . foundations of socialist communal living*: Paul Betts, 'Private Property and Public Culture: A Forgotten Chapter of East European Communist Life', *Histoire@Politique*, no. 7 (2009)

– *fixated on property*: Inga Markovits, *Justice in Lüritz: Experiencing Socialist Law in East Germany* (2006; English translation, Princeton, NJ: Princeton University Press, 2010), p. 26

204 *tiny enclaves of self-determination*: Markovits, *Justice in Lüritz*, p. 40

– *utopia . . . where art seemed to actually be about experimental lifestyles*:

Jonathan Jones, 'The Closure of Berlin's Tacheles Squat Is a Sad Day for Alternative Art', *Guardian*, 5 September 2012

205 *an extraordinary place and space*: amtacheles.de

207 *By 1921 thirty thousand families*: Andreas Rumpfhuber, 'Vienna's "Wild Settlers" Kickstart a Social Housing Revolution', *Guardian*, 8 April 2016

– *It is not the individual house*: Rumpfhuber, 'Vienna's "Wild Settlers"'

– *Karl-Marx-Hof*: Owen Hatherley, 'Vienna's Karl Marx Hof: Architecture as Politics and Ideology', *Guardian*, 27 April 2015

208 *Sixty per cent of the city's population*: Rumpfhuber, 'Vienna's "Wild Settlers"'

11. COMMUNITY AND COOPERATION

211 *I often have to explain to people*: These and following quotations are from residents speaking to the film-maker Adam Tanaka for his 2018 documentary *City in a City*

212 *The high cost of hideousness*: Peter Blake, 'The High Cost of Hideousness', *New York* magazine, 19 August 1968, quoted in James Nevius, 'Co-op City at 50', *Curbed New York*, 5 December 2018

– *The spirits of the tenants*: quoted in Nevius, 'Co-op City at 50'

– *In a city whose median home price recently surpassed $800,000*: Adam Tanaka, 'Co-op City: How New York Made Large-Scale Affordable Housing Work', *Bloomberg*, 3 January 2019

– *If we have extra cash*: Tanaka, *City in a City*

– *You don't own in the same sense*: Tanaka, *City in a City*

214 *Just name a service*: Tanaka, *City in a City*

– *mixture of all kinds of cultures*: Tanaka, *City in a City*

– *in sharp contrast . . . to the segregation*: Tanaka, 'Co-op City'

215 *valued for their ongoing use as habitation*: quoted in Nevius, 'Co-op City at 50'

– *what labour with good, effective, progressive leadership*: John F. Kennedy, speech to Penn South Co-operative, New York, 19 May 1962

216 *In 1975 the complex defaulted*: 'State Moves to Foreclose Mortgage on Co-op City', *New York Times*, 5 August 1975

– residents started a thirteen-month rent strike: 'Co-op City Rent Strike Ended by Accord', *New York Times*, 30 June 1976

216 *The idea of Co-op City is wonderful*: Samuel G. Freedman, 'Co-op City, a Refuge in Transition', *New York Times*, 25 June 1986

217 *A further enormous refinancing*: 'NY's Co-Op City Receives $621.5 Million Loan', Affordable Housing Finance, 4 December 2012

218 *You've got the cardboard box*: Tanaka, *City in a City*
  – *Many shareholders . . . have chosen to stay put*: Tanaka, *City in a City*

220 *kollektivhus*: Pernilla Hagbert et al. (eds), *Contemporary Co-housing in Europe: Towards Sustainable Cities?* (Abingdon: Routledge, 2020), Kindle edition, p. 38
  – *the Stacken community*: Hagbert et al., *Contemporary Co-housing*, p. 38

222 *The fate of the New Communities experiment*: International Independence Institute, *The Community Land Trust: A Guide to a New Model of Land Tenure in America* (Cambridge, MA: Center for Community Economic Development, 1972), p. 23

223 *a legal entity, a quasi-public body*: International Independence Institute, *The Community Land Trust*, p. 1
  – *distinguishe[d] between land with its natural resources*: International Independence Institute, *The Community Land Trust*, p. 2
  – *land belongs to god*: International Independence Institute, *The Community Land Trust*, p. xiii

224 *unearned increment*: Ebenezer Howard, *Garden Cities of Tomorrow* (London: Sonnenschien, 1902), p. 16
  – *several other inspirations*: International Independence Institute, *The Community Land Trust*, pp. 7–9
  – *moshav shitufi*: International Independence Institute, *The Community Land Trust*, p. 9
  – *communists*: Allen G. Breed, 'Black Farmers' Lawsuit Revives a Dream', *Washington Post*, 6 December 2001

225 *it hurt so much*: Breed, 'Black Farmers' Lawsuit'
  – *permanent affordability*: Jake Blumgart, 'How Bernie Sanders Made Burlington Affordable', *Slate*, 19 January 2016
  – *the only socially equitable and fiscally prudent way*: John Emmeus Davis, Line Algoed and María E. Hernández-Torrales (eds), *On Common Ground: International Perspectives on the Community Land Trust* (Madison, WI: Terra Nostra Press, 2020), Kindle p. 484

226 *A group was formed called HALT*: Blumgart, 'How Bernie Sanders'
  – *In 1985 the trust helped its first resident*: Davis et al., *On Common Ground*, Kindle p. 494

226 *We don't understand*: Blumgart, 'How Bernie Sanders'

227 *six hundred shared-ownership homes*: Davis et al., *On Common Ground*, Kindle pp. 494–5

  – *remains a niche model*: Blumgart, 'How Bernie Sanders'

  – *St Clement's Hospital*: Davis et al., *On Common Ground*, Kindle pp. 527–48

228 *Granby Four Streets*: Aditya Chakrabortty, 'How One Community Beat the System, and Rebuilt Their Shattered Streets', *Guardian*, 14 February 2018

  – *one or two hundred homes per year*: interview with Tom Chance, April 2022

12. THE VISIBLE HAND

233 *There's no beginning and there's no end*: Quotations by Milton Keynes residents are from Milton Keynes People's Stories, Living Archive, 2017

234 *It was brought into being*: informative accounts of the making of Milton Keynes include Terence Bendixson and John Platt, *Milton Keynes: Image and Reality* (London: Granta, 1992); Ian Wray, 'Milton Keynes, the Making of a New City', *Geography*, vol. 101, no. 3 (2016), pp. 116–24

235 *garden cities*: Howard, *Garden Cities of To-morrow*

  – *crystal palace*: Howard, *Garden Cities of To-morrow*, Kindle p. 11

236 *healthy, natural and economic*: Howard, *Garden Cities of To-morrow*, Kindle p. 10

  – *raise the standard of health and comfort*: Howard, *Garden Cities of To-morrow*, Kindle p. 10

  – *old, crowded, chaotic slum-towns*: Howard, *Garden Cities of To-morrow*, Kindle p. 66

  – *all the advantages of a most great and beautiful city*: Howard, *Garden Cities of To-morrow*, Kindle p. 95

  – *in pawn to the owners of its soil*: Howard, *Garden Cities of To-morrow*, Kindle p. 105

  – *because the people in their collective capacity own the land*: Howard, *Garden Cities of To-morrow*, Kindle p. 95

  – *Though Communism is an excellent principle*: Howard, *Garden Cities of To-morrow*, Kindle p. 68

237 *It is not the area of rights that is contracted*: Howard, *Garden Cities of To-morrow*, Kindle p. 14

238 *community without propinquity*: Melvin M. Webber, 'The Urban Place and the Nonplace Urban Realm', in Webber et al. (eds), *Explorations into Urban Structure* (Philadelphia: University of Pennsylvania Press, 1964)

240 *lit an all-night bonfire*: Patrick Barkham, 'The Struggle for the Soul of Milton Keynes', *Guardian*, 3 May 2016

241 *simple fact of housing . . . 2.8 million people*: 'A New Future for New Towns', TCPA, August 2021

242 *youthful energy, enthusiasm, and social sharing*: Boughton, *Municipal Dreams*, p. 85

243 aspiration to treat all its citizens equitably: Boughton, *Municipal Dreams*, p. 6

243 *The first council homes in Britain*: Boughton, *Municipal Dreams*, p. 13

244 *the most abominable state of filth*: Boughton, *Municipal Dreams*, p. 11
   – *pestilential human rookeries*: Boughton, *Municipal Dreams*, p. 12
   – *remediable causes*: Boughton, *Municipal Dreams*, p. 11
   – *vice and sensuality*: Boughton, *Municipal Dreams*, p. 12
   – *Housing of the Working Classes Act*: Boughton, *Municipal Dreams*, pp. 16–17
   – *Boundary Estate in Shoreditch*: Boughton, *Municipal Dreams*, p. 21
   – *one painful and monotonous round*: *Illustrated London News*, 24 October 1863

245 *cottage suburbs*: Boughton, *Municipal Dreams*, p. 24
   – *homes fit for heroes*: Boughton, *Municipal Dreams*, p. 34
   – *Becontree Estate*: Boughton, *Municipal Dreams*, pp. 33, 36
   – *Stalag Luft III camp*: Boughton, *Municipal Dreams*, p. 71

246 *to solve, first, the housing difficulties*: Nye Bevan, speech to the House of Commons as Minister of Health, 17 October 1945, *Hansard*, vol. 414
   – *We shall be judged*: quoted in Boughton, *Municipal Dreams*, p. 94
   – *living tapestry of a mixed community*: Nye Bevan, speech to the House of Commons as Minister of Health, 16 October 1949, *Hansard*, vol. 462

247 *a wholly evil thing*: quoted in Boughton, *Municipal Dreams*, p. 96
   – *a maximum of 20 per cent*: Boughton, *Municipal Dreams*, p. 93

247 *more than eight hundred thousand council homes*: Boughton, *Municipal Dreams*, p. 105

– *Housing is not a question of Conservatism or Socialism*: Macmillan first made this statement in an article written in September 1925, and revived it as a campaign slogan in 1951. Alistair Horne, *Macmillan: The Official Biography* (London: Macmillan, 1988; electronic edition 2012), Kindle location 1509

– *more homes of all tenures were built*: '50 Years of the English Housing Survey', Department for Communities and Local Government (2017), p. 9, table 244

248 *Loddon Rural District Council*: 'Tayler and Green and Loddon Rural District Council, Parts I and II', municipaldreams.wordpress.com, 10/17 December 2019

249 *Alton Estate in Roehampton*: Boughton, *Municipal Dreams*, pp. 117–18

250 *To anyone who doesn't live on one*: Lynsey Hanley, *Estates: An Intimate History* (London: Granta, 2007; repr. 2017), p. 5

251 *When cities were still filled with slums*: Hanley, *Estates*, p. 3

– *it would inevitably tend to make that class depend*: Boughton, *Municipal Dreams*, p. 16

252 *dream of holding a fair and equitable stake*: Hanley, *Estates*, p. 11

– *didn't matter*: Hanley, *Estates*, p. 11

13. IMAGINE A COUNTRY

260 *absorption*: Oliver Letwin, 'Independent Review of Build Out, Final Report', Ministry of Housing, Communities and Local Government, 2018

254 *Golf courses . . . take up almost as much space*: Pete Jefferys, 'A Fair Way? Do We Prioritise Golf or Homes?', Shelter, 11 November 2013. This statistic has been challenged by some sources, and reaffirmed by Shelter and others. It varies depending on methodologies used – for example whether gardens and driveways are included in the area of housing, or car parks and ancillary buildings are included with golf courses. However, it illustrates a basic truth, which is that housing and golf courses occupy a comparable amount of land.

– *a historic city called Uxcester*: URBED, 'Uxcester Garden City', submission to the Wolfson Economics Prize, 2014

264 *farmland around the city*: URBED, 'Uxcester Garden City', p. 2

265 *For every hectare of development*: URBED, 'Uxcester Garden City', p. 2
   - *satellite extensions*: URBED, 'Uxcester Garden City', p. 2
   - *twenty times its current agricultural value*: URBED, 'Uxcester Garden City', p. 3

270 *according to one estimate £23.4 billion*: 'Meeting Housing Demand', House of Lords Built Environment Committee, 10 January 2022, p. 5
   - *80 per cent of the population live in state-provided housing*: Adam Majendie, 'Why Singapore Has One of the Highest Home Ownership Rates', Bloomberg.com, 8 July 2020

14. HOW TO SOLVE A HOUSING CRISIS

273 *a radical plan*: 'Deputy Prime Minister on Changes to National Planning Policy', https://www.gov.uk/government/speeches/deputy-prime-minister-on-changes-to-national-planning-policy.

274 *the houses that Hitler's bombs blew down*: https://speakola.com/political/nye-bevan-post-war-reconstruction-housing-1946.
   - *A 1 per cent increase in stock*: 'Analysis of the Determinants of House Price Changes', https://assets.publishing.service.gov.uk/media/5ad0a75ee5274a76be66c25c/OFF_SEN_Ad_Hoc_SFR_House_prices_v_PDF.pdf.
   - *A 2018 report*: 'Independent Review of Build Out: Final Report', https://www.gov.uk/government/publications/independent-review-of-build-out-final-report.

275 *a rate of building 300,000 homes a year*: Sophus O. S. E. zu Ermgassen et al., 'A Home for All within Planetary Boundaries', *Ecological Economics*, November 2022, https://www.sciencedirect.com/science/article/pii/S0921800922002245.

276 *According to research published by the London School of Economics*: Ian Gough et al., 'Fair Decarbonisation of Housing in the UK: A Sufficiency Approach', March 2024, https://sticerd.lse.ac.uk/dps/case/cp/casepaper232.pdf.

278 *While developers in Lower Manhattan have made good business*: D. T. Max, 'Can Turning Office Towers into Apartments Save Downtowns?', *New Yorker*, 29 April 2024, https://www.newyorker.

com/magazine/2024/05/06/can-turning-office-towers-into-apartments-save-downtowns.

278 *In the Îlot Saint-Germain development in Paris*: Jon Astbury, 'Parisian Office Blocks Transformed into Îlot Saint-Germain Social Housing', *Dezeen*, 3 May 2024, https://www.dezeen.com/2024/05/03/ilot-saint-germain-social-housing.

  — *new homes could be built on golf courses*: https://rcka.co.uk/our-projects/holes-to-homes.

  — *spare land around rural train stations*: https://ruralstations.russellcurtis.co.uk.

279 *the development of Houlton on the edge of Rugby*: Rowan Moore, 'Houlton Rugby: A New Town That's Sending Out All the Right Signals', *Observer*, 18 September 2022, https://www.theguardian.com/artanddesign/2022/sep/18/houlton-new-town-review-rugby-urban-and-civic-david-lock.

280 *living tapestry of a mixed community*: 'Housing Bill', *Hansard*, 16 March 1949, https://api.parliament.uk/historic-hansard/commons/1949/mar/16/housing-bill.

  — *devastating impact*: 'Securing the Future of Council Housing', September 2024, https://www.southwark.gov.uk/sites/default/files/2024-10/Securing-the-Future-of-Council-Housing.pdf.

  — *including the mayor of Greater Manchester*: Gemma Sherlock, 'Andy Burnham Wants to Suspend Right to Buy Scheme', BBC News, 7 May 2024, https://www.bbc.com/news/articles/c88z93vm0y5o.

SELECT BIBLIOGRAPHY

Al, Stefan, *The Strip: Las Vegas and the Architecture of the American Dream* (Cambridge MA: MIT Press, 2017)

Barrett, Wayne, *Trump: The Greatest Show on Earth, the Deals, the Downfall, the Reinvention* (New York: Regan Arts, 1992)

Bendixson, Terence, and John Platt, *Milton Keynes: Image and Reality* (London: Granta, 1992)

Biswas, Suptendu P., *Gurgaon to Gurugram: A Short Biography* (New Delhi: Rupa Publications, 2021)

Boughton, John, *Municipal Dreams: The Rise and Fall of Council Housing* (London: Verso, 2018)

Bullough, Oliver, *Moneyland: Why Thieves and Crooks Now Rule the World and How to Take it Back* (London: Profile, 2018)

Christophers, Brett, *Rentier Capitalism: Who Owns the Economy and Who Pays for It?* (London: Verso, 2022)

Colenutt, Bob, *The Property Lobby: The Hidden Reality behind the Housing Crisis* (Bristol: Policy Press, 2012)

Davis, John Emmeus, Line Algoed and María E. Hernández-Torrales (eds), *On Common Ground: International Perspectives on the Community Land Trust* (Madison, WI: Terra Nostra Press, 2020)

De Soto, Hernando, *The Other Path: The Economic Answer to Terrorism* (New York: Harper and Row, 1989)

De Soto, Hernando, *The Mystery of Capital: Why Capitalism Triumphs in the West and Fails Everywhere Else* (New York: Basic Books, 2000)

Deamer, Peggy (ed.), *Architecture and Capitalism: 1845 to the Present* (London: Routledge, 2013)

Dorling, Danny, *All That Is Solid: The Great Housing Disaster* (London: Allen Lane, 2014)

Federici, Silvia, *Caliban and the Witch: Women, the Body and Primitive Accumulation* (New York: Autonomedia, 2004)

Gans, Herbert J., *The Levittowners: Ways of Life and Politics in a New Suburban Community* (1967; repr. New York: Columbia, 1982)

George, Henry, *Progress and Poverty* (New York, 1879)

Glaeser, Edward, *Triumph of the City: How Urban Spaces Make Us Human* (London: Macmillan, 2011)

Golby, Joel, *London Rental Opportunity of the Week* (vice.com, 2016–23)

Greer, Allan, *Property and Dispossession: Natives, Empires and Land in Early Modern North America* (Cambridge: Cambridge University Press, 2018)

Hagbert, Pernilla, Henrik Gutzon Larsen, Håkan Thörn and Cathrin Wasshede (eds), *Contemporary Co-housing in Europe: Towards Sustainable Cities?* (Abingdon: Routledge, 2020)

Halligan, Liam, *Home Truths: The UK's Chronic Housing Shortage* (London: Biteback, 2019)

Hanley, Lynsey, *Estates: An Intimate History* (London: Granta, 2007)

Hill, Christopher, *The World Turned Upside Down: Radical Ideas during the English Revolution* (1972; repr. Harmondsworth: Penguin, 1975)

Howard, Ebenezer, *Garden Cities of To-morrow* (London: Sonnenschien, 1902)

International Independence Institute, *The Community Land Trust: A Guide to a New Model of Land Tenure in America* (Cambridge MA: Center for Community Economic Development, 1972)

Lea, David, *Property Rights, Indigenous People and the Developing World: Issues from Aboriginal Entitlement to Intellectual Ownership Rights* (Leiden: Martinus Nijhoff, 2008)

Lewis, Michael, *The Big Short: Inside the Doomsday Machine* (London: Allen Lane, 2010)

Linebaugh, Peter, and Marcus Rediker, *The Many-Headed Hydra: The Hidden History of the Revolutionary Atlantic* (London: Verso, 2000)

Linklater, Andro, *Owning the Earth: The Transforming History of Land Ownership* (London: Bloomsbury, 2014)

Locke, John, *Two Treatises of Government* (London, 1689)

Marriott, Oliver, *The Property Boom* (London: Hamish Hamilton, 1967)

Marx, Karl *Grundrisse: Foundations of the Critique of Political Economy*, trans. Martin Nicolaus (Harmondsworth: Penguin, 1973)

Marx, Karl, and Friedrich Engels, *The Communist Manifesto* (1848)

Mazzucato, Mariana, *The Value of Everything: Making and Taking in the Global Economy* (London: Allen Lane, 2018)

Oldenburg, Veena Talwar, *Gurgaon: From Mythic Village to Millennium City* (Noida: HarperCollins Publishers India, 2018)

Ostrom, Elinor, *Governing the Commons: The Evolution of Institutions for Collective Action* (1990; repr. Cambridge: Cambridge University Press, 2015)

Proudhon, Pierre-Joseph, *What Is Property? An Inquiry into the Principle of Right and Government* (1840), ed. and trans. Donald R. Kelley and Bonnie G. Smith (Cambridge: Cambridge University Press, 1994)

Rasmussen, Steen Eiler, *London: the Unique City* (1934; repr. Cambridge, MA: MIT Press, 1982)

Ryan-Collins, Josh, Toby Lloyd and Laurie Macfarlane, *Rethinking the Economics of Land and Housing* (London: Zed Books, 2017)

Ryan-Collins, Josh, *Why Can't You Afford a Home?* (Cambridge: Polity Press, 2019)

Sassen, Saskia, *Expulsions: Brutality and Complexity in the Global Economy* (Cambridge, MA: Belknap Press, 2014)

Shaxson, Nicholas, *Treasure Islands: Tax Havens and the Men who Stole the World* (London: Bodley Head, 2011)

Shrubsole, Guy, *Who Owns England? How We Lost Our Green & Pleasant Land & How to Take It Back* (London: William Collins, 2019)

Singh, K. P., *Whatever the Odds: The Incredible Story behind DLF* (Noida: HarperCollins Publishers India, 2011)

Skelton, Noel, *Constructive Conservatism* (Edinburgh: Blackwood, 1924)

Standing, Guy, *Plunder of the Commons: A Manifesto for Sharing Public Wealth* (London: Pelican, 2019)

Trump, Donald J., with Tony Schwartz, *Trump: The Art of the Deal* (New York: Random House, 1987)

URBED, 'Uxcester Garden City, Submission to the Wolfson Economics Prize' (2014)

Webber, Melvin M., 'The Urban Place and the Nonplace Urban Realm', in Webber et al. (eds), *Explorations into Urban Structure* (Philadelphia: University of Pennsylvania Press, 1964)

Wright Sr, John A., *Kinloch, Missouri's First Black City* (Charleston, SC: Arcadia 2000)

ACKNOWLEDGEMENTS

Patrick Walsh at PEW literary for unstinting encouragement and wisdom

Laura Hassan at Faber for faith, patience and insight, and Fred Baty, Kate Ward, Robert Davies, Sarah Barlow, Lauren Nicoll, Jonny Pelham, Colette Levitt and Jess Kim

Those who read drafts, and gave insight and guidance, who helped in crucial ways, and the friends, family and colleagues who, often without knowing, have sparked ideas and opened up vistas. Including (but not only):

David Bass, Carolyn Steel, Richard Wentworth, Richard Cohen, Transparency International, MK Gallery, Town and Country Planning Assocation, Aradhana Seth, Malavika Talukder, Amit Krishn Gulati, Rakesh Rana, Bruce Palling, Vibhuti Sachdev, Kankan Kataria, Adam Tanaka, Roger Connah, Luke Harding, Liza Fior, Eva Franch i Gilabert, Niall Hobhouse, Sean Griffiths, Eyal Weizman, Nigel Hugill, Marie Coulon.

My editors at the *Observer*

Dad and Lizzie, who have gone

Felix and Stella, Mum, Charlotte and Charles

All known Mulreadys, in particular Ned, Sally and Seamus

And Molly.

Thank you

IMAGE CREDITS

p. x–xi © Panos Pictures

p. 17 courtesy of *St. Louis Argus*

p. 19 (*top*) courtesy of the State Museum of Pennsylvania, Pennsylvania Historical and Museum Commission; (*bottom*) Patti McConville / Alamy Stock Photo

p. 40 (*top*) PA Images / Alamy Stock Photo; (*bottom*) © Bex Wade

p. 60 courtesy of George D. McDowell/Special Collections Research Center, Temple University Libraries, Philadelphia, Pa.

p. 87 courtesy of Nevada State Museum, Las Vegas

p. 91 Kim Petersen / Alamy Stock Photo

p. 98–9 © Iwan Baan Studio

p. 108 Photo by NY Daily News Archive via Getty Images

p. 121–2 © Rowan Moore

p. 153 courtesy of the BLM General Land Office Records

p. 166 (*bottom*) PA Images / Alamy Stock Photo

p. 206 (*top*) AH! Siedlung Rosenhügel; (*bottom*) B. O'Kane / Alamy Stock Photo

p. 213 © Adam Tanaka

p. 221 (*top*) photo by Dawn Makarios, courtesy of New Communities; (*bottom*) photo by Mtamanika Youngblood, courtesy of New Communities

p. 239 © Estate of Helmut Jacoby Courtesy Eve Happold Walker

INDEX

Page references in *italics* denote illustrations

Abercrombie, Patrick, 246
Adams, John, 23, 28, 151
Adelson, Sheldon, 92, 97
AIG FP, 84
Al, Stefan, 93
Al Maktoum, Mohammed, 105
Albayrak, Berat, 112
Aliyev, Heydar, 102
Aliyev, Ilham, 102
Aliyev family, 102, 103–4, 105
Aliyeva, Mehriban, 102
Ansal, 120
Ashley, Lord, 147
Australia, 154
Azerbaijan, 93, 101–5

Baku, Azerbaijan, 93, 101–2
Bannon, Steve, 113
Barker, Kate, 51
Barrett, Wayne, 107
Baturina, Yelena, 105
Beame, Abe, 107
bedroom tax, UK, 50
Berkeley, St Louis, 31
Berlin, post-1945, 203–5
Bevan, Nye, 246–7, 270
Bhasin, Pramod, 125
Big Short, The, 83–4
Biswas, Suptendu, 123, 124, 132
Bolton, John, 112
Bragdon, Kathleen, 149
Bridgewater, Duke of, 26, 29
Brill Building, New York, *19*, 21–2

Britain *see also* housing policies (Britain); property-owning democracy: council housing, 243–52; decent homes and society scenario, 255–7; Diggers and Levellers campaigns, 163–5, *166*, 167; enclosure impacts, 26, 27–8, 142–5, 200–1; feudal system, 142, 144–5, 199–200; foreign capital and property, 47, 171; homeowning and countryside myths, 257–9; house and garden ideal, 38–9; housing inequalities, present trends, 37–8, *40*; landowners and industrialisation, 25–9; property prices, inflationary effects, 43–8, 56–8, 76–8, 258–9; women's rights and witch hunts, 156–7
Broughton, John, 243
Brown, Michael, 31
Burlington Community Land Trust, 225–7
Burnham, Andy, 280
Bush, George W., 23

Canada, 174
casino capitalism, 94–6
Castle, Philip, 240
Champlain Housing Trust, 227, 229
Chance, Tom, 228
Charles V, Emperor, 156
China, 23–4, 92–3
co-housing: *kollektivhus*, Sweden, 220, 222; principles, 219, 228
collateralised debt obligation (CDOs), 84–5, 94

Collective, London, 220
collective living projects, 219–20
common land (commons): communal resource, 199; enclosure debate, 200–1; governance, good and bad forms, 201–3
communal ownership: Berlin squats, post-1945, 204–5; common land (commons), 199–200; De Soto's theories, 24; Vienna's 'wild settlers,' 205, 206, 207
community land trusts: Burlington Community Land Trust, 225–7; National CLT Network, UK, 228; New Communities Inc. project, 221, 222–5; residency criticisms, 228–9; UK city projects, 227–8
compulsory purchase: discriminatory clearance, US, 30, 31, 242–3; kleptocratic state abuse, 105, 112; social benefit and value uplift, 234, 237–8, 247
Co-op City, New York: benefits over aesthetics, 211–12; cultural diversity, 214, 216; development history, 215–17; shared ownership, 212, 213, 214, 216, 217, 218
cooperative housing: benefits and challenges, 218–19, 228; Co-op City, New York, 212–18; New York initiatives, 214–15
Cotton, John, Rev., 146
council housing, Britain: achievements and criticisms, 251, 252; early schemes, 243–4; forms and specifications, 248–9; legislation and policies, 244, 246–8; London estates, 244–5, 246; policy aims, 243; rural districts, 248; 'sink estates' 249–50
COVID-19 pandemic, 47, 261, 262
Crawley, 54, 55
credit default swaps, 84
Cromwell, Oliver, 165
Curtis, Russell, 278

Cylich, Bernie, 211, 212

D'Antonio, Michael, 107
de Freitas, Michael (Michael X), 65–6
de Soto, Hernando, 24, 82–3, 175
Deripaska, Oleg, 171
developer kings: Azerbaijan elite families, 102–5; Donald and Fred Trump, 105–7, 108, 109–10; elite enrichment, prime objective, 113–14; power and politics, 1, 104–5, 109–10, 114–16; public funds, private property interests, 102, 104, 111–12, 114–15; Recep Tayyip Erdoğan, 93, 110–12
Dickinson, John, 15
Diggers (radicals), 163–4, 200
District of Columbia Redevelopment Land Agency, 30
DLF, 120, 128–9
Doğan, Aydin, 113
Dorling, Danny, 44
Drexel Burnham Lambert, 94

Eden, Anthony, 41
Ellenborough, Baron, 170
eminent domain, 30, 31, 215, 242
enclosure and land clearance: Australian occupation, 154; Britain's winners/losers, 26, 27–8, 142–5, 200; common land (commons), 199–203; US colonisation, theoretical arguments, 147–50, 155; US demarcation ordinances, 150–2, 153, 154, 155; women's rights and witch hunts, 156–7
Engels, Friedrich, 188–9
English Charter of the Forest 1217, 199–200
Erdoğan, Recep Tayyip, 105, 110–13

Fairburn, Jeff, 47
Federici, Silvia, 156–7
Ferguson, Missouri, 31–2
feudal system, 142, 144–5, 199–200

Flamingo Casino, Las Vegas, 86, *87*
Fleming, Owen, 244
Foster, Norman, 88
France, 174, 187
Friedman, Milton, 23

gaming cities, development, 86, *87*, 88–90
Gandhi, Rajiv, 129–30
Gandhi, Sanjay, 129
Gans, Herbert, 18, 20
garden cities: developments and influence, 237, 238, 240, 245; funding and financial management, 236–7; planning practices, 235–6; URBED's modern vision, 264–6
George, Henry, 184–6, 189, 223, 234
Glaeser, Edward, 21, 22
Golby, Joel, 75
Goldman Sachs, 84
Goodman, Oscar, 95
Green, David, 248
Greer, Allan, 149, 150, 202–3
Gurgaon/Gurugram: commercial expansion under Gandhi family, 129–30; 'controlled areas', developers exploitation, 126–9, 131, 133; non-cohesive architecture, 123–5; pre-development 'poor district', 125–6; private enclaves, neighbouring deprivation, 120, *122*, 123; private enclaves, promoted benefits, 119–20, 123, 131–2; private/public boundaries, *121–2*, 124, 131–2; social separation issues, 132–3

Hadid, Zaha, 101–2
Halligan, Liam, 48, 51
Hamilton, Alexander, 151
Hanley, Lynsey, 250, 252
Hardin, Garrett, 201
Harding, Luke, 103
Harlow, 54, 55
Harrison, William, 144

Haryana Urban Development Authority (HUDA), 126, 128
Heatherwick, Thomas, 134
help to buy scheme, 47, 261, 262
Herzog & de Meuron, 205
Heseltine, Michael, 41–2
Heydar Aliyev Centre, Baku, 101–2
Hezer, Ismet, 110–11, 115
Holzer, Jenny, 88
home makeover phenomenon, 64–5, 67–9
Home Owners Loan Corporation, 29–30
home ownership, Britain: generational gains and unattainability, 71–5; government induced divisions, 47, 50–1, 57–8, 258–9, 261–3; home makeover trend, 64–5; 'market value' phenomenon, 44–5; renters' financial barriers, 48–9, 71–3; socioeconomic motivations, 51–2, 285–6; Thatcher's 'right to buy' policy, 41–3, 280
housing crisis (Britain), solutions analysis: 'brown field' sites, 266; construction/space efficiencies, 260–1, 267; fiscal and financial incentives, 261–2, 267–8; garden city on greenbelt proposal, 264–6; homeworking/city commute, 266–7; land supply, release issues, 263–4; socioeconomic divisions, 258–9; state provision and financing, 268–70; unrestrained market issues, 259–60, 268
housing policies (Britain), Conservative: COVID-19 tax breaks, 47, 261, 262; help to buy scheme, 47, 261, 262; housing benefit restrictions, 49; local authority housing, 244; mortgage liberalisation, 42–3, 46, 261; permitted development, toxic conversions, 53–6; post-1945 council houses, 247, 249; social

housing reductions, 49–50, 250–1;
socioeconomic divisions, 50–2;
Thatcher's 'right to buy' policy, *40*,
41–4, 49, 250
housing policies (Britain), Labour:
'buy to let' scheme, 46; post-
1945 council houses, 246–7, 249;
socioeconomic divisions, 50–1
Houston, 134
Howard, Ebenezer, 224, 235–7
Huang, Yukon, 24

Iceberg House trend, 67–9
India: developers' political allies, 129–
30, 131, 133–4; Gurgaon private
enclaves, 119–20, *121–2*, 123–5,
131–2; planning laws, developer
manipulation, 126–8

Jackson, Kenneth, 30
Jacoby, Helmut, 238, *239*
Jefferson, Thomas, 5, 151, 157, 183,
190–1, 287
Johnson, Boris, 52

Kazan, Abraham, 214–15
Kennedy, John F., 215
King, Carole, 21
Kinloch, Missouri, 15–16, *17*, 30–1,
32, 242
Koolhaas, Rem, 88
Kushner, Jared, 112, 113

Lal, Bansi, 129
land (property) ownership:
colonisation and enclosure
145–8; development inequalities,
184–7; divine allocation, 141–2;
egalitarian solution challenges,
189–90; feudal system to enclosure
acquisitions, 142–5; modern
exclusivity, 141; property as
capital, Communist view, 188–9;
'Property is theft', Proudhon's
critique, 187–8

Land Ceiling Act 1976 (India), 126,
127–8
Lansky, Meyer, 90
Las Vegas: casino capitalism, 94–6;
casino developments, 86, *87*, 88–9;
development fundamentals, 89–90;
enterprise, growth and influence,
90, *91*, 92–4
Le Corbusier, 211–12
Leeds, Quarry Hill Estate, 248
Lefcourt, Abraham E., 22
Levellers, 164–5, 167
Levitt, William, 23, 30, 61
Levitt and Sons, 18
Levittown, New Jersey, 18, *19*, 20
Levittowns, 29, 30, 61–2
Lewis, Michael, 83–4
Libeskind, Daniel, 88
Lin, Maya, 88
Linebaugh, Peter, 155
Linklater, Andro, 141–2, 144, 158
Liverpool: first council homes 1869,
243–4; Granby Four Streets CLT,
228
Locke, John: Native Americans
misdescribed, 149–50, 169; rights
to life, labour and property, 25,
82, 144, 167–9; US colonisation,
theoretical argument, 28, 147–50,
169–70; Western society, influence
on, 169–70, 171–2
Loddon Rural District Council, 248
London: Alton Estate, Roehampton,
249; Becontree Estate, 245, 248;
'beds in sheds', 69; Boundary
Estate, Shoreditch, 244–5, 249;
city expansion, 27; Collective
project, 220; County Council's
housebuilding, 244–6, 248; 'ghost
streets', 69; Greater London
Plan 1944, 246; Iceberg House
phenomenon, 67–9; investment
apartments, 71–2; multiple
occupancy 'favelas', 69; Notting
Hill's gentrification, 65–7; Old

Oak Estate, Hammersmith, 245;
permitted development policies,
54–6; property prices, inflationary
effects, 47–8, 50–1, 67–71; St
Clement's Hospital CLT, 227–8;
unattainable ownership, personal
case, 71–5; Vauxhall's luxury
enclave, 134
Luzhkov, Yury, 105

Macau, 92
Macmillan, Harold, 247
Maddox, Lester, 224
Madison, James, 151, 158, 179
Mammadov family, 103, 104–5, 114
Mandelson, Peter, 65, 67
Markovits, Inga, 203–4
Marshall, Colin, 29
Martinez, Melquiades R., 23
Maruti Motors Ltd, 129
Marx, Karl, 82, 176, 188–9
May, Theresa, 51
Meng, Xiaosu, 23–4
Milken, Michael, 94
Milton Keynes: planning inspiration/
innovations, 238, 239, 240;
residential benefits, 233–4, 242;
state investment and planning,
234–5, 241
Moore, Rowan, 50–1, 285–7
More, Thomas, 143
Moses, Richard, 215
Mumford, Lewis, 18
Myers, William and Daisy, 30, 60,
61–2

Narkomfin project, Moscow, 220
National Association of Realtors, 61
Neilson, Kathy, 226
Neurath, Otto, 207
New Communities Inc., Georgia, 221,
222–3
new towns, UK: garden city concept
and influence, 235–7; government
Acts, 237; Milton Keynes's creation,
233–5, 238, 239, 240–1; planning
criticisms, 241; residential benefits,
233–4, 241–2; state investment and
planning, 234–5, 237–8, 242
New York: Co-op City, 211–12, 213,
214–18; cooperative housing
movement, 214–15; Hudson Yards,
94, 134; Mitchell–Lama housing
scheme, 215: property, investment
lure, 106–7, 217–18: Trump
developments, 105–7, 217
Notting Hill (film), 66

Oppenheim Group, 81–2
Organised Crime and Corruption
Reporting Project, 104
Ostrom, Elinor, 201–2
Overton, Richard, 164–5, 177

Pan, Jingyuan, 21
Patrick, Diane, 211
Patterson, Maureen and James, 40,
41–2
permitted development, 53–6
Persimmon, 47
Peru, 24
Picasso, Pablo, 88
Policy Exchange, 52
Ponzi scheme, 45–6
Powell, Alena, 211, 214
Progress and Poverty (George), 184–6
property: and financial speculation,
84-5; decent homes and society
scenario, 255–7; developer
power and politics, 85–6, 105,
109–10, 114–16, 133–5; exploitive
capital, 188–9; ideological
divides, 203–4; natural and
abstract concepts, 3–4, 5–6,
82–3; slavery, colonial justification,
155–6, 157–9; socioeconomic and
emotional relations, 6–8, 62–3;
socioeconomic challenges/benefits,
6–8, 32–3, 191–3, 251–2, 287–9;
voting rights link, 29

property, rights and entitlement: Communist critique, 188–9; Diggers' communal advocacy, 163–4; human rights declarations, references to, 173–5, 187; Jefferson's usufruct idea, 190–1; landowners and industrialisation, 25–9; legal and political devices, 177–8, 192; legal construction, 177; Levellers' natural, individual rights, 164–5, 167; Locke's retention through labour, 25, 82, 167–9; natural right, flawed reasoning, 173, 175–6; possession, fundamental ideals, 191–3; 'possession', Proudhon's concept, 188, 190; privilege, flawed reasoning, 170–2; Proudhon's critique, 187–8; situational based practices/customs, 172–3; socio-economic divisions, 178–9; Soto's boundaries argument, 175–6; US colonisation, Locke's justification, 147–50, 169–70

property value: cultural obsession, Britain, 63–4; entitlement defence, 62–3, 77; generational gains and unattainability, 71–5; gentrification opportunities, 66–7; home makeover trend, 64–5; housebuilders' market controls, 47, 260, 263, 268; Iceberg House phenomenon, 67–9; London investment extremes, 67–71, 75; micro-tycoons, benefits/pressures, 75–8; race and proprietorship, 61–2

property-owning democracy: British embodiment, 2, 32–3, 170; concept principles, 39, 41; government induced divisions, 41–58, 258–9, 261–3; Thatcher's housing policies and impacts, *40*, 41–4

Proudhon, Pierre-Joseph, 187–8, 189, 190

Public Land Survey System (USA), 25, 29, 152, 169, 186

Raban, Jonathan, 66

race, property and discrimination, 15–16, *17*, 29–32, *60*, 61–2

Rachman, Peter, 65–6

Rasmussen, Steen Eiler, 38–9

Ravitch, Richard, 106, 107

Rayner, Angela, 273

real estate, USA: casino capitalism, 94–6; imagery and reality TV, 81–2; Las Vegas, gaming city developments, 86, *87*, 88–90, *91*, 93–4; subprime mortgage crisis and consequences, 83–5; Trump's vision, 96–7

Rediker, Marcus, 155

'redlining', 29

Rees, Peter, 67–71

restrictive covenants, 61–2

Rich, Nathan, 124–5

Rifkind, Hugo, 51

Robbins, Bob, 226–7

Rocha, Guy, 95

Rockefeller, Nelson, 215

Roosevelt, Franklin D., 23

Ryer, Lillian, 216–17

Sanders, Bernie, 225–6

Selling Sunset, 81–2

Siegel, Bugsy, 86

Silkin, Lewis, 241

Singapore, 92, 269, 270

Singh, Kushal Pal, 125, 126, 128–30

Skelton, Noel, 39, 41

slavery, colonial justification, 155–6, 157–9

Smith, John, Captain, 145–6, 147

social housing: council owned benefits, 73–4; permitted development, toxic conversions, 53–6; public funding, reduction impacts, 49–51

squats: Berlin, post-1945, 204–5; rights, De Soto's theories, 24

St George's Hill, Surrey, 163–4, *166*, 171

Standing, Guy, 142, 199

Stein, Seth, 67

Stevenage, 241
Stiglitz, Joseph, 2
sub-prime mortgage crisis, 46, 83–5
Sweden, 220, 222, 269

Tacheles, 204–5
Tanaka, Adam, 211, 212, 218
Tayler, Herbert, 248
Tecumseh, 223
Temporary Autonomous Zones, 204
terra nullius, 154
Thatcher, Denis, 241
Thatcher, Margaret: housing policies
    and impacts, *40*, 41–4, 46, 49,
    250–1, 261; Milton Keynes
    opening, 241; 'property-owning
    democracy', 32–3
Thiers, Adolphe, 170
Trump, Donald: Atlantic City casinos,
    110; Baku developments, 102–3;
    behavioural traits, 96–7; father's
    connections and legacy, 107, 109;
    New York developments, fortunate
    start, 105–7, *108;* Turkey,
    favourable dealings, 112–13
Trump, Fred, 107, 109, 110, 114
Turkey: Burj Al Babas chateaux, 93,
    111; Erdoğan's 'urban renewal',
    110–12, 115; Trump's Presidential
    dealings, 112–13

UN Universal Declaration of Human
    Rights, 174
unearned increment, 224, 265, 270
Unitech, 120
United Housing Federation, 215
United Nations (UN), 174
United States (USA): black people,
    proprietorship discrimination,
    15–16, *17,* 29–32, *60,* 61–2; Brill
    Building, New York, *19,* 21–2;

colonisation and enclosure, 146–8,
    150; colonisation and property
    rights, 4, 15, 28–9, 145–6, 149–51,
    169–70, 173–4; cooperative
    housing, New York, 211–12, *213,*
    214–18; frontier development
    and inequalities, 184–7; Kinloch,
    Missouri, 15–16, *17,* 30–1,
    32, 242; Levittown, suburban
    dreams, 18, *19,* 20, 29; Native
    Americans' displacement, 28, 152,
    154, 202–3; Native Americans'
    misrepresentation, 149–50; New
    Communities Inc., Georgia, *221,*
    222–5; ownership and freedom,
    23; public housing law, 243; Public
    Land Survey System, 25, 29, 152,
    169, 186; rights declarations and
    property, 173–4, 183; settled
    territories, land demarcation,
    150–2, *153,* 155; slavery, colonial
    justification, 155–6, 157–9; sub-
    prime mortgage crisis, 46, 83–5
URBED, Uxcester proposal, 264–6
Utopia (More), 143

Viñoly, Rafael, 88
Vice magazine, 75
Vienna: social housing, *206,* 207–8,
    243; 'wild settlers' settlements, 205,
    206, 207

Webber, Melvin, 238
Welch, Jack, 130
Wetherell, W. D., 20
Winstanley, Gerrard, 163–4
Winthrop, John, 146–7, 154
Wright, John, A. Sr., 16
Wynn, Steve, 88, 94

Yalçındağ, Mehmet Ali, 112–13